Fabio Schillaci
Architectural Renderings
Construction and Design Manual

*To Julienne and
my family*

Fabio Schillaci
Architectural Renderings
Construction and Design Manual

A John Wiley and Sons, Ltd, Publication

Foreword

Most people think of architectural rendering as something new and unique to the computer. This is not the whole truth. A "render" is any depiction or interpretation that evokes something that already exists or that is yet to exist. It doesn't matter if it is made digitally or by hand. We should not separate the digital from the hand-made, because both processes stem from the same line of evolution. The modern digital render could not have come into being without the earlier drawing.

In the light of the debate about representation and whether digital technologies have altered the drawing paradigm, I asked Fabrizio Avella to write about the history of architectural representation for this book, and to focus especially on the tools and how they have changed the discipline over the course of the centuries. Avella's essay is a very important summary which serves to demonstrate that the logic applied down the ages by the masters in hand-drawing is the same as that applied today in the digital software.

So if that is true, why then is there still so much reluctance to accept the digital paradigm? This was the question I put to Augusto Romano Burelli. He was very critical about contemporary modes of computer use, pointing out that the problem lies not with the tool, but in the way we use it: the computer is today becoming the end rather than the

means. Using computers implies accepting the risks inherent in progress, but we should need to understand those risks in order to control the tool and not to get wy out of our depth. That is what happened to the ancient Greeks who built the Olimpieion in the colony of Akragas – today's Agrigento in Italy. They tried to build a temple which was too ambitious for the technical skills of the time, and so it collapsed around the heads of its architects. Such is the sin of hubris, arrogance, that Burelli reveals through incredible drawings which reconstruct the architecture of the temple from the few ruins that have survived. Quite the opposite of hubris are two works by Fiorenzo Bertan and his students at IUAV in Venice, which use computer and digital technologies to reconstruct the Palladian Ponte di Rialto through a Canaletto "Capriccio", which renders with objectivity a completely out of scale architectural vision, and to represent the old Venetian boat "Sampierota" by using the computer to document its manufacture and to transmit it to the next generation, thus saving the hand-crafted art for posterity.

When I began to research this book, I had the opportunity to search out some of the world's most interesting architectural rendering studios. Because of my relative lack of professional experience, I was astonished to discover that the most famous architectural companies in the world were outsourcing their rendering instead of doing it themselves. This led me – largely over the internet – to discover a huge number of specialist offices doing architectural rendering. I invited fourteen of the best to present and explain their work in the book. They were largely enthusiastic about my invitation, and gave me the motivation to continue with the project. Each office agreed to publish its best images and to answer my questions about their work, philosophy and process. This was a big opportunity for me to learn, and it is this knowledge that I want to pass on to you. Although each office works digitally, they do it in different ways. Their presentation goes from hand to computer, capturing a new way of thinking – and consequently drawing – rather than simply posing and solving some technical issues. The projects showcased in these pages go some way to thank all the offices and to congratulate them on their outstanding work. While I am sure you will already be familiar with some renderings because they are very famous, you will most probably ignore the name of their creators.

Generally people do not understand what rendering means, and underestimate the work involved. Thus, in conclusion, I decided to illustrate the making of render through my own work. The aim of this section is to show the process and the amount of work behind the rendering. While even for the professional renderer this will not be a comprehensive tutorial, I feel sure it will help beginners and clients to understand more about our work and skills. I hope, too, that this will also open architecture students' minds to the huge potential of digital technologies.

Fabio Schillaci

Fabrizio Avella
**Drawing between history and
digital innovation**

Fabrizio Avella

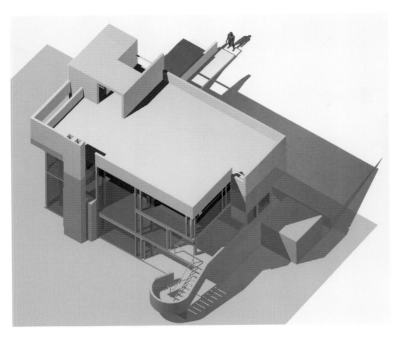

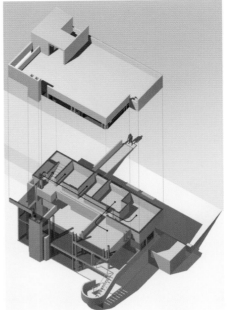

Bernardo Augello,
Smith House by Richard Meier,
2006

The introduction of digital processing techniques in architectural drawing has, in recent years, shaken the foundations of the discipline of drawing. The aim of this essay is to determine what, conceptually, has remained unchanged compared to the conventions of drawing by hand and how far digital rendering has become the new intellectual approach. Considering technique as a dimension that creates thought with a set of bi-univocal reports, one wonders if and how the use of new skills can influence and change the way we represent – and, therefore, think – about architecture. In order to do this, it is necessary to reflect on the codes of the methods and techniques of representation, focusing on those aspects which can help us understand whether and how these codes have been subverted or incorporated in the processes of digital drawing.

The plan

It is very difficult to determine how long the plan has been used to describe architecture. The first method of representation mentioned by Vitruvius is *iconography*, the footprint of an object left on the soil, and traces of this method are found as early as 7200 BC.[1]

The plan is a drawing that requires a high level of abstraction on the part of those who carry it out and who have to interpret it: basically we need to visualize what an object could look like when viewed from a point of infinite distance, after it has been cut horizontally by a large plane and had its upper part removed.

The sequence of images taken from a study by Bernardo Augello of some buildings by Richard Meier shows the process leading to the drafting of a plan.

Yet, despite probably being the most analogical and least mimetic design invented by man, the plan remains the most familiar and easy to interpret even for the inexperienced eye and even for those unused to drawing diagrams. Subway maps, information boards for tourists and diagrams of emergency exits to public buildings are all drawn in plan; estate agents provide photos and plans, but never an axonometric section; any client, even if untrained, can

1 The first evidence of what we call a plan is visible in a drawing on a wall in Catal Höyuk (Turkey), dated to between 7200 and 6800 BC.

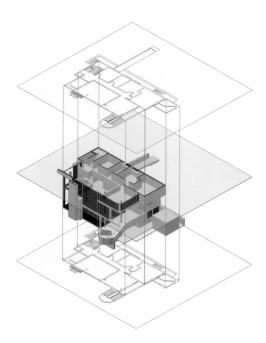

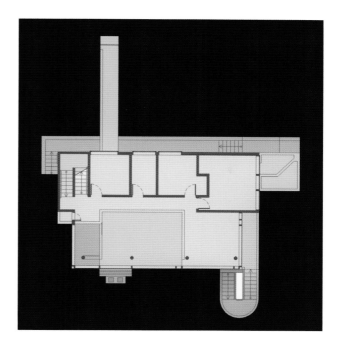

Bernardo Augello,
Smith House by Richard Meier,
2006

understand the intentions of the architect by looking at the plans of a project.

It is not easy to determine the reasons for this familiarity, but certainly anyone who has studied design has been introduced early to this kind of drawing. The Greek temples are classified as *monoptera, pseudo-diptera, diptera*, depending on how many rows of columns surround the naos, or hexastyle, octostyle depending on the number of columns on the main façade, while the Christian churches are sorted between those with a central plan and those with a longitudinal plan.

The plan was also well known and used in Roman times. Besides the afore mentioned Vitruvius, there survive fragments of a stone plan of imperial Rome, dated to between AD 203 and 211. The *Forma Urbis* or *Marble Map of Rome* is a set of marble slabs showing a rectangular portion of the city measuring 4.3 by 3.2 kilometers, on a scale which reduces the plan to approximately 18 × 13 meters.[2] The excellent construction technique and the accuracy of the survey appear even more remarkable given the tools available at the time, so corroborating the idea that a very high quality of representation was already being coded and implemented.

The easy stroke for the wall is not misleading, as it is probably the result of the scale of the drawing and the available technology. Consider that the plan was created by cutting marble slabs with a stylus, where the size of the representation did not allow for exact scale reproduction of the thickness of the walls. A representation of walls by parallel signs can be seen in the plan of a portion of the Temple of Castor and Pollux, constructed prior to the *Forma Urbis*, which displays a rendering technique quite similar to the one used today.

The simplification of graphics in the *marmorea plan* is most probably the result of the limit imposed by the technique of the time rather than a simplification of the code.

The work becomes even more impressive when one considers that the first perfect planimetric representation in orthogonal projection with an acceptable level of accuracy is not due to appear until thirteen centuries later, when Leonardo da Vinci drew the map of Imola in 1502. Considering that apart from the plan of Imola, pseudo-perspective or pseudo-axonometric representations in topographic maps are not found until the seventeenth century, the scientific nature of *Forma Urbis* is even more extraordinary. It is most probable that the plan was also used in medieval times, but it is not until the fifteenth century that codes closer to our contemporary ones start to appear. It is worth noting, in this respect, the survey of the Diocletian Baths by Giuliano da Sangallo, in which is clearly visible the distinction between the cut portions of the wall and the projection of the vaults above.

---

2   For a detailed description of the Forma Urbis Romae cf. Mario Docci, Diego Maestri, *Storia del rilievo architettonico e urbano*, Laterza, Bari (Italy), 1993, ch. I, *L'antichità*.

Forma Urbis Romae, AD 203–211
Tav. 53 della Forma Urbis Roma,
Stanford University e Sovraintendenza ai Beni Culturali
del Comune di Roma,
Rome (Italy)

*Pianta del Tempio di Castore e Polluce presso il circo
Flaminio*, 2nd century AD
Museo Nazionale Romano, inv. 365105,
Rome (Italy)

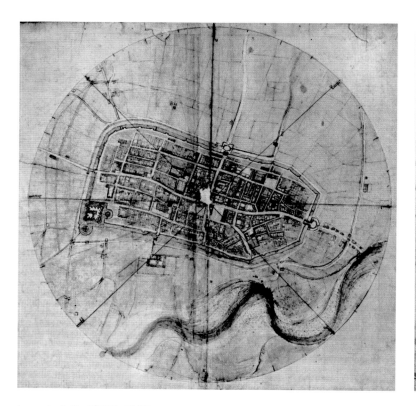

Leonardo da Vinci (1452–1519),
Pianta di Imola (Italy), 1502
Windsor Castle, Royal Library, RL 12284r,
Windsor (UK)

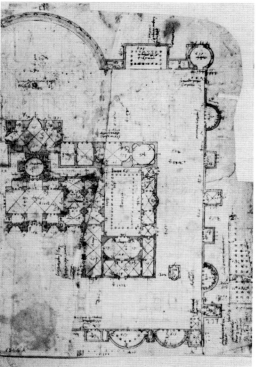

Giuliano da Sangallo (1445–1516),
Pianta delle terme di Diocleziano a Roma (Italy),
date unknown
Gabinetto delle Stampe degli Uffizi, Florence (Italy),
Photo: Pineider

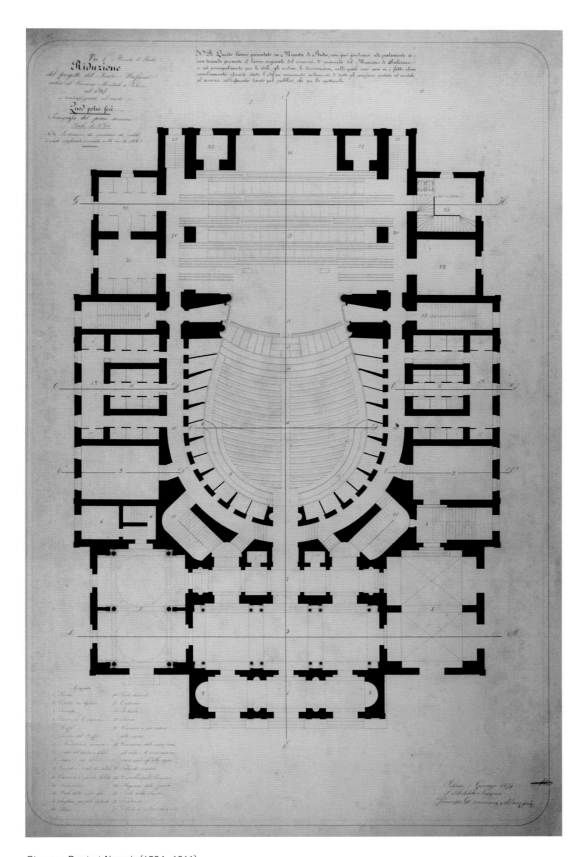

Giuseppe Damiani Almeyda (1834–1911),
Project for Teatro Massimo in Palermo.
Plan of the first floor, 1874
Archivio Damiani, Palermo (Italy)
Photo: Fabrizio Avella,
post-processing: Fabrizio Avella,
Giuseppe Dalli Cardillo

The reproduction of the plan did not undergo any specific innovations in the following centuries, except for refinements to techniques for distinguishing between the drawing of the section parts and the projection parts.

From a purely theoretical point of view, there is no difference between the plan of Teatro Massimo in Palermo by Giuseppe Damiani Almeyda, and the plan study of Casa Smith by Richard Meier, achieved through a common CAD software: both plans sought to cut the building with a secant plane positioned at a certain height, to remove the top and look at the remaining portion from an infinite distance from above. They both also reveal the choices made by the designer to distinguish clearly the portions of wall cut from what, by contrast, is represented in the orthogonal projection.

The descriptive power of the plan – perhaps determined by its abstract, low mimetic nature – was so strong that it was subsequently chosen to define the typological characteristics of architecture. Consider, for example, the tables of Durand,[3] and, more recently, the interesting essay by Carlos Martí Aris on the concept of type in architecture. In both cases, the purpose of defining architectural types leads to an extensive use of the plan as fully sufficient to define the types in question.[4] Moreover, the shock waves created by the formal and spatial Modern Movement were not able to undermine the importance of the plan since even Le Corbusier felt the need to identify it as one of the five principles which generate architecture. Still today, despite the fact that we have entirely abandoned the idea of typology and accepted that contemporary architecture moves toward complex forms, the plan remains among the forms of representation still used and all BIM programs provide more or less automatic procedures for extracting plans from three-dimensional models, regardless of the complexity of their configuration.[5]

3   Jean-Nicolas-Louis Durand, *Recueil et Parallele des edifices de Tout Genre, Anciens et Modernes*, 1801, and *Précis des leçons d'architecture données à l'école polytechnique*, Paris (France), 1805.

4   See Carlos Martí Aris, *Le variazioni dell'identità: Il tipo in architettura*, Città Studi, Milan (Italy), 1998 (1st. ed. 1990).

5   Building Information Modelling is a system which associates vectorial entities and parametric information (such as composition of the wall, type of profile of a frame or glass, etc. ... to a graphical-numerical database that handles both vectorial and parametrical information with the possibility of bi-univocal variations.

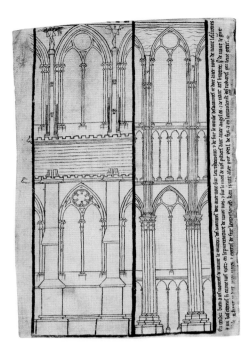

Villard de Honnecourt, *Front view and section of the nave of the cathedral of Reims*, c. 1220/1235
From *Livre de Portraiture*, Codex ms. Fr. 19093,
Fol. 31. National Library of France, Paris (France)

Façade of Strasbourg Cathedral
("Plan A1"), c.1275
Musée de l'Œuvre Notre-Dame,
Inv. No. 2, Strasbourg (France)

Orthogonal projections and flat section

Almost all the texts dealing with the history of representation pay tribute to the original section of the nave of the cathedral of Reims, dated around 1230, and described in the *Livre de Portraiture* by Villard de Honnecourt. Commenting on its importance, Frommel notes how the role of the architect evolved in the Gothic period to incorporate that of the master builder or head of the building site, a job which required considerable technical expertise. His need to visualise the building required not only *in-situ* sketches, but also accurate drawings to organize the project.[1] Such a drawing is additionally interesting because it fits together the exterior view of the building (the façade) with the interior view (the section), juxtaposing façade and section to highlight similarities and variations, revealing an analytical capacity on the part of the architect.

Another outstanding example of Gothic architecture is given on the design of the façade of the cathedral in Strasbourg,

dated between 1250 and 1260, which shows more correct orthographical projection than that on the sheet of Palinsesto of Reims. These drawings represent the earliest surviving European examples of sections and façades rendered on parchment using a projective code similar to our modern era. Certainly, the complexity of the Gothic construction site and the considerable emphasis given to constituent elements such as doors, windows, pinnacles, and the refined geometries which they underpin brought an understandable legitimacy to the systematic use of the front view. The method was probably already known and used. Consider, for example, that Vitruvius had already combined orthography, now called elevation, with iconography, "the drawing in plan". Nor does lack of evidence necessarily mean that there was no "orthographic" drawing during the early Middle Ages.

The importance of these medieval drawings should be attributed not to the fact that they reveal the use of this system during the Middle Ages, but rather to the fact that they represent the rare few pieces of evidence that have survived. While we have evidence for the existence of the plan in Roman times, there is no equivalent to the front elevation with a clearly identifiable code similar to the one existing today.

There may be several reasons for this. We should recall that, in medieval construction sites, the *magister* (master) made "ephemeral" drawings on non-durable media, such as boards

---

1 "If the architecture of the Romanesque buildings was of relatively simple design, the Gothic (with its transparency, logical structure, and geometric ornament) requires a more elegant and precise design. [...] No previous era, in fact, had tried to achieve a similar correspondence between exterior and interior, and had so closely linked together the individual elements of the body of the building by means of axes and frames. [...] It was only through training and using such a graphical method for designing, during the first half of the twelfth century, that it was possible for the architect to develop in the modern sense, fixing designs regardless of their realization and transmitting them to artisans to carry out the work", in C. L. Frommel, *Sulla nascita del disegno architettonico*, in H. Millon and V. Magnago Lampugnani (ed.), *Rinascimento da Brunelleschi a Michelangelo*, Bompiani, Milan (Italy), 1994, p. 101.

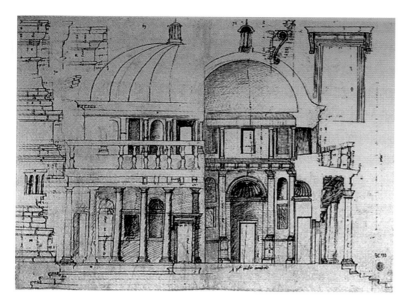

Anonymous French artist, *Tempietto di San Pietro in Montorio*, date unknown
Cod. Destailleur D, I, Hdz. 4151, Fol. 103 recto,
Staatliche Museen, Kunstbibliothek, Berlin (Germany)

surrounded by wooden planks, where he would "draw" – or better scribble – with a steel or wooden stylus on a layer of lime. These drawings were actually an empirical tool for solving problems of construction. They were necessary for the *magister* in order to communicate with apprentices. Once the problem was solved, the drawing could be removed and the "sheet" could be reused.

The elevation drawing, like the plan, underwent refinement during the Renaissance. One reason for this may lie in the education of the Renaissance architect, which included the study of buildings in order to grasp compositional rules and codes. Orthogonal projection proved to be even more effective for pictorial reproduction of ancient buildings because it allowed the representation and description of the architectural order with geometrical accuracy.

If an architect begins to use a method of representation in order to understand ancient architecture, it is likely that he will also apply it to his own constructions. Referring to specific essays on the role of drawing tools for developing architecture from the early Renaissance, it is useful to follow some progression.[2] In the fifteenth century, the need to control the design process through drawing was already understood, and it is no coincidence that contemporary treatises devote space to specific ideas on the methods of representation.

In *De re aedificatoria* Leon Battista Alberti feels the need to give specific guidance for architectural drawing that is intended for construction only, without yielding to the temptation of providing pictorial representations.[3] Unlike the artist, the architect needs a metric precision and he must strive to design "the shape and extent of each front and each side using real angles and non-variable lines: like one who wants his work to be judged not on a deceptive semblance, but precisely on the basis of verifiable measurements".[4]

In the early Renaissance, despite its strong value for "measuring" space, the perspective was not used in architecture because it often produced an "illusory appearance" and for three-dimensional representation wooden models were preferred, as they were indispensable tools for the verification of what was to be built, and their construction formed an important stage of the design process.

2 See W. Lotz, *La rappresentazione degli interni nei disegni architettonici del Rinascimento*, in *Studi sull'architettura italiana del Rinascimento*, Electa, Milan (Italy), 1989, (Original title *Studies in the Italian Renaissance*, Massachusetts 1977).

3 "The overall architecture consists of the drawing and construction. Concerning the drawing, its whole purpose and method is to find an exact and satisfactory way to fit together and connect lines and angles, through which the look of the building is fully defined. The function of the drawing is to assign to the buildings and their parts an appropriate location, an exact proportion, a convenient and harmonious order, so that the whole shape of the building rests entirely in the design itself." [Author's translation] In R. Bonelli and P. Portoghesi (eds.), *Leon Battista Alberti, L'Architettura (De re aedificatoria)*, Book I [Il Disegno], Polifilo Edizioni, Milan (Italy), 1966, p. 18.

4 Ibid, Book II [materials], chap. I, p. 98. We recommend a comparison with the perspective method used by Bramante: A. Bruschi, *Bramante*, Laterza, Bari (Italy), 1990, I ed. Thames and Hudson, London (UK), 1973, pp. 13–32.

Thus, the model became a method of representation,[5] also praised by Leon Battista Alberti, who appreciated its metrical accuracy to the point of considering it one means of expenditure control: a sort of three-dimensional cost estimate.[6]

Thus, a method for architectural design emerged: the use of detailed and metrically controllable drawings. These needs were met by the plan, by the elevation in orthogonal projection, and by the wooden model in scale which allowed three-dimensional control even before the invention of axonometric projection.

However, the process is not linear and there is a phase in which the earlier perspective studies re-enter the vocabulary of architectural drawing: this is the case with those drawings where pseudo-perspective betrays a lack of control in the process of rationalization of the orthogonal projection. Look at the section and elevation of Bramante's Tempietto of San Pietro in Montorio; while the elevation drawing on the left depicting the front is quite correct, the section succumbs to the temptation of perspective in the drawing of the external ambulatory, whose columns are viewed from an angle.

A mixture of orthogonal projection and perspective is far from rare in architectural drawing during the Renaissance, but there is a progressive refinement of the method and a greater respect for heartfelt Albertian prescription.

The orthogonal triad, which involves the combined and closely correlated use of plan, elevation and section is thus an achievement of the mature Renaissance. Raphael, in the letter sent in 1519 to Leo X, gives very specific guidelines for the drawing of architecture:

"The drawing, and thus the building relevant to the architect, is divided into three parts, the first of which is the plan, or we say the 'plan drawing', the second is the outside wall … the third is the inside wall … which is as necessary as the other two, and is made in the plan with parallel lines – like the outside wall – and shows half of the building inside, as if it were divided in half."

Although not all historians agree on the attribution of the famous letter to Leo X, it is, however, very probable that the author meant the need for control of construction through clear and shared graphic signs, with notations, that do not lead to perspectival distortion. Undoubtedly a strong impetus to codify the orthogonal projection was the construction of St. Peter's Basilica in Rome. Control of such an ambitious and complex project

5 "Even if the architects of the Renaissance were not the first to use the architectural models, they still built them with much more methodology and correctness than any predecessor." [Author's translation] In H. A. Millon, *I modelli architettonici nel Rinascimento*, in H. Millon and V. Magnago Lampugnani, op. cit., p. 19.

6 "I never tire of recommending what the best architects used to do: thinking and rethinking the work to be undertaken as a whole and the extent of its individual parts, using not only drawings and sketches, but also models made of wood and other material, consulting experts. Only after such a thorough examination can we address the cost and supervision of construction." [Author's translation] In R. Bonelli and P. Portoghesi (eds.), *Leon Battista Alberti*, op. cit., Book II [*I materiali*], chap. I, p. 96.

Antonio da Sangallo il Giovane (1484–1546),
Progetto per San Pietro, 1516
Galleria degli Uffizi, A 66,
Florence (Italy)

had to be supported by precise, metrically controllable graphics. Given the magnitude of the work, the design complexity and its symbolic importance, the site was the perfect opportunity to codify the architectural drawing. Here, therefore, the requirement of the plan, of the "outside wall" and "inside wall", is that of the elevation and of the section. The need to design according to these parameters was felt by Raphael, who grappled with the complexity of the work and who understood that he could not use perspective to address and solve the complex problems of the construction of St. Peter's. The role played by Antonio da Sangallo the Younger in coding the section and the orthogonal projection is underlined by Wolfgang Lotz, who reminds us of Sangallo's education as a "*faber lignarius*" (a carpenter): a non-philosophical education which can be seen in Sangallo's strength in implementing a drawing method more useful to a carpenter than a painter.[7] He introduced (or re-introduced) it in the drawing of architecture giving it an importance equal to that of perspective, which, while effectively describing space, is not ideal for metrically controlling the size of a column or a wall, or for controlling the architectural

order.[8] Marking some of the stages of this long and winding path, we may stop at Leon Battista Alberti, who suggested the use of the plan and model as methods for accurate representation of architecture, at the letter to Leo X, in which the author relied on the accuracy of the orthogonal projection and the vertical section, and at Antonio da Sangallo the Younger, who seems to collect these suggestions and implement the use of the section for the construction of St. Peter's.

Here, then, plan, elevation and section – the orthogonal triad – are as closely related one to another as the legs of a three-legged stool, describing the building with the precision of a surgeon in order to monitor its construction. This code was enhanced with a special type of projection in which half the elevation was accompanied by half the cross section. This method, which assumes perfect symmetry in the building, may have been the result of practical needs: the cost of paper, although not comparable to that of parchment, was still high, and, in addition to the use of both sides of the sheet, the representation can be optimized by putting

7   "The drawings we possess today suggest that Antonio da Sangallo the Younger, the youngest apprentice of Raphael for the construction of St. Peter Basilica, was the first to use orthogonal projections to represent an interior through the section." [Author's translation] In Wolfgang Lotz, *Studies in Italian Renaissance Architecture*, Cambridge, Massachusetts (USA), MIT Press, 1977, op. cit., p. 37.

8   "Before his appointment as *coadjutore* [close to Raphael during the construction of St. Peter Basilica], Sangallo had worked on St Peter's as *faber lignarius* and *carpentarius*. He is the only major architect of the Renaissance in Rome who came from the ranks of craftsmen. Unlike Bramante, Raphael and Peruzzi, who had all started out as painters, Sangallo had not studied perspective during his education. [...] It is probable that Peruzzi, as a painter, considered the orthogonal projections inadequate for the purpose of representation, while Sangallo, a good craftsman, must have immediately grasped the benefits of greater clarity and legibility." [Author's translation] Ibid.

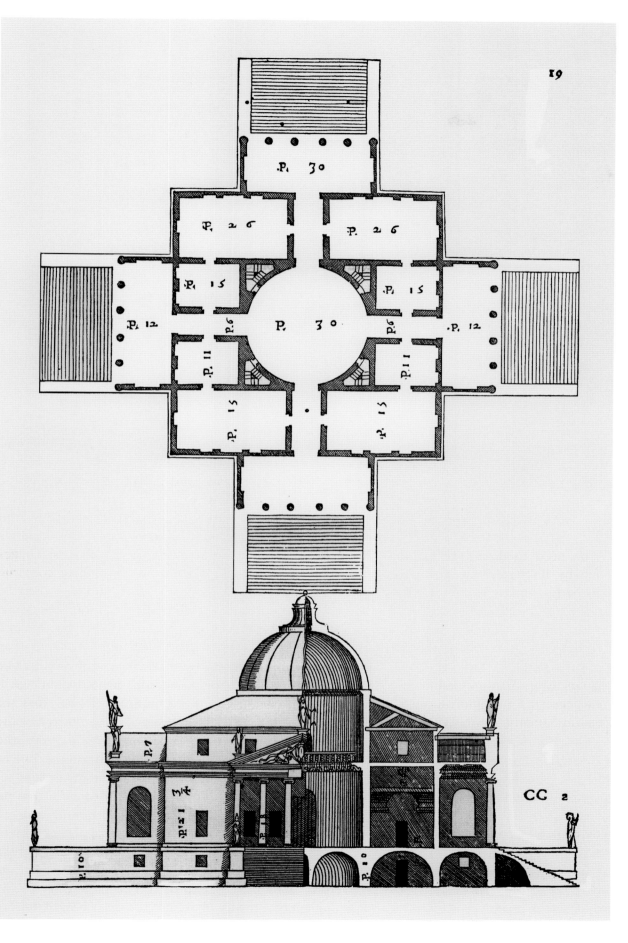

Andrea Palladio (1508–1580),
La Rotonda, 1570
From *I quattro libri dell'architettura*
(Libro Secondo),
Venice (Italy)

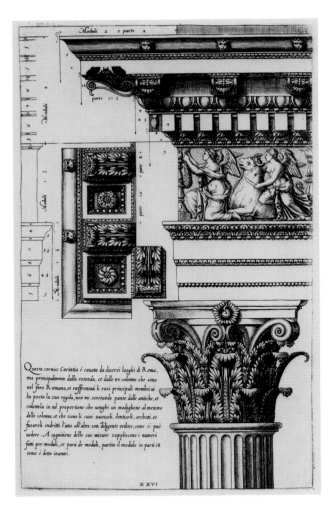

Jacopo Barozzi da Vignola (1507–1573),
Trabeazione e capitello di ordine corinzio, 1562
From *Regola delli cinque ordini dell'architettura*, tav. XXVI,
Rome (Italy)

Vincenzo Scamozzi (1552–1616),
Elementi decorativi di architettura di ordine dorico, 1615
From *L'idea dell'architettura universale*, Parte II, Libro VI,
Venice (Italy)

together the two portions of the building. The axial symmetry also ensures that the information contained in this type of drawing is comprehensive.

What we today call the theory of architecture owes its force to the Renaissance, entirely independently of the architecture itself: a set of theoretical concepts which acted as perfect models, a set of rules underlying a new idea of architecture that is not necessarily indebted to real buildings of the past.

One way to convey the theory of architecture, and one which owed much to the possibilities afforded by printing on paper and the new techniques of graphic representation, was the treatise, which made extensive use of the triad (plan, elevation and section), and which proved a powerful medium for the dissemination and study of the theory of architecture. We will see later some of the reasons behind the development of the treatise; for now it is important to note how the orthogonal triad became a shared set of rules: the techniques of engraving had changed and shaken off the uncertainties of the pseudo-perspective of the early Renaissance.

Taken together, these projective methods lend themselves perfectly to the description and control of the founding parameters of Renaissance architecture: *ordo, dispositio, symmetria, proportio* of the whole and its parts. The regular pattern of plan and type, the proportional pattern in elevation, and the proportional order need a precise system of representation; conversely, a codified system of representation allows the development of a theory of architecture based on that order.

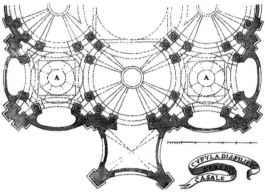

Guarino Guarini (1624–1683),
Chiesa di San Filippo Neri a Casale, 1737
From *Architettura Civile*, tav. XXV,
Turin (Italy)

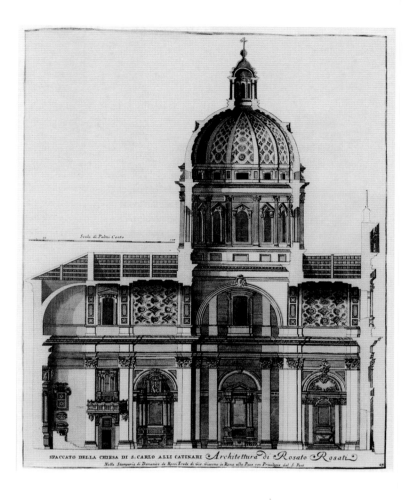

Domenico De Rossi (1659–1730),
Chiesa di San Carlo ai Catinari, 1721
From *Studio d'Architettura Civile*, III, fol. 23
Photo: Biblioteca Hertziana,
Rome (Italy)

The planimetric design, the description of architecture via orthogonal projection, and, if necessary, the "inside wall" are together capable of providing clear guidance for the configuration of architecture. Axonometric projection, perspective, mimetic simulations of space are not necessary: the specifications of the plan, and the signs of the "inside wall" are enough fully to describe a work of architecture without giving rise to misunderstanding or misinterpretation. Plan, section and elevation remained substantially unchanged during the Baroque and late-Baroque periods, as well as in treatises until the twentieth century, having been included in the Mongian code which is still widely in use today.

It could be the very power of the code of the orthogonal projection, reinforced by the work of Gaspard Monge, that allowed these elements to remain current until the early decades of the twentieth century: the concept of "façade", "front elevation" and "side elevation" as well as the permanence of the architectural orders.

Giuseppe Damiani Almeyda (1834–1911),
*Progetto per il teatro Massimo di Palermo,
prospetto principale*, 1874
Archivio Damiani, Palermo (Italy)
Photo: Fabrizio Avella, post-processing:
Fabrizio Avella, Giuseppe Dalli Cardillo

Gran Caffè
Particolare del Padiglione centrale

Giuseppe Damiani Almeyda (1834 – 1911),
Padiglione centrale del Gran Caffé, prospetto, 1890
From *Istituzioni Architettoniche*,
Archivio Damiani, Palermo (Italy)

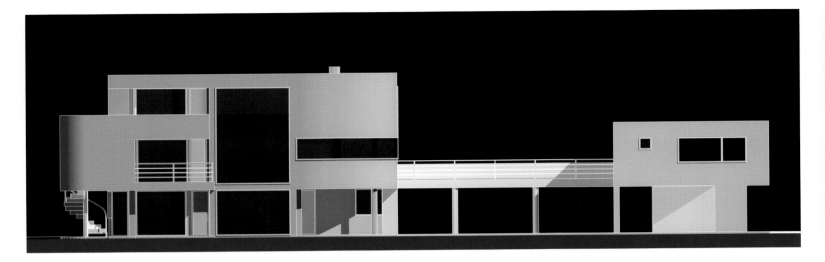

Bernardo Agnello,
Saltzman House by Richard Meier,
elevation, 2006

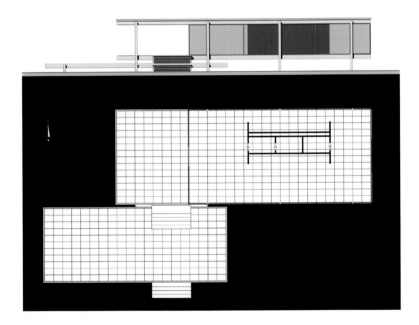

Fabrizio Avella,
Farnsworth House by Mies van der Rohe,
plan and elevation, 2006

The "drawing, the outside wall and the inside wall" is therefore also a form of thought. Even the concept of the modern movement, based as it is on orthogonal planes, has not weakened this position: Le Corbusier felt the need to include the free plan among his five points and to control the Modulor in the elevation; the plan and the elevation lend themselves both to "classicism" and to the proportional severity of Mies van der Rohe.

As to the influence of the system of projection on conceptualization in architecture, Vittorio Gregotti has this to say: "As a first rough approximation we can say that the systems of representation that we used are generally related to the structure of Euclidean space and its geometric representation for projections and sections, a system that has some significant limitations." [9]

The system of orthogonal projections, in fact, is able to represent architecture when it has certain characteristics: the façade of a Renaissance church is drawn on a plane parallel to the front, perpendicular to the main axis. The sections lie on vertical planes parallel to those of the elevations and any elevation belongs to planes which are all perpendicular to the plan. This system of projections reproduces (and inspires) features such as *axiality* and *perpendicularity* between axes and planes, referring to axes x, y, z, which are orthogonal to each other. These features, though within complex space systems, are still present in many examples of modern and contemporary architecture. The spatial, formal and volumetric complexity of the emblematic architecture of the twentieth century from Rietveld to Loos, from Mies to Meier is, however, to be considered as a highly structured system of orthogonal planes. As far as digital design is concerned, nothing new was introduced apart from a procedural point of view: the elevation is not a drawing to be attached to the plan, which generates the information needed for its construction, but is one of the infinite elaborations that can be drawn from a three-dimensional model. It is a two-dimensional set of three-dimensional information. It can be realized as an autonomous two-dimensional model, but the tendency is to cut it from a three-dimensional model and submit it to a subsequent post-processing, where information can be added, such as dimensions, notations or other technical data.

9   V. Gregotti, *I materiali dell'architettura*, Feltrinelli, Milan (Italy), 1966, pp. 28–29.
[Author's translation]

Perspective

Anyone wishing to discover the genesis of perspective can draw on essays of unsurpassed virtuosity: from the now "classic" essay by Erwin Panofsky *Perspective as Symbolic Form*,[1] to the most recent work by Martin Kemp, *The Science of Art*,[2] to Henry Millon and Vittorio Lampugnani Magnago's, *Rinascimento da Brunelleschi a Michelangelo. La rappresentazione dell'architettura*,[3] to name only the most famous. Beyond the various approaches of the works cited and of other essays on the subject, it seems that today we can agree on some points. First of all, as we have seen for orthogonal projections, the perspective as we know it is the result of a long process of codification, which received a strong impetus in the early fifteenth century. This is not to say that it did not exist earlier: Panofsky points out that every era had its own perspective, a system to represent the depth of space. From the vertical axis perspective with "fish bone" vanishing point perspective, to the mere juxtaposition of an array of Byzantine plans, sufficient to understand what is "in front" and what "behind", each era chose its own way of representing space. Even masters of painting such as Giotto and Lorenzetti had begun to explore different ways of representing the volume and placement of figures in the depths of space to overcome the long-standing problem of the representation of the n dimensions of phenomenal reality on the two-dimensional surface to be painted. Interest in perspective was very strong in both the pictorial and architectural fields and the two areas overlapped in the fifteenth century, losing their disciplinary boundaries: it is not clear whether the perspective was borrowed from pictorial studies or if painting absorbed a method developed to draw a rational space like that of the Renaissance. Early studies on the definition of a method can be seen in the work of one architect, Filippo Brunelleschi, who in 1413 drew on a board the famous Baptistery of Florence; Leon Battista Alberti wrote about perspective in his *De Pictura* of 1436, to emphasize the fact that perspective does not belong solely to architectural design. The ideal city of Baltimora is dated after 1470, but it is hard to know whether it is a framework or an architectural representation. *De prospectiva pingendi* by Piero della Francesca was produced in 1482 during his stay in Rimini and after

1 Erwin Panofsky, *La prospettiva come forma simbolica*, Feltrinelli, Milan (Italy), 1995, [original title: *Die Perspektive als "symbolische Form"*, Leipzig – Berlin 1927] I ed. it. Milan (Italy) 1961.

2 Martin Kemp, *La scienza dell'arte, Prospettiva e percezione visiva da Brunelleschi a Seurat*, Gruppo Editoriale Giunti, Florence (Italy), 1994 [original title: *The Science of Art: Optical Themes in Western Art from Brunelleschi to Seurat*, Yale University Press, London and New Haven 1990].

3 Henry Millon, Vittorio Magnago Lampugnani (ed.), *Rinascimento da Brunelleschi a Michelangelo. La rappresentazione dell'architettura*, Bompiani, Milan (Italy), 1994.

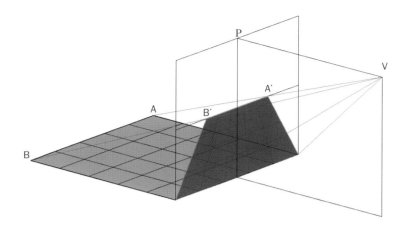

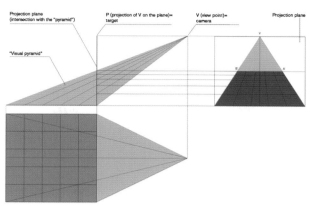

Fabrizio Avella, *Construction of a perspective*
(axonometric diagram)

Fabrizio Avella, *Perspective construction according to
the method of Leon Battista Alberti*

completion of his major paintings, which are often framed in architectural spaces, and, in the same year, the presence of Donato Bramante in Milan is documented for the construction of the choir of Santa Maria in San Satiro, which thanks to the use of perspective was able to simulate a depth similar to that of the transepts, deceptively expanding a relatively small space.

One could go on but it suffices to highlight the following: the *perspectiva artificialis*[4] focuses on the positioning of a point of view from a measurable distance, coinciding with the eye of the observer, from which the visual rays start and, when intersected by a plane, give life to the representation of perspective. Point of view (V), projected perpendicular to the framework, determines the position of principal point (P), i.e. the vanishing point of lines perpendicular to the plane. Studies by Brunelleschi, the method of L.B. Alberti ("Intersection of the visual pyramid"), the experiments of Albrecht Dürer, the optical chamber of Canaletto, all are based on the same concept: given a centre of projection, the image of infinite points in space can be determined if, interposing a plane between this centre and objects in space, it is possible to draw (on the plane) the intersection between the plane and the "pyramid" of visual rays. To reassure the supporters of innovation: the concept is identical to that encoded in the algorithms underlying the perspective view in a CAD program: the centre of projection, or point of view, coincides with the camera, its projection on the plane coincides with the target. The perspective which is created with a CAD program perfectly follows the rules codified by Brunelleschi and Alberti. This can be verified by drawing a regular pattern and obtaining its perspective according to the Albertian method of intersection of the visual pyramid: the viewpoint is positioned at V and its projection on a representation at P. According to Alberti's method, to obtain the perspective of a regular pattern made of squares it is sufficient to find the intersection of visual rays (red) with the perspective plane cutting the "pyramid" of visual rays convergent in the point of view (V). The frontal view of the framework shows that these intersections will come together as you move toward the horizon line. The intersection with the traces of straight lines perpendicular to the framework and, therefore, convergent at the "central" vanishing point, will result in the perspective. The perspective path shown in the figure will be extracted.

4 Thus defined to distinguish it from the *perspectiva naturalis*, which concerned the technique for rendering the depth of natural landscapes. Note in this regard Leonardo's theory that it is necessary to lighten the hills and decrease the saturation of colour as we move away from the representation framework.

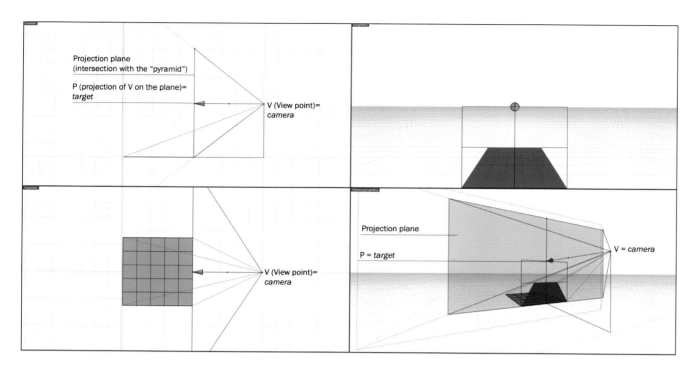

Fabrizio Avella, *Perspective construction according to the method of Leon Battista Alberti performed with a CAD software*

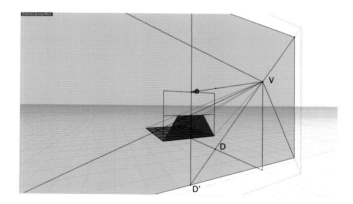

Fabrizio Avella, *Perspective scheme which extends the width of the visual field*

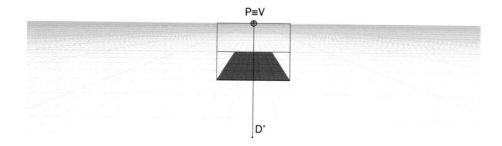

Fabrizio Avella, *Perspective of the previous scheme*

Essay > Fabrizio Avella

Albrecht Dürer (1471–1528),
Man Drawing a Lute, 1525
Bibliothèque Nationale de France,
Paris (France)

Albrecht Dürer (1471–1528),
Man Drawing a Reclining Woman, 1525
Bibliothèque Nationale de France,
Paris (France)

If a camera is placed in correspondence with the point of view and what in many programs is called the target is placed at the projection on the point of view, you can see how the two constructions coincide perfectly.

It should be noted, however, that if one extends the field of view of the plane of projection, marked in blue, over the ground line, on a monitor the perspective view will make the parts placed in front of the projection plane visible, resulting in distorted perspective or aberration. You can, for example, vertically extend the framework to include the projection of point D in front of the framework itself. The effect is shown in the figure, where D' is the projection of D at the bottom of the perspective view. Again, construction perspective follows all of the rules of descriptive geometry that continue to have importance and meaning.

However, even if the software applies an algorithm that would have pleased Brunelleschi, Alberti, Dürer and Monge, it is easy to find today perspectives with horrible aberrations which provide a distorted representation of space. This happens for one simple reason: the construction of perspective is made intuitively and without control. Let us momentarily reconsider the Renaissance perspective: in order to draw it, it is essential to have perfect control of the positioning of the view in the plan; the plane was often positioned vertically and it was always possible to determine the position of the point on the perspective from the

combination of planimetric and altimetric information.[5] A system of thought such as that of the Renaissance focused on the "central perspective", that is the perspective where the point of view, and hence the vanishing point, was centrally located in the composition. It was the human eye, placed at "the centre" of humanist thought.

5 Leaving aside for the time being the perspective construction achieved by means of optical rooms or other tools. For the use of auxiliary tools for mechanical construction, cf. Kemp, *The Science of Art*, op. cit.

Raffaello Sanzio (1483–1520),
Studio di prospettiva, date unknown
Galleria degli Uffizi,
Florence (Italy)

Fabrizio Avella,
Farnsworth House by Mies van der Rohe,
perspective, 2006

Denise Ippolito,
House N by Sou Fujimoto, 2008

The central perspective may also have the advantage of enhancing the asymmetry, as in the drawing of the Farnsworth House by Mies van der Rohe, where the glass window on the left side balances the right wall with the chimney. The centrality of perspective in this case also serves to highlight the spatial rhythm of the perspective through the use of the rigid pattern of tiles in the floor. It is probably no coincidence that the Renaissance principles of drawing describe the simple space of modern architecture as well, since both classical and modern architecture converge in the quest for simplicity. Contrastingly, the central and "centered" perspective in House N by Sou Fujimoto shows strong asymmetry of the architecture, albeit in a highly rational composition characterized by orthogonal planes.

Even if most of the Renaissance architects (and artists) started drawing a lot of perspective with a central vanishing point, they soon felt the need to break this symmetry.

In the same way, the "rule" of order was changed, broken and transformed by architects such as Palladio and Bramante,[6] even the centrality of the perfect design or iconic composition is called into question: the vanishing point can therefore be decentralized, as in Cigoli's perspectives, or be placed almost in line with the floor, as in Galli Bibiena's drawings; in some cases it even goes outside the sheet, which would

6 See the remains of the volute of the angular capitel at the cloister of Santa Maria della Pace, a solution that probably would have horrified Alberti.

hardly have been an acceptable solution for Leon Battista Alberti and Piero della Francesca.

The perspective is always "with one only vanishing point", but the image is cropped so as to decentralize the positioning. Perspectives made in this way give a sense of dynamic space, the eye runs towards the vanishing point and the weight of the image becomes unbalanced, a condition which was attractive to artists who were beginning to think about a new, non-static idea of space that would lead to Baroque and late Baroque compositions.

The decentralization of the vanishing point is a criterion that went on to be used until the twentieth century, where representation accentuated the longitudinal axis of the space, whatever the style or other architectural features. A new variable came into play: the rotation of the plane of projection. The world is changing its image. It is possible to maintain, perfectly undisturbed, already existing conditions, as long as the eye does not look over a wall, or at a compositional axis, but toward a corner, then something extraordinary happens: there are now two vansihing points, the space becomes faster, and the calm, reassuring symmetry of the Renaissance is overtaken by the complexity of space in the Baroque era.

If, then, architecture is conceived as a composition of volumes that do not necessarily follow rhythmic and axial compositions, if space is no longer marked by the constant

Ludovico Cardi, called Cigoli (1559–1613),
Prospettiva di un passaggio, date unknown
Galleria degli Uffizi,
Florence (Italy)

Hans Vredeman de Vries (1527–1609),
Hall with colonnades on two floors, c. 1560
Albertina Gallery,
Vienna (Austria)

Paul Landriani (1755–1839),
Ingresso ad una galleria con imponente scalone,
date unknown
Castello Sforzesco,
Milan (Italy)

Paul Landriani (1755–1839),
Interno monumentale con soffitto cassettonato,
date unknown
Castello Sforzesco,
Milan (Italy)

Ferdinando Galli Bibiena (1657–1743),
Prospettiva di un interno con passaggi multipli di arcate sorrette da pilastri a bugnato, date unknown
Accademia di San Luca,
Rome (Italy)

repetition of parallel planes, then looking in a corner is a good way to obtain a lot of information and capture the essence and articulation of those volumes. Although the concept of space had not yet been upset by the Modern Movement, the first decades of the twentieth century were undoubtedly fertile in generating new concepts of composition and volumetric space, thanks also to the accidental perspective which became the preferred method for three-dimensional representation until axonometric projection was invented. The factory at Purmerend, by Jacobus Johannes Pieter Oud, consists of simple volumes, perfectly rendered by using accidental perspective,[7] which was even successful in representing the *Fallingwater House* by Frank Lloyd Wright or *La Maison Spatiale* by Jean Gorin. This is not to posit a similarity between those architectures, but to highlight the effectiveness of this method for rendering them (even if they present different features). This method was also ideal for rendering the futuristic perspectives of Antonio Sant'Elia, Mario Chiattone and Tullio Crali, whose architectural visions yearned for buildings with complex volumes and the expressive power of the cultural revolution that spread across Europe during those years.

Chernikhov's choice of perspective shows without any doubt some similarities, at least with regard to the representation of utopia.

Just as rotating the framework of an azimuthal angle is enough to change the outcome of a perspective, rotating the framework on a vertical plane changes something again, the result is a sloping perspective, a device which is particularly suitable for drawing large vertical buildings.

7 It is worth remembering that the distinction between perspective with one or two vanishing points is simply the result of a nomenclature, which can, however, give rise to ambiguity: the perspective construction always follows the same laws, it is only the relationships between point of view, plane and objects that determine different perspectives.

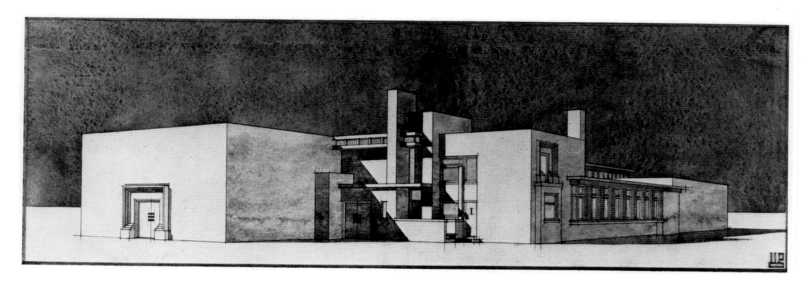

Jacobus Johannes Pieter Oud (1890–1963),
Factory at Purmerend, 1919
Nederlands Documentatiecentrum voor de Bouwkunst,
Amsterdam (the Netherlands)

Frank Lloyd Wright (1867–1959),
The House on a Waterfall – Fallingwater (*Kaufmann House*), 1935–37
Frank Lloyd Wright Foundation,
Taliesin, Wisconsin (USA)

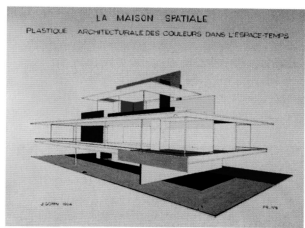

Jean Gorin (1899–1981),
La Maison Spatiale, 1964
Musée National d'Art Moderne – Centre Pompidou,
Paris (France)

Tullio Crali (1910–2000), *Palazzo delle scienze*, 1930
MART, Museo d'Arte Moderna e Contemporanea di
Trento e Rovereto,
Rovereto (Italy)

Antonio Sant'Elia (1888–1916), *La città nuova.
Casamento con ascensori esterni, galleria, passaggio
coperto, su tre piani stradali*, 1914
Museo Civico di Palazzo Volpi,
Como (Italy)

Mario Chiattone (1891–1957),
Construzioni per una metropoli moderna, 1914
Università di Pisa, Dipartimento di Storia dell'Arte,
Gabinetto di disegni e stampe,
Pisa (Italy)

Fabrizio Avella, *Tensione*, 2005

Page 37:
Yakov G. Chernikhov (1889–1951)
Composition No. 86
From *Architectural Fantasies: 101 Compositions*
Gouache on paper, 24,2 cm × 30,3 cm,
Collection Dmitry Y. Chernikhov (Russia)

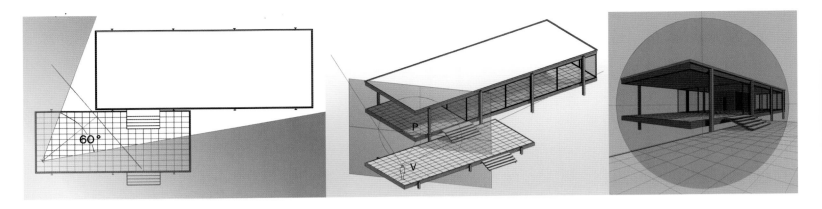

Fabrizio Avella,
Farnsworth House by Mies van der Rohe,
perspective studies, 2007

From these considerations it emerges that the perspective is not simply a mechanical operation aiming at a three-dimensional view on the plan, it is also – and perhaps above all – an expressive code. It is seen as the variation of the concept of space; it changes the settings of the perspective, the positioning of the main point, or the rotation of the perspective's plane. One wonders what has changed today in the perspective representation in digital drawing. Considering that the algorithm that handles the setting of the perspective with CAD programs follows a logic in line with the constructions of Alberti and Brunelleschi, one can't blame the loss in perspectival representation on these programmes. If fault is to be found in the programming, it is in the simulation of the photo, which, apart from having many things in common with the perspective, actually introduces parameters such as convexity of the lens outside the flat representation. That means that if we want to render the perspective of a three-dimensional model, we do not need directly to settle the position of the projection plane, its rotation or its inclination. Often the only operation required is the positioning of the camera (coinciding with the point of view or centre of projection) and a target (projection of the point of view on the plane), but in doing so the plane disappears from view. Alternatively, it is even easier to "orbit" around an object and change the setting from "parallel" to "prospective". Almost no CAD user

worries about how the perspective is created, and begins to flounder between the various zoom parameters, distance and pan until a view that comes close to that expected is obtained. The results are often disappointing. Among the most common are the distortion of the perspective and the inclination of the framework. Distortion happens when too extensive a portion of the visual field is included in the framework. Inclination of the framework often happens because, while fixing the camera, one does not see the plane itself (because most CAD software does not visualize it). Yet it is actually very simple to obtain a pleasant and controlled perspective.

We begin from the perspective's plane: CAD software, it is said, does not allow you to visualize the perspective's plane, which is essential for the manual construction. How do you solve the problem? Noting that the right vector joining the camera (the point of view, V) with the target (projection point of view on the framework, P) is none other than the main visual axis that, by definition, is perpendicular to the plane, we can determine the camera-target axis, i.e. the vector VP and indirectly but entirely accurately, the positioning of the plane. We must, however, decide what portion of the model we want to render. According to an empirical rule for manual construction, we should draw the portion of the object that is included in the dihedral angle whose apex is the centre of projection. This angle, about 60°, is defined as an

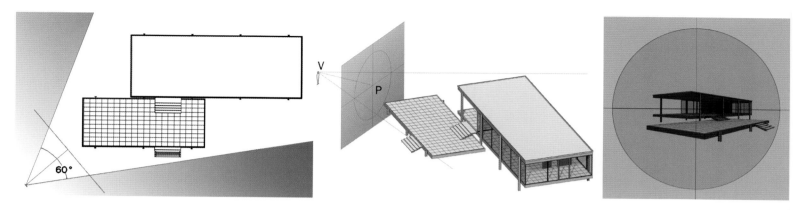

Fabrizio Avella,
Farnsworth House by Mies van der Rohe,
perspective studies, 2007

optical cone: on the inside, the peripheral distortions doesn't cause distortion in the perspective view.[8] As you move away, the perspective suffers distortions which become, at times, unbearable to the eye. The succession of figures that render some perspectives of *Farnsworth House* by Mies van der Rohe allows us to observe how, to increase the visible portion and avoid peripheral distortion, we just need to apply a simple trick: move the projection centre (the view point) away from the model, while keeping the camera-target distance unchanged. This will avoid the damaging effects of the zoom function, which often automatically changes the distance of the point of view from the plane, so increasing the visible portion, but also including those portions which present peripheral distortion.

The same considerations apply to the plane inclination. If the inclination of the plane can be useful, for example, when rendering a skyscraper seen from below, the same will probably not be true for rendering a horizontal building. The perspectives with vertical plane, easier to draw by hand than the ones with tilted plane, are, paradoxically, less immediate in CAD software, because it is not easy to control the positioning. It is true that in reality our visual axis is rarely perfectly horizontal, but the charm of perspectives with vertical plane is perhaps due to the abstraction of this particular condition. As we noted, the perspectives of Sant'Elia, Chiattone and Chernikhov, whilst their buildings are drawn with vertical development, are not drawn with tilted plane. Moreover, the perspective with vertical plane respects a very strong natural condition: the perpendicularity of the axis of the human body to the earth, resulting in visual horizontality. It is, therefore, necessary to choose which effect you wish to obtain and, again, this can be done through the control of the camera-target: locating the two points in space on the same coordinate of the z-axis, the camera-target axis will be horizontal and, consequently, the drawing will be vertical. Tilting the axis tilts the drawing, too. Simple. What has failed in the common digital drawing is the need for a priori thinking that involves choices about "what" to see, "how" to see it, and "why" see it in one way rather than another.

8   This rule does not actually have a scientific basis, but is determined by experience and not intended as a rigid prescription. We can simply observe that the perspective which covers a visual field determined in this way has a pleasing visual effect, while those with a huge visual field present unpleasant distortions.

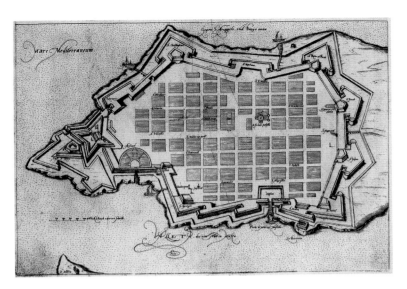

Daniel Speckle (1536–1589), *Valletta map*, 1589
From *Architectura von Vestungen*,
Tab. 15 before fol. 84 (ed. 1608),
Strasbourg (France)

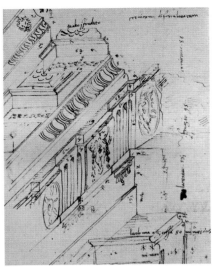

Antonio da Sangallo il Giovane (1484–1546),
Dettaglio di trabeazione, date unknown
Gabinetto delle stampe degli Uffizi,
Florence (Italy)

The axonometric projection

A brief history of axonometric projection requires us to recall the impact that the introduction of gunpowder had on military strategy in Europe, both in terms of attack and defence. The defensive strategy involved the need to redesign the system of city walls. An attack carried out with ladders and arrows could be effectively contained by high, relatively thin walls, but the advent of long-range artillery required a reconfiguration of the walls, which were transformed into low, wide embankments contained by thick, solid walls to absorb the pounding of artillery fire. The study of ballistics also provided some guidance on geometric trajectories, giving preference to bastions with sloping walls, which were very effective in diverting projectiles while simultaneously allowing the insertion of defensive positions. The form of the fortifications was complicated, the perimeters of fortified towns became jagged, geometrically they became triangular, hexagonal, pentagonal. In elevation drawings the walls had to be well designed: their profiles had to be tilted to contain the embankment and to absorb and deflect projectiles; and the study of the ditches and the distance between the outer and internal walls demanded attention too.

Thus the control parameters become numerous and complex and require new methods of representation. As in the case of religious architecture, the wooden model can perform this task perfectly, but presents certain difficulties as it is normally cumbersome and not always easy to transport.

One can try, then, to draw a complex object on a flat surface, like a model but without the distortions that occur in perspective. One can try to obtain a design that may include planimetric indications of the plan and altimetric ones of the profile.

If such a method existed it would have considerable advantages: it could completely control the planimetric form and model – how the walls would react to an offensive, how troops could move along the walls, and how the walls relate to the road layout and the city behind. One could also understand precisely what elevated forms should be used in order to minimize the risks. It is therefore a matter of putting together information about the plan with information about the profile.[1] Hence, what is called today – not by chance – military axonometric projection, originates where heights are shown in accurate proportions on

1 "Plans and profiles, generally distinct drawings, merge into a single representation, thus finding – as Lorini said – a graphical, projective and permanent trick, able to combine formal and metric reliability with a three-dimensional view of the object. [...] The resulting image is similar to a bird's eye view of a model on which it is possible to make measurements and ballistic simulations." [Author's translation] In Domenico Mediati, *L'occhio del mondo. Per una semiotica del punto di vista*, Rubettino Editore, Soveria Mannelli 2008, p. 133.

Giuliano da Sangallo (1445–1516),
Macchine per ingegneria, date unknown
Biblioteca Apostolica Vaticana,
Vatican City

a layout scheme lacking in angular and metric distortions.[2] Simple. Inspired. Effective.

It is likely, however, that axonometric projection had little success because, as already mentioned, the requirements of the Renaissance architect were perfectly satisfied by the orthogonal triad, the wooden model and perspective. The axonometric projection was unnecessary and, ultimately, useless; it added little to the design of architecture in its entirety for an eye used to the possibility of "real-time orbit" around the wooden model. The "3D view" was, in the Renaissance, entrusted to the wooden model for proper control of the scale dimension, and to the prospective for spatial simulation. The axonometric projection might have been suitable, at best, for the design of architectural detail and machines.

---

2   "Thus, the engineer or architect becomes a simple designer of architectural principles of organization dictated by the commander. The terrain of dialogue must be, therefore, common among the subjects involved in the project [...]. There is thus a need to find methods of representation that, with greater adherence to the forms of real space, provide reliable support for the decisions of princes, troops and gunners." [Author's translation] Ibid.

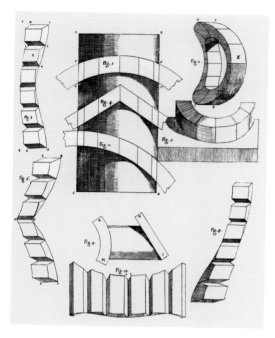

Guarino Guarini (1624–1683),
Scomposizione in conci di porzione cilindriche, 1737
From *Architettura Civile*, tab. XXXI,
Turin (Italy)

When, however, the architect becomes a military planner, an adequate system of representation is developed. Remember too that in the sixteenth century Italy was the scene of continuous fighting between European powers, fragmented into many political entities involved in a frenzied game of alliances, betrayals, campaigns and counter-attacks: a perfect laboratory for the development of increasingly sophisticated defensive architecture and rapid and effective ways of designing it.

To see the axonometric projection enter into the design of civil and religious architecture, one needs to wait until the seventeenth century. For the Baroque architect it is no longer sufficient to determine the type, the architectural system and order, he is no longer content with the Platonic solid approach, but feels the need to intersect, overlap, and warp simple forms in search of complex spaces.

But the workmen are unprepared; the architects stress their ability to build the project: if it is true that the plan, elevation and perspective still work well for describing general information, architectural order and spatial effect in the Baroque, it is also true that any one of those techniques was sufficient to describe the way to cut the stones and how to put them together to obtain the complex three-dimensional forms of the Baroque building.

Once again a graphic method is needed to solve new and complex problems. Once again architects need to match the information coming from the plan with that resulting from the elevations; they need to understand how to position a form with precision without running the risk of juxtaposing pieces with faces that do not match. The architect must be able to tell the craftsman exactly how to carve the stone in a way the craftsman can understand. But before reaching this stage, the architect must be able to very accurately conceptualize the shape of the individual stone and its positioning in the determination of the overall shape.

Today we call this science *stone carving*, and it can be said that in the post-Renaissance era it introduced the use of axonometric projection to the graphic language of the architect even in a non-military context, contributing to disciplines that converge in this respect in what we now call descriptive geometry.

Architectural treatises are enriched by this form of representation and it becomes customary to insert tables explaining how to obtain the intersection of curved, spherical and conical surfaces and everything else necessary to turn into stone the fervent imaginations of Baroque and late Baroque architects. The axonometric projection, sometimes shaded, now carried equal weight with the plans and prospect views, but only to elucidate the technical and constructive aspects. Until the nineteenth century axonometric projection remains, however, an effective way to represent the components of architecture, of construction and the geometry of portions of buildings, but not yet architecture in its entirety. It is the method Auguste Choisy used, as decribed in the tables of his famous *L'art de bâtir chez les Romains* and *L'art de bâtir chez les Byzantins* and Jean-Baptiste Rondelet in his *Traité théorique et pratique de l'art de bâtir*.

In architectural design, the capacity of axonometric projection to describe the components and volumetric relations of an object is a feature that meets the needs of a burgeoning reality in the nineteenth century: that of industrial production. A machine cannot be designed by drawing a perspective (because of its misleading visuals) and must be represented with total accuracy in all its components, to show how these should be assembled as well as indicating what the machine should look like once assembled.[3] The technical drawing becomes an instrument of thought and control, an essential component of the production process, functional to the precision requirements of mechanized production.[4] Since then the axonometric projection design associated with the planning and performance of industrial products has been continuously applied. Even today kits for model building and the explanations for the assembly of kits, toys and electrical components are drawn in axonometric projection.

The moment the axonometric projection moves from a military to a civilian context, it loses its ability to control the design and becomes a code of expression for drawing components, parts, whether these are made out of stone, wood, steel or cast iron.

To see the axonometric projection become a method of representation capable of describing the entire architectural complex (and not just one part of it) one must wait until for the conceptualization to be assailed by the profound transformation, ushered in by a world war that destroys the architectural status quo so that concepts such as architectural order, rhythm of a façade, and decorative motifs are swept away by the irrepressible force of Futurism, Cubism, and the Modern Movement.

3 "A house whose walls are not perfectly parallel, and that do not conform to the project, is not less habitable. For the world of machine these inaccuracies are almost always fatal. A distortion of only a few tenths of a millimeter is sufficient to annul a rotational motion while even a microscopic defect in the construction of a cannon can cause it to explode. It is therefore no coincidence that the kind of representation that in 1852 M.H. Meyer called for the first time axonometric projection, has its origin in the mechanical world." [Author's translation] In M. Scolari, *Aforismi e considerazioni sul disegno*, in Rassegna (Rappresentazioni), Year IV, No. 9 March 1982, Bologna (Italy), p. 79.

4 "Nor are we surprised to see that, when William Farish in 1820 inaugurated the studies about axonometric projection (On isometrical Perspective), the first speaker and the addressee is not the world of architecture but that of the machine." Ibid.

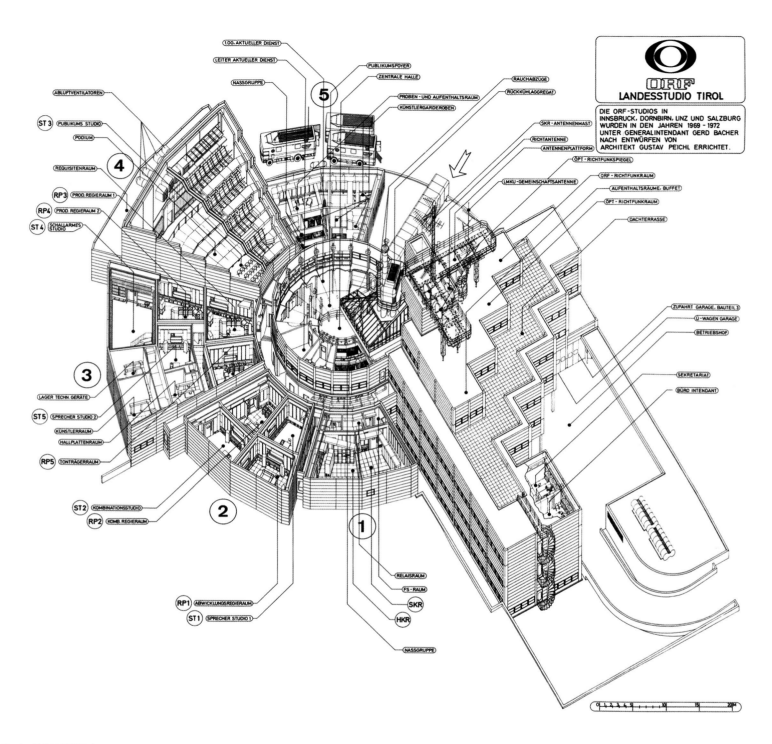

LEITER AKTUELLER DIENST
1.OG. AKTUELLER DIENST
NASSGRUPPE
PUBLIKUMSFOYER
ZENTRALE HALLE
PROBEN - UND AUFENTHALTSRAUM
KÜNSTLERGARDEROBEN
RAUCHABZÜGE
RÜCKKÜHLAGGREGAT
ABLUFTVENTILATOREN
SKR - ANTENNENMAST
RICHTANTENNE
ANTENNENPLATTFORM
ÖPT - RICHTFUNKSPIEGEL
ORF - RICHTFUNKRAUM
LMKU - GEMEINSCHAFTSANTENNE
AUFENTHALTSRÄUME, BUFFET
ÖPT - RICHTFUNKRAUM
DACHTERRASSE
ST 3 PUBLIKUMS STUDIO
PODIUM
REQUISITENRAUM
RP3 PROD. REGIERAUM 1
RP4 PROD. REGIERAUM 2
ST 4 SCHALLARMES STUDIO
ZUFAHRT GARAGE, BAUTEIL 3
Ü - WAGEN GARAGE
BETRIEBSHOF
SEKRETARIAT
BÜRO INTENDANT
LAGER TECHN. GERÄTE
ST 5 SPRECHER STUDIO 2
KÜNSTLERRAUM
HALLPLATTENRAUM
RP5 TONTRÄGERRAUM
ST2 KOMBINATIONSSTUDIO
RP2 KOMB. REGIERAUM
RELAISRAUM
FS - RAUM
SKR
HKR
RP1 ABWICKLUNGSREGIERAUM
ST1 SPRECHER STUDIO 1
NASSGRUPPE

ORF
LANDESSTUDIO TIROL

DIE ORF-STUDIOS IN INNSBRUCK, DORNBIRN, LINZ UND SALZBURG WURDEN IN DEN JAHREN 1969 - 1972 UNTER GENERALINTENDANT GERD BACHER NACH ENTWÜRFEN VON ARCHITEKT GUSTAV PEICHL ERRICHTET.

Gustav Peichl (1928–),
ORF regional studio Tyrol, 1969
Innsbruck (Austria)

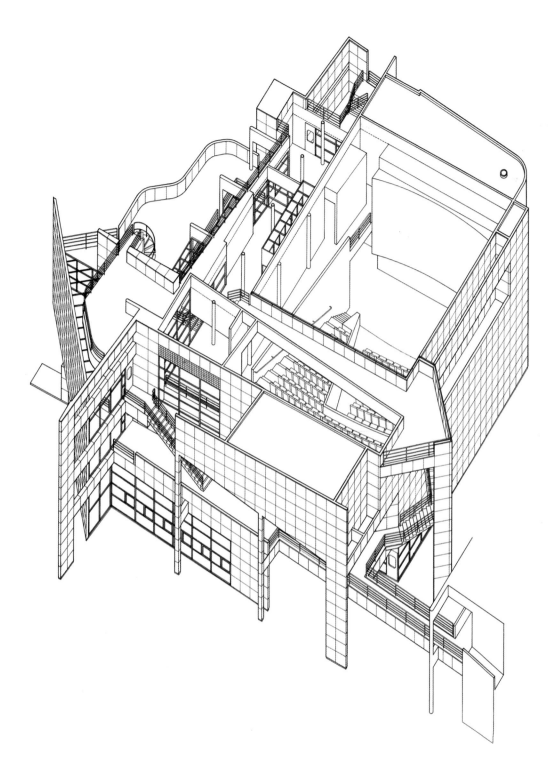

Richard Meier (1934–) and Partners,
The Atheneum, 1976
New Harmony, Indiana (USA)

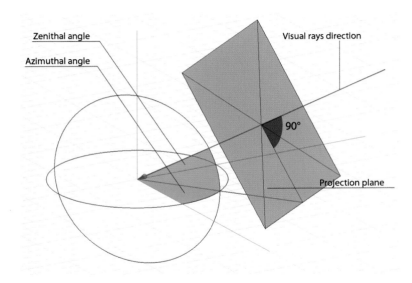

Fabrizio Avella,
Projective conditions of orthogonal axonometric projection with CAD software

Everything is called into question politically: democracy, economic growth, the visual arts, literature.

The point of view and perspective disappear from painting. Pictorial space is no longer measurable. Architectural order is banished: it is not appropriate in a world that seems to reject the order of things. It seems, moreover, that after fanciful interpretations made by architects and imitators from the Renaissance onwards, architectural order no longer seemed to serve any purpose.

The beginning of the twentieth century offered fertile ground for the displacing of axonometric projection from the design of machines to that of architecture. This occurred for several reasons: in the Modern Movement, architecture is considered a "living machine". If I have to draw a car, I need a method already successfully tested in the design of machines. Modern architecture rejects "style", order, decoration, façade,[5] in favour of a concept of space and form that tends to trap, intersect and split simple volumes, collecting the pieces in new compositions and re-assembling them, preferably on plans and Cartesian systems.[6] The axonometric projection is perfect: a machine is designed with no decorative frills, which are now considered superfluous, it decomposes the elements, provides the cold lucidity of mechanics, and allows the composition of pieces to be observed with detachment. Again, a perfect union between method of representation and thought. The method has been passed down to us and is included among those available to design technique. But we need to clarify precisely what type of axonometric projection we mean. While the axonometric construction drawn by hand may vary between oblique and orthogonal axonometric projection, almost all programs for digital design will use orthogonal axonometric projection. The reason is simple: the algorithm that manages orthogonal projection is also perfectly applicable to axonometric projection in the sense that the calculation for drawing an object on the projection plane depends on the relationship between projecting rays and plane, not between framework and object position. It is totally irrelevant, therefore, whether the plane is perpendicular or oblique with respect to the face of an object;

5 "The supremacy of the façade, the unquestioned dominant architectural expression of the past, has finally been set aside thanks to a method of representation that does not propose a dominant point of view but prefers the control of stereometric definition rather than the decoration of façade [...] The axonometric projection will thus – according to the hypothesis supported by Bois and Reichlin – become a 'symbolic form' for the movements of the early twentieth century avant-garde, a sort of antagonist to perspective, the vehicle of a changed relationship between space and architecture." [Author's translation] Ibid., p. 170.

6 "There is no doubting the usefulness of an axonometric projection system of representation in the process of defining the architectural form. The dual function – metric definition and volumetric control – gives it a crucial role in different stages of design. In a cultural context such as modernism, in which the architectural language was dominated by stereometry, axonometric projection becomes the primary tool of expression for architects." [Author's translation] In Domenico Mediati, *L'occhio del mondo. Per una semiotica del punto di vista*, Rubbettino Editore, Soveria Mannelli, Catanzaro (Italy), 2008, op. cit., p. 165.

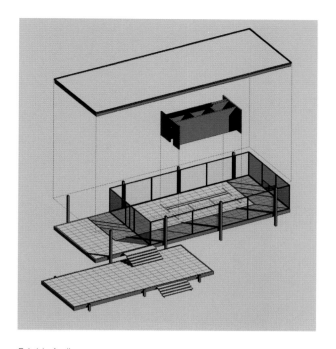

Fabrizio Avella,
Farnsworth House of Mies van der Rohe,
axonometric projection, 2006

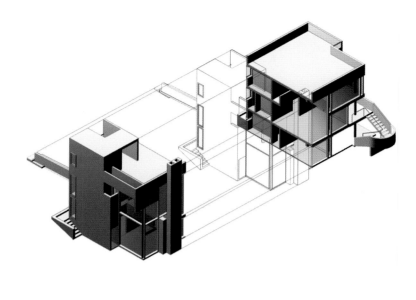

Bernardo Augello,
Smith House by Richard Meier,
axonometric projection, 2006

the planar orthogonal projection can simply be considered a special case of generic orthogonal projection. The mathematical relationship that determines the calculation of the reduction factors on the axes is a trigonometric function depending on the azimuthal and zenithal angles that define the visual axis and, consequently, the positioning of the plane. A projection in elevation, therefore, is fully described by the algorithm that handles this function, in which the direction of view axis is perpendicular to the plane in which the elevation lies. A plan is the result of a visual axis perpendicular to the horizontal plane. Nothing new. All you need is a basic knowledge of descriptive geometry to know that orthogonal projections and orthogonal axonometric projections have identical projective conditions.

The problem of "digital thinking" is that axonometric projection is not consciously chosen as a form of expression, but is only one of the ways that someone has predetermined for us to see an object in three dimensions.

What remains, however, is the ultimate usefulness of viewing an object from different points of view without undergoing the laborious axonometric construction that design by hand entails.

Paper

This brief and necessarily incomplete overview of methods of representation cannot end without considering what is a determining factor for the history of drawing: the introduction of paper into Europe. The fact is anything but minor and involves not merely a technical change in habits: the implications are indeed far-reaching.

It was mentioned how on medieval building sites ephemeral media were used for the preparation of construction drawings where the drawing was used to explain a specific detail or part of the building, and was no longer needed once what it signified had been completed. It is hardly surprising that this approach paid little attention to projective accuracy, which was probably not considered necessary for providing effective and qualitative information.

Drawings that served not a functional purpose but for some reason had to preserve and pass on information, were executed on parchment, which was very expensive and required laborious preparation.[1] The introduction of paper in the fourteenth century did not immediately undermine the use of parchment due to its initial high cost and because, as always,

---

1 "Before the arrival of what is destined to become the medium par excellence of every kind and class of drawings, for those works intended to last, artists had available only parchment, a material which required long and laborious processes of manufacture." [Author's translation] In Anna Maria Petrioli Tofani, 'I materiali e le tecniche', in AA. VV. *Il disegno, forme, tecniche, significati*, Amilcare Pizzi Editore, Milan (Italy) 1991, p. 191.

new techniques and new habits need time before they supersede those already tried and tested. The practice of using appropriately prepared wooden tables for inscribing with a metal stylus was still widespread among artists in the fifteenth century. In 1437, Cennini Cennino described in detail the preparation of wooden tables on which lay a mixture of crushed animal bones, which were first incinerated in a furnace and then mixed with saliva and smoothed to provide a surface which could be marked using a metal stylus. Once a drawing was finished with, the table could be used again by removing the substrate and spreading out a new one. Paper has, however, significant advantages and by the mid-fifteenth century papyrus was already being used, if almost exclusively for special occasions.[2] Having a medium on which to execute a drawing that can continue to exist even after it has performed its function means that the same drawing may become the subject of study by others as well as the executer. Having paper means being able to draw from the monuments of antiquity, which was an essential component of architecture education during the Renaissance. The increasing availability of paper, and at a more reasonable price, facilitated the development of project proposals and of coding architectural orders. These conditions meant that architects began to use architectural drawing not only when building something new, but also as part of their education, for studying existing architecture, giving rise to the discipline that today we call architectural surveying, and to conceptualization of the design process.[3]

Paper makes a unique contribution to the theory of the birth of architecture, a study unthinkable without the help of the drawing; and probably you can now appreciate how the discipline of drawing does not necessarily require the creation of a painting, a fresco, a statue, or a building.[4]

Now think about another aspect: it was seen that both medieval construction site and preparatory techniques for painting required to trace signs on a surface, bounded or not, that was actually flat. The use of paper lying on a table does not call into question this consolidated habit: it continues to provide a flat surface to draw. Likewise painting on canvas should be considered as a form of drawing on a flat surface.

2   "The decline of parchment can be said to begin at the end of the fourteenth century, and within fifty years it had been supplanted by paper in virtually every sector of use." [Author's translation] Ibid., p. 193.

3   "When you look at it in general in historical perspective, we see that the spread of drawing as an artistic process becomes common in the European area only after the middle of the fifteenth century [...]. I believe that it is no exaggeration to say that the availability of this or that type of medium, and especially the introduction and vicissitudes of paper and its diffusion on the European continent, have played a vital role of conceptualization, as we have seen." [Author's translation] Ibidem, p. 191.

4   "It is only with the arrival of paper from the East [...] that drawing can be said to enter the stage of history." [Author's translation] Ibid., p. 198.

Perhaps these aspects, together with other considerations of conceptual levels, prompted fifteenth-century designers to try to codify the drawings on the plane. Perhaps, these were the reasons that led to the codification of what we know today as flat projection methods. Perhaps this mental practice has as its logical corollary of Cartesian space. Perhaps.

Paper certainly plays an important role in the growth of the discipline of architectural drawing and in the encoding of methods of representation. Paper goes down in price. In addition to the historic mills of Fabriano, other paper mills are set up. The techniques optimize the process. People realize that in addition to executing the drawing, you can also reproduce drawings, not only by means of a copy, but also through techniques that allow several copies to be obtained using a matrix. At the beginning of the fifteenth century Johannes Gensfleisch (better known as Gutenberg) develops printing techniques. Now text can be reproduced without the hard work of copyist scribes. Paper grows ever cheaper, methods of representation begin their arduous path to codification, the techniques of reproduction such as woodcut and *intaglio* allow a number of copies of a drawing etched with a stylus into a slab of wood or copper to be reproduced on paper, the study of classical architecture teaches that orders are categories to be interpreted: here are all the ingredients for a potentially explosive mixture.

It is the birth of the treatise: architecture is studied not only through the observation of classical monuments, but also through books, from the pages of treatises containing various "modern" interpretations. Architectural drawing in the Renaissance is not confined to building, but becomes an instrument of knowledge and interpretation of architectural thinking, a new language that needs shared coding, which provides rules to be respected as it becomes a page that can be accessed at a later date. Nor does its communication load end with the resolution of a construction problem, it goes still further. It cannot therefore afford the randomness of spoken language, it needs precise grammatical and syntactical rules. Such coding reached completion with the work of Gaspard Monge, who, while not having invented the methods of representation, certainly played an important role in their definition, classification and nomenclature. He imposed order on what had already happened, clearly defining the codes that are still in use today.

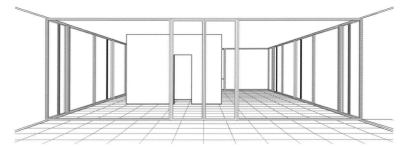

Fabrizio Avella,
Farnsworth House by Mies van der Rohe,
axonometric projection, 2006

Karl Friedrich Schinkel (1781–1841),
Hall of Neues Museum Berlin (Germany), c. 1828
From *Sammlung architectonischer Entwürfe,
enthaltend theils Werke, welche ausgeführt sind,
theils Gegenstände, deren Ausführung beabsichtigt
wurde*, ed. Karl Friedrich Schinkel, Berlin 1828,
Notebook 18, p. 103.

Techniques

Just as thought influences technique, so technique influences thought. The two chase each other along circular paths in which one becomes the offspring of the other. Coming to the end of these thoughts about drawing we must not neglect its technical realization, in its purely instrumental-material aspect and embracing of expressive technique, taking into account the semantic implications that the choice of a technique entails. Perhaps the most immediate way to draw is to leave a mark, a trace on a surface: with a piece of wood on wet sand, a finger on a fogged glass, a pencil on a sheet of paper.

In this case, the non figure has the same background as the figure: the barest outline serves to distinguish what is the form from what is the surrounding space, but the background is the same, the grain and the colour of the medium do not change.[1] For someone who draws, feeling the need to describe the plasticity of the object is not necessary, it suffices to give information about its shape and dimensions. The drawing is analytical, schematic, descriptive of crucial points but entirely disinterested in the plastic, volumetric or material.

It is the preferred technique of technical drawing, of executive drawing, little inclined to research chromatic character. The person in control, a designer, for example, transmits to the recipient (a builder, a workman, a carpenter, a blacksmith), simple and essential information to tell him where to build a wall, at what height and end to insert the frame, how to fit two pieces of wood, where and how to put a hole in a metal pillar.[2] At this stage it is not necessary to know that the wall will be plastered and painted red, that the wood will be teak or rosewood, or that the metal will undergo a process of satin chrome. In the drawing the focus is on the form as abstract concept, on the model as a reproduction of an idea, a concept, not necessarily reported or projected in the real world.

One of the aspects that require such a choice is related to the techniques used to create and reproduce the drawing. It is no coincidence that such an expressive criterion has been used, for example, for reproduction techniques that "hollow out" such as a woodcut, where the printing plate is carved in relief, leaving what will be the stroke of the drawing. The artist carves the part that will not be drawn, the "line" is obtained by subtraction of matter and it is therefore already very difficult to achieve an apparent

---

1   Of the symbolic role of the board, de Rubertis writes: "This calls into question just what is and will remain forever in history the mysterious charm of the line: to express forms through their margins, to allow us to guess the contents by describing the container, to neglect the object and focus attention on its limit." [Author's translation] In Roberto de Rubertis, *Il disegno dell'architettura*, Carocci, Rome (Italy), 2002 (I ed. Rome 1994), p. 32.

2   "In the Middle Ages and Renaissance architects showed their preference for the drawing made up of lines. The geometric graphic language lends itself to agile and encrypted communication between professionals engaged in the construction process." Ibid., p. 213.

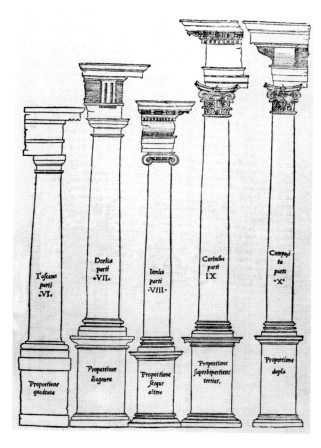

Sebastiano Serlio (1475–1554),
Ordini di colonne, 1619
From *Tutte l'opere d'architettura et prospettiva*,
book IV, p. III,
Venice (Italy)

James Stirling (1926–1992),
Derby City Centre, 1970
Drawing by Leon Krier

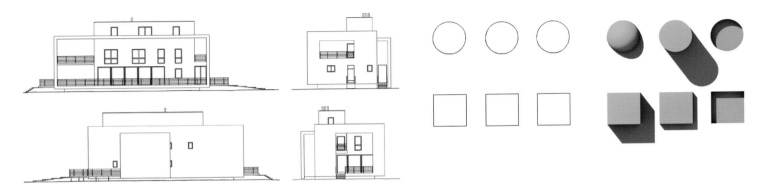

Carmela Volpe,
Mumelter (Taberhof) House by Werner Tscholl, 2006

Fabrizio Avella,
Study of shadows

contour drawing.[3] Adding information would only make the technique even more cumbersome and, in fact, Renaissance woodcuts in many treatises often represent drawings of architectural orders only in outline.[4] There are, in fact, woodcuts showing shadows that contravene this rule, as in the case of the treatise by Scamozzi, but it is easier to find images, as in the treatise by Serlio, that simply describe only an outline.

More recently the same result can be achieved by drawing on a sheet of glossy paper with China pens or ink pens, while in the digital environment you can use the "hidden" visualization technique which allows you to hide everything that is in the background relative to the positioning point of view – and therefore "hidden" to the eyes of the observer. The apparent contour drawing is restricted to distinguishing the limits of the object; it does not give any other information. You can then add the shadows, introducing into the architectural drawings techniques already used

in preparatory drawings for painting: charcoal drawing, white lead, and even blood become part of the lexicon as the architect provides an excellent introduction to a new parameter: shadow. By simulating the presence of a light source something changes: the volume is no longer just a form distinct from other forms and from the space in which it is immersed. It projects and casts shadows on itself, on another volume, on its support. Its edginess is manifested more clearly and becomes more recognizable than the soft roundness of the ball that it is next to. Moreover, even in spoken language we use the term "shed light on something" to intimate clear understanding of something hitherto obscure. But for the sake of clarity there need to be shadows to give us information.[5] The forms remain abstract but are no longer described only by straight or curved sections. Three squares and three circles on a white field: the shadows tell us that the first is a hemisphere, the second a cylinder, the third a hole, and the squares are the projection of two blocks of different heights and a hole in square form. The shadows tell us the roundness of the surface, the height of solids and the depth of the holes.

3 "The drawings of façades of Palladian buildings are pen on paper in order to accurately measure the relationship between architectural members as well as to offer the right level of schematization necessary for woodcut." [Author's translation] Ibidem.

4 "The woodcut illustrations found in the editions of Renaissance treatises were a particularly appropriate system for obtaining the desired images. The ideal was a universal harmony in architecture and the need for essential and simple images. [...] The technique of carving poses technical limits to the quality and quantity of the lines, preventing the transposition of the effects of shade and grain of the materials. The images so made present architectures without body, without colour, without material, they are scientific images, representations of ideas to support an idea." [Author's translation] Ibidem, p. 223.

5 The perceptual experience enables us to receive information stemming from the differences between the parts in shadow and the illuminated parts of an object: "We could not otherwise estimate, as humans, the distance that separates us from the objects if light did not illuminate them and project shadows, thus suggesting to us the idea of a three-dimensional perception." [Author's translation] In Agostino De Rosa, *Tutta la luce del mondo*, in *XY Dimensioni del disegno*, Rome (Italy), 2005, Volume 9, p. 63.

Shadows add a lot of information: what remains to be determined is how to represent them. To this end, it is useful to distinguish drawings that do not need to be reproduced from those which should be. If today, in fact, given available reproductive techniques, the distinction is negligible, in previous eras reproducibility became a parameter choice for technique and, consequently, graphic rendering suffered. The problem can be easily seen in the original editions of the treatises, in which the drawings were to be reproduced to complement and explain the text. The desired effect can be achieved thanks to the spread of "relief" techniques, including the *etching*, a technique used for the reproduction of images of the treatise by Vignola, which allow for a more subtle and dotted drawing. Unlike the woodcut, the drawing is reproduced using signs that actually will be inked, removing with a metal tip (hence the name, in some cases, "puntasecca") a thin layer of wax that covered the plate. Metal parts that were no longer protected by wax corroded when immersed in a mixture of water and nitric acid. After cleaning and inking, the paper surface was pressed to the plate. For this procedure, the lines can be made with very fine tips which results in a reduced thickness of the final mark. However, in the treatises drawings appear with their shadows achieved by means of a combination of parallel lines, sometimes overlapping and cross-hatched, which thicken in darker areas and thin out in the lighter ones. A similar effect, visible in the Perrault's table, was obtained by reproducing a matrix engraved on copper.

The problem does not exist when there is no need to reproduce the drawing; in this case you can use pen or Indian ink on paper and get the shading by using pencil, charcoal, watercolour or tempera. An example of this is the drawing by Ludovico Cardi (Cigoli), made with pen and brown ink with watercolour on white paper. The shadows can be homogeneous and their intensity obtained by varying the dilution of the colour. Shading is widely used in digital design to simulate the presence of light sources. The total absence of problems in the reproduction of shaded images means that not only are the shadows produced by homogeneous background hatching, but you can even achieve very good levels of shading simulation on curved surfaces with nuances that range from intense black to white, passing through a wide spectrum of grey.

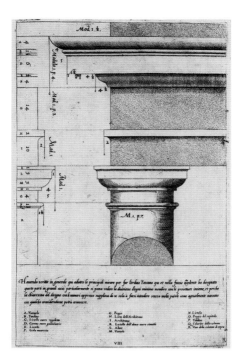

Jacopo Barozzi da Vignola (1507–1573),
Trabeazione e capitello di ordine toscano con
indicazione precisa del modulo, 1562
From *Regola delli cinque ordine d'architettura*, tav. VIII,
Rome (Italy)

Claude Perrault (1613–1688),
Base, capital and entablature and details
of ionic column, 1683
From *Ordonnance des cinq espèces de colonnes*
selon la méthode des anciens, tab. 4,
Paris (France)

Ludovico Cardi, called Cigoli (1559–1613),
Disegno per apparato effimero, date unknown
Galleria degli Uffizi,
Florence (Italy)

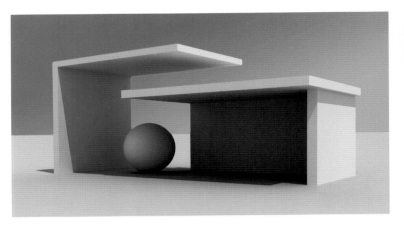

Giuseppe Dalli Cardillo,
Study of shadows, 2008

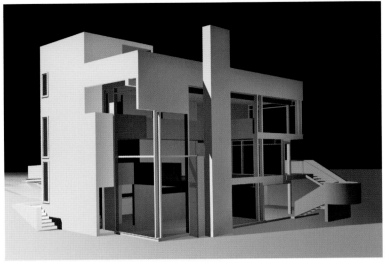

Bernardo Augello,
Smith House by Richard Meier,
shaded perspective, 2006

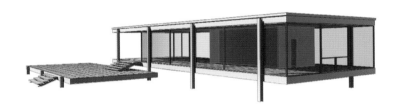

Fabrizio Avella,
Farnsworth House by Mies van der Rohe,
shaded perspective, 2006

The different rendering engines also allow the simulation of clear shade that simulates the sharp light of the sun on a beautiful day, or nuanced, as obtained from diffused light or from the interaction of light sources, and many more different reflections of light rays.[6]

6 The calculation of the shade net is obtained through the technique of ray tracing, and the nuances of shadows can be achieved by engines that work out the global illumination, which calculates not only the incidence effects of rays projected from the light source but also from their reflection on these surfaces, according to an algorithm that calculates the light absorbed and reflected.

But shadow might not be enough: colour might be needed. Where there are no problems with reproduction or where *chromo-lithographic* techniques permit, the design of architecture is enriched by the use of colour. The techniques employed, in some cases borrowed from painting, have been numerous, ranging from drawing to watercolour to tempera to coloured pencils. Watercolour is much favoured, as it allows various intensities of colour, more or less saturated depending on the amount of colour and dilution, and produces a good drawing on paper of appropriate

Giuseppe Damiani Almeyda (1834–1911),
*Project for the Teatro Massimo in Palermo,
front elevation*, detail, 1874
Archivio Damiani, Palermo (Italy)
Photo: Fabrizio Avella, post-processing:
Fabrizio Avella, Giuseppe Dalli Cardillo

Otto Wagner (1841–1918),
Villa Wagner, 1905
Historical Museum of the City of Vienna,
Vienna (Austria)

thickness; nor do any distortions occur, as they would with other types of paint. Tempera, used more rarely in architectural drawings, allows similar results, but with very diluted paint used very carefully. The *façade* of the competition project for the Teatro Massimo by Damiani Almeyda, from the second half of the eighteenth century, and the perspective of Wagner's villa, from the beginning of the twentieth, are two examples of successful drawing on watercolour paper.

Another technique that spread in the twentieth century was that of gouache, which allowed for the creation of uniform coloured surfaces and of shadows.[7] Like the techniques for watercolour and tempera, it could be used on drawings in pencil, pen or ink on paper or cardboard.

7 Gouache is a type of tempera made brighter by the addition of pigments such as chalk or white lead, and more dense by mixing with gum arabic.

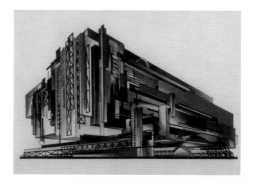

Yakov Chernikhov (1889–1951),
Hydroelectric power station, From *Fundamentals of
Modern Architecture*, tab. 149, 1931
Yakov Chernikhov International Foundation
Moscow (Russia)

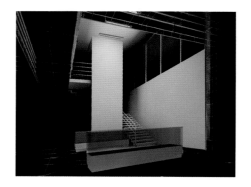

Fabrizio Avella, Guglielmo Acciaro,
Pepe Vasquez Reina,
Archaeological Museum of Corciano (Italy), 2002

Chromatic simulation has already been included in digital drawing simply by means of colouring volumes or surfaces which are transformed into polygonal surfaces by the rendering engine. The image of the museum at Corciano was obtained via insertion of light sources and colouration of the faces of the solids used for modelling. On the individual faces it is visible the effect of light rays that make the tone darker, and dark grey if the surface is entirely deprived of colour. The use of colour in manual drawing has opened the way for an additional level of information: material simulation. Just as colour can be used to obtain the shade of a wall, so it can be used to simulate the material aspects. Borrowing from painting, the nineteenth century architect surveyed the expressive possibilities of colour to produce not only differing degrees of brightness and colour saturation depending on how well it is illuminated, but also to simulate the characteristics of material surfaces. In this way they could capture the tones of textures of stone, wood, marble, decorated walls and even marble slabs for flooring, as in the splendid drawing of a burial chapel by Damiani Almeyda. Polychrome design became widely used after the archaeological excavations at Pompeii where the wonderful colours of the frescoes of the building became the model for much architecture of the nineteenth century. The technique also lends itself to the representation of highly ornamented architecture, as with the experiments of what today is called *Eclecticism*, but it was also effective for the design of Art Nouveau ornaments.

At the beginning of the nineteenth century, Alois Senefelder, who had already invented lithography in 1796, perfected the process and laid the foundations for *chromo lithography*, which allowed the reproduction of shades and nuances. Chromatic simulation falls therefore, within the limits of reproductive technology and colour can be achieved even

Cappella sepolerale di congregati
Prospetto principale e pianta

Giuseppe Damiani Almeyda (1834–1911),
Cappella sepolcrale, 1890
From *Istituzioni Architettoniche*, Archivio Damiani,
Palermo (Italy)

Anthony Saladino,
Chiesa di San Lorenzo in Trapani (Italy),
rendering by Mirco Cannella, 2007

when we know that it must be reproduced for educational or teaching purposes.

The colourful design suffers a setback with the advent of the Modern Movement, which bans, among other things, decoration and does not like the colour, preferring simple volumes, preferably white, or, at most, unplastered material or concrete. Such a simple architecture does not need to be drawn in colour. A contour drawing with, at most, a bit of shade is enough to show the volumetric composition. Today, the colourful and "mimetic" drawing has taken the place it deserves thanks to the introduction of techniques for rendering which, in addition to simulating the impact of rays of light, can simulate the material aspect via calculating engines. The rendering engine allows the simulation of material aspects, such as reflection, mirrored reflection, grain,[8] a matte or shiny appearance. Besides the technique allows for the simulation of textures,[9] so that you can faithfully reproduce patterns on materials such as wood or marble veins, the pattern of a wall of bricks, the irregularity of a wall of stone, etc.

Even an untrained eye can recognize, in the drawings, that in some cases the figure is more abstract, analytical, with a code that requires more interpretative skills on the part of the observer, while in other cases, the similarity with the perception is greater and the drawing is more mimetic.[10] Between mimesis and the symbol there may be different levels, and codes may overlap mimetic analogue codes. It may happen, for example, that an interior by Mies can be described by overlapping the design in black and white (perfect for the representation of modular scanning), with images of furniture and outside vegetation, whose realism, achieved through photographic superimposition emphasizes the transparency of glass surfaces. The shapes of people, cut from photographs and, therefore, operating as a mimetic code, may be incorporated into designs that deliberately have cartoon-like graphics: conversely, the photo of a panel, from the mimetic code, positioned on an interactive wall of a display module may co-exist with the black silhouettes of stylized human figures.

8 The grain, which is necessary to reveal aspects of materials such as concrete, plaster and rough surfaces, is obtained in relief through operations of bumping or displacement, in which a map of light or dark pixels is interpreted by associating to light colours the parts in relief and to dark colours the hollow parts. The reaction to light rays determines the illusion of shading holes and of increasing brightness of the parts in relief.

9 The texture is a raster image that is associated with one or more sides of a polygonal model.

10 On the notion of the iconic and mimesis in drawing please see Roberto de Rubertis, *Il disegno iconico*, in Roberto de Rubertis, op. cit.

Denise Ippolito,
Interior of a residence, 2007

Fabrizio Avella,
Farnsworth House by Mies van der Rohe, perspective, 2006

Angela Finocchiaro,
Housing, 2007

Giuseppe Dalli Cardillo,
Banca Popolare di Lodi (Italy) by Renzo Piano, perspective, 2006

Denise Ippolito,
Conference room, 2007

Giuseppe Dalli Cardillo,
Banca Popolare di Lodi (Italy) by Renzo Piano, perspective, 2006

Angela Finocchiaro,
Housing, 2007

Claudia Di Carlo, Giuseppe Trapani, Luca Viccica,
Modulo espositivo, 2008

Or perfectly simulated stone walls co-exist with trees that stand out against an unreal white sky.

The balance of possibilities may also serve to indicate a technique which is very far from accurate mimesis. The surfaces show strange striations, or hatches which are thickened where the light changes to shadow without any indication of the real materials or colours that will be perceived in that space.

Aldo Baldo, Giuseppe Dalli Cardillo,
Salvatore Mandracchia,
*Restoration of the Ospedale dei Bianchi in
Corleone (Italy)*, 2007

Ernesto Basile, *Palazzo per l'esposizione nazionale di arti e industrie in Palermo*, c. 1891
Archivio Basile, Università degli studi di Palermo,
Facoltá di architettura,
Palermo (Italy)

To conclude our exploration of the techniques of representation we will consider a symbolic drawing by Ernesto Basile: the elevation of the National Palace of Arts and Industries of Palermo, in which mimetic code and analogical code co-exist in the image almost perfectly. You can virtually see the different levels of attention paid by the architect to the study of the façade: from the geometric trace to the play of geometric projection of light decorative bands; from the penumbra of the voids to the chromatic valences determined by pigmentation or by different materials assumed for the columns or for the building's structure.

Permanence and variations in computer science design

In this essay I chose to address the complex problem of two-dimensional representation by distinguishing the representation methods from the techniques of construction. The two are not separable for the proper interpretation of an image, but the distinction may be useful to identify similarities and innovations in digital vis-à-vis manual drawing. With regard to the methods of representation, we have already seen how computer technologies for flat representation have not introduced any changes to the codes already known: a section of a modern building is conceptually similar to the section of St. Peter's by Antonio da Sangallo the Younger, just as a front elevation is obtained by algorithms that use identical projective parameters to those shown and used in the façade of the Rotonda di Palladio. In respect to axonometric projection, we have already seen what the limitations of digital drawing are; it does not allow, except in rare cases, the development of oblique axonometric projection. In fact, this limitation has a negligible impact on the draftsman: oblique axonometric projection had significant advantages during the construction phases as it allowed the entities to be kept in true shape and size, limiting dimensional changes to the oblique axes. It was easy, therefore, to build and control three-dimensional elements. If, however, it is possible to achieve orthogonal axonometric projection without undue effort, the loss of oblique axonometric projection seems to be a small price to pay. The problem of post-dimensional control, a user-friendly solution for the oblique axonometric projection where simple factors were used (1 : 2, 1 : 1), can be overcome through the many commands for distance analysis, angles, areas available in CAD programs. As for perspective, we have seen that it is easy to demonstrate that the algorithm for calculating the perspective is actually quite close to that of Brunelleschi and Alberti, and even to Monge. What has changed profoundly is the implementation procedure and the concept of the geometric model. In hand drawing, each drawing is a two-dimensional model of a multi-dimensional reality: a plan, an elevation, a perspective, are two-dimensional transpositions of a multi-dimensional object, drawn according to a shared code of descriptive geometry which today we call methods of representation. The use of different models that are related to one another forces you to think carefully about the method you are using, whether or not it is appropriate for expressing the meaning and describing the right information. We saw how historically this has resulted in a long and arduous path of choice of coding methods. We have also noted that the method was also associated with a particular mode of thought. To paraphrase Panofsky, the plan, the section, the orthogonal projections, the axonometric projection, the perspectives are all "symbolic forms". Even if you have only made a cube with a CAD program you will know that the process is reversed: it constructs a model in a virtually infinite space, from which infinite projections are derived. It is not necessary, therefore, to think too hard about which method of representation you are using. The important thing is to see the object. It is not uncommon to see talented modellers who manage to obtain models of even complex shapes that do not pose a problem if they are looking at the object in axonometric projection or perspective. Ironically, the ease of immediacy of visualisation has generated a digital split from the building of the model and its representation. A problem that is easily seen when teaching requires the teacher to get the students to understand that even if they make a perfect model, the exercise is not complete, they still have to "draw" it. In hand-drawing, construction and manual representation of the model are simultaneous. In computerized design they are not: building and monitor display coincide, but the representation is left to a stage where some control is lost. The process can be legitimate when it passes directly from a CAD model to a CAD or CNC implementation,[1] which does not need any drawing on paper and representation in a not too distant future, and will allow numerically controlled sites. Then

1 Computer Aided Manufacturing, Computer Numerical Control.

we could argue about the utility of disciplinary issues. Considering that, for various reasons, the static plan representation could be needed for a long time, it was necessary to come up with some reflections. For those who have experienced physical pain and strained their eyesight trying to build an axonometric projection or a perspective, the thought of having infinite points of view of a model in a matter of seconds is simply breathtaking. What is vital is to ensure that the representation of a digital model is created after the brain has been switched on – remembering that representing means choosing and so avoiding someone or something else (the program or the limits on its use) choosing for us. The positive aspects of digital design include the "revenge" of the perspective, thanks to its "ease" of execution. You look back at architecture "from below" and not just in axonometric projection (whose manual construction is more immediate), something which can only be good for a design in which man is "inside" architecture, not simply looking at his absurdly shaped shiny technological object from infinity.[2] The drive towards the prospect is also a desire for immersive viewing. Panofsky had already raised the issue of limitation of the perspective plan, and one might wonder whether the computer cannot refine the passing of this method. Projection systems on cylindrical surfaces are already on the market, and it is possible that these systems may become widely available in the near future. Nor should the possibility of spherical projection systems be ruled out. The impetus could come from the display systems for virtual simulation in military operations and for video games. Development has begun and it is already possible to find projectors or helmets with monoscopic or stereoscopic displays with viewing angles of 150°, a value near the horizontal view of our eyes. As for the techniques of representation, the reasoning to be done is between technique and thought: if I can paint colour, I can think of colours; if I want to make a white object, I choose to leave the colours in the tray. Thanks to rendering, the drawing goes back to being "in colour", and this is wonderful. Thanks to rendering the photorealism often becomes the end, and that is not necessarily so wonderful. One thing is certain: the concept of the model is changing and, therefore, the way it summarizes reality. The model is no longer a set of abstract geometric shapes that combine to reproduce an idea: Renaissance design and Alberti's wooden model were not concerned with providing additional information. They described the shape and that was already sufficient to give the necessary information. The authority, the Pope, the duke or lord, knew that implementation would involve the

2 This essay does not address the implications of digital design on the genesis of shape, as this is too broad a topic and unrelated to the immediate discussions. To understand the development of shape, I refer readers to the essay by Livio Sacchi, *Il digitale: un bilancio*, in "Ikhnos, Analisi grafica e storia della rappresentazione", Lombardi editore, Syracuse (Italy), 2008.

choice of stone, plaster, wood, paintings, frescoes to change that work into abstract spaces, floors, sometimes columns. There was no need to render.

Today, the wooden model is no longer enough. At the conclusion of a process that began with the eighteenth-century *vedutistica*, architectural design is enhanced by the pictorial meanings that horrified Alberti, but, inevitably, are irresistibly attractive. Today a customer, often far less educated in the arts than the Renaissance patron, is unable to interpret an abstract design. The culture of the image in which we are immersed has lost the commonsense capacity of abstraction, we must look to understand and we must see something that is as close as possible to reality. Manufacturers of video games began a race a long time ago to obtain the most realistic result; TVs now have a resolution that can be compared to a view through the microscope. No longer satisfied with seeing a football match, we must see the beads of sweat on the player, each individual hair and the tattoo printed on the shoulder when the player takes off his shirt, rejoicing after a goal. Even the animation industry has introduced, within a few years, increasingly sophisticated techniques aimed at realistic representation: we have all been fans of Nemo's father and we have forgiven Dori for her thoughtlessness; we hoped for the victory of the Incredibles, and we hoped that Scrat in "Ice Age: Dawn of the Dinosaurs" would finally get his acorn.

All this surrounded by beautiful scenery where the ocean depths, tropical forests and glaciers were presented with impeccable craftsmanship. So the speed of innovation that is occurring in Research and Development related to realism and virtual reality is normal and expected. The problem is that we are confusing media with the goal. The representation cannot do without symbolic codes and photorealism cannot be the ultimate goal. Hoping not to share the same fate as the protagonists of "Until the End of the World" by Wim Wenders,[3] we will soon be users of immersive visualization systems and display systems will diffuse to increase reality: we will be able to see a digital model overlapped perfectly with phenomenal reality through displays with semi-transparent lenses. The method is already widely used in industrial design, and is likely to expand rapidly to the visualization of architecture. In this way, our desire for realism will be satisfied and we will not be able to distinguish what really exists from what is the fruit of our imagination. Perhaps all this follows an atavistic impulse towards mimetic reproduction: efforts to obtain drawings in perspective, the techniques of reproduction, photography, first in black and white, then colour, Muybridge's attempts to reproduce motion, cartoons, the growth of video games from

---

3 One of the themes of the film by Wim Wenders, released in 1991, was testing a visor, intended to show pictures to a blind mother of the protagonist. Viewing virtual images progressively leads people to detach from reality.

aseptic white rectangles on a black background bouncing a rectangular white ball to football video-games that reproduce the appearance of real players, and moreover, deliver the pursuit of realism. It is truly extraordinary dealing with reproductions, not only visual, which can simulate reality. The historic success of Madame Tussaud's wax work museum in London is one of many confirmations that the concept of the faithful copy is fascinating to man. Perhaps it is a way of feeling capable of owning reality,[4] rather than being subjected to it: the higher the degree of "precision" with which I reproduce reality, the greater the illusion of control and possibly, too, the lower the sense of frustration I face when I realize that however sophisticated technologies become, reality is not reproducible.

But man needs symbol, abstraction. Perhaps this awareness of the introduction of new techniques will lead to new forms of abstraction. In fact, our need to create symbols to represent codes of non-immediate interpretation is equally powerful. None of the techniques mentioned affect the success of The Simpsons, or South Park, and we will continue to watch with pleasure the Pink Panther cartoons and Mickey Mouse.

It seems disappointing, then, that the digital representation is unable to resolve the dilemmas: mimesis or abstraction? Hyperrealism or new areas of expression? Icon or metaphor? Finally, if the model is no longer an immutable object but can become an information system that interacts with the user, surely I must be able to exert even greater control over its construction and its representation, be it analogic or iconic, symbolic or mimetic, static or dynamic. Whatever its result, I must know how to control, how to manage the model. The possibilities of digital representation are enormous and are influencing the way we interpret and represent reality, whether existing or potential. What does not change, and what we should always bear in mind, is that to draw – to represent – means to choose, to decide. Better do it with awareness.

---

4   Franco Rella said: "Men have traced lines, expressed words, have constructed codes and composed figures, to give meaning to what, at first sight, was as confused as a tangled and impenetrable forest." In Franco Rella, *Immagini e figure del pensiero*, in "Rassegna (Rappresentazioni)", Year IV, No. 9, March 1982, Editrice C.I.P.I.A., Bologna (Italy), p. 75.

Augusto Romano Burelli
Architectural drawing in the age of
digital reproduction

**The Disappearance of
the Original in the Age of Digital Reproduction**
Drawings: A. R. Burelli, 2005
*Techniques: Graphite, red pencil, red ink and blood on
Schoellershammer paper*

Computer assisted drawing is homogenized to other drawings, replicable by other authors, it can be infinitely manipu-
lated without us noticing. There is no longer an original to
use as a reference, nor a single author recognizable for his
mastery or graphical ability.

It is the triumph of the "varied copy", the "non-identical"
serial reproduction, a kind of "retouched" photographic
reproduction without the first shot; a technique that prom-
ises the freedom of the tools within the cold confines of the
digital technology. The "varied copy" is the radical break-
ing of the criterion of authenticity as "individual style".

Two "identical" exhibitions are now open in Venice and on
the Rhine: "Mors et Renovatio der Antike".

DAS TRIUMPH DER "VERÄNDERLICHEN KOPIE"

DIE ORIGINALZEICHNUNG
IST IM PROZESSOR ELEKTRONISCH AUFGELÖST .DIESER REPRODUZIERT SIE.
DIE ZEICHNUNG IST JETZT EINE FOTOGRAPHISCHE REPRODUKTION,"RETUSCHIERT,"
OHNE ERSTE AUFNAHME.
FEHLENDE AUTENTITÄT ALS STIL DES INDIVIDUUMS

ZWEI IDENTISCHE AUSSTELLUNGEN VON ZEICHNUNGEN FINDEN SIMULTAN IN VENEDIG UND AM RHEIN STATT:
« MORS ET RENOVATIO DER ANTIKE : DAS HEIDELBERGER SCHLOSS »

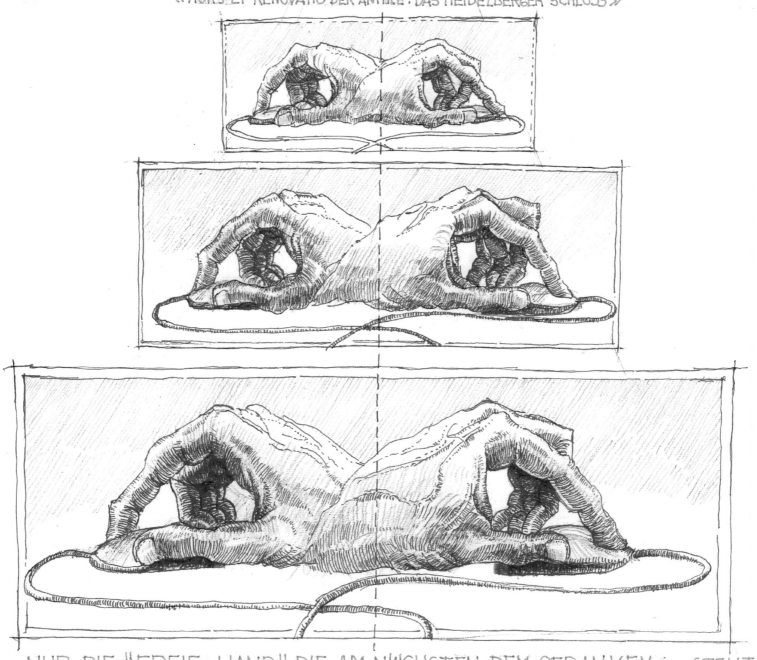

NUR DIE "FREIE HAND", DIE AM NÄCHSTEN DEM GEDANKEN STEHT,
KANN DIE ARCHITEKTEN RETTEN.

**J. S. Bach, in copying "Magnificat"
by Caldara, saved it: the original is gone.
Did he perhaps improve it?
Probably yes …**

Computer assisted design has broken into architecture in an unpredictable, noisy way. It has imperiously installed itself in the world of representation, changing the roles: the computer is now assisting the architect, not his design. In the name of liberation from the slavery of manual design, it has introduced another, more subtle, type of slavery, which concerns the architect closely.

The computer came to the architect as a tool for "absolute accuracy" in his work. This has led him to the "infinite detailing", which no longer allows uncertainty or procrastination in the name of accuracy to be achieved later. The conception, the parts and the details simultaneously knock at his door. The once slow, laborious process of configuring, making the constructive idea explicit has been brutally shortened.

Another minor trauma has affected design: the conceptual representation of an idea of architecture is no longer needed, people demand the "real" from the beginning of a project.

The speed with which electronic media can transform plans, sections, elevations into perspectives, where it is possible to change the point of view at will, is prodigious. Speed and precision have created a dependence on tools, which if on a higher spiritual level, is analogous to the medieval belief in witches. It is no accident that the "absolute devotion" expected from the computer turned into idolization in Eastern and Indian operators, who are not protected by Greek logos in the way we are.

The criticism of the intrusiveness of computers into the world of "form" is an abdication in the face of the challenge of the times, assert some fans of electronic representation. We must realize that the success of the media has been so persuasive and pervasive as to cause the total destruction of authenticity as "individual style", and the architect seems to have accepted that violence almost as liberating fact.

The phenomenon of infinite manipulation of the "form" is a corollary of the "question of technology" ("Die Frage nach der Technik") according to which the technique is no longer just a "medium", a tool which man uses for his own purposes.[1] "Technology has transformed man inwardly: the aims that he may achieve are already determined technically."[2] Electronic media, the father of absolute precision, came to architects in the most seductive way. It wants to persuade them with a paradox: "Only some of you will be able to use all my artifices and thus become artists: <u>everyone</u> come in to be part of this elite."

1 The famous conference on technique at the Bayerische Akademie der schönen Künste, Munich (Germany), held in the summer of 1953, was attended by Martin Heidegger, Friedrich Georg Jünger, Werner Heisenberg, Ernst Jünger and José Ortega y Gasset. Heidegger concluded his speech with a statement that brought him extended applause: "For questioning is the piety of thought." ("Denn das Fragen ist die Frömmigkeit des Denkens.")

2 Friedrich Georg Jünger: "… weil die Technik den Menschen bereits innerlich verwandelt hat, sind die Zwecke, die er sich setzen kann, bereits technisch determiniert."

In a seminar in Berlin fifteen years ago I supported the following thesis: "In the past, a bad architect drew his weak ideas poorly, now he conceives the same weak ideas, but he represents them in a sensational, or at least attractive way" and this fact gratifies him, satisfies him and prompts him to continue. It was a shock for many mediocre architects to find themselves artists at fifty! They thought they had become part of the promised elite, where a giant circle of incapable architects hold each others' hands, rescued by computer graphics. The situation is similar to that of intellectuals without much intellect, described by Hans-Georg Gadamer, as part of the great "smart circuit" of the Internet.

During the same period, however, the great German manufacturers of compasses and drawing boards and, above all, the prestigious Kuhlmann factory, which provided the precision needed for "freehand drawing", closed their doors for good.

The technique of electronic reproducibility has also disrupted the process of designing, developing and drafting the details of the architectural project. It has forced the architect to obey the keyboard, favouring a "perverse synecdoche". It appears subtly to suggest: "Give me the first part and I'll design the whole." It is a simple and quick process, which undermines the idea in its embryonic state, piercing it with its details. Right from its conception it is convenient to repeat a detail which already has been studied, to appease its electronic thirst for precision, detail that can be taken from a previous project, so that something blasphemous now adheres to the motto "God is in the details".[3]

I remember that in 1994 for the competition for the Museum Island in Berlin the architect Hans Kollhoff presented the façade of the Altes Museum by Schinkel with golden eagles aligned over the top of the cornice, replicated via the computer with absolute precision. I was impressed, just as I was struck by the accuracy of the capitals and cast iron railings. I thought back fondly to the efforts of the designer who in 1825 drew all those eagles with his pen, almost identical to one another as time slowly passed. I began to think that architecture had been afflicted by an infection of the media and that the only medicine for the architect against the epidemic was: to build!

The fact that the detail can be designed by isolating it on a computer screen without keeping your eye on the plan or the façade led me to suspect that the technique of electronic representation was seriously attacking the basic principle of architecture of Humanism, taken up by the Greeks, reaching us through Vitruvius, that the part is not separable from the whole: rather it must contain the DNA, the essential building blocks, of the whole.

3 "Der liebe Gott steckt im Detail": the motto is attributed to Mies van der Rohe but probably comes from the texts of St. Thomas Aquinas he had in his library.

What can't we do without?

At one time, students seeking admission to the Faculty of Architecture were only required to pass a drawing test – which proved an obstacle for Albert Speer and his friend Walters in their attempt to gain admission to the School in Berlin of Poelzig, Gropius and Mies. What test should we require of those seeking to enter modern schools of architecture? How can we rediscover that free-hand drawing is by far the fastest tool for keeping track of one's thoughts, so rapidly that no one, nothing, will ever manage to equal it? How can we keep in mind that the architect's hand is the organ immediately in contact with his brain, as Descartes said? While from their new heights, the new Cassandras of contemporary architecture continue to launch their prophecies:
– "It is not true that you 'think' the architecture the way you would like to represent it!"
– In architecture "ugliness" has a great aesthetic future!
In their words Adorno's aphorism "There is no continuum that leads from ugliness to beauty through the median; what is in the middle is always ugly" loses all meaning.[4] With these new axioms, the new Cassandras encourage students to look at "what is in the middle": "ugliness", an educational program that does not represent any problem for them.
If you exclude "beauty" from architecture as a dated category, anyone can easily excel at what contrasts with it.

Let us ask ourselves if electronic design has destroyed, or just shaken to the core, a principle hitherto considered immutable, that of "learning by replicating", on which the "education" of any artistic profession was built.
If, as common sense tells us, we learn a language by repeating the words spoken by others, how can we learn, if not in the same way, about architecture which, as collective art, is itself a language?[5] Even with the computer we learn by replicating, or rather it leads us to continuous replication, it is the "triumph of the copied."
We must not forget that until Le Corbusier, architects perfected their figurative sensitivity by redesigning the architecture of the past; they interpreted and remembered through their conceptual sketches in travel notebooks. Not even the advent of photography eliminated this type of education, causing Heidegger, watching the tourists who photographed the ruins at Delphi, to write, "They throw away their memory to entrust it to a technically produced image."[6]
"Learning by replicating" is also a way of learning at your computer keyboard, because it is essentially based on the principle of replication, here called "copy and paste".

4 T. W. Adorno, *Ästhetische Theorie*, Suhrkamp, Frankfurt am Main (Germany), 1973, p. 334.

5 Remember Herder's aphorism: "Man is a biologically weak being that has language as compensation."

6 M. Heidegger, "Sie werfen ihr Gedächtnis weg in das technisch hergestellte Bild." In: *Aufenthalte*, Vittorio Klostermann, Frankfurt am Main (Germany), 1989, p. 32.

The great speed and accuracy of electronic design, however, are subject to stringent constraints. Thousands of architects design at the same time, all over the world, different projects using only four or five different software programs. This is a tremendous reduction of freedom of expression, a negative influence on their manual skill and sensitivity that should make them think. And in fact they are rebelling, by unloading their resentment on the "form" which does not have any fault.

The architects, usually egocentric, debate, chained by an absolute homogenization: that of designing their renders differently with just a few programs. They seek a style of design never tried before, untouched, but alas everything is already in the keyboard, the possibilities are few, only those permitted by the CAD software used. However, there is something more serious: some architects, accepting American standards of productivity and costs, outsource their projects to offices specialized in renders. So between a talented architect and a mediocre one, the excellence of the extravagance in their designs cannot be distinguished.

As I flicked through the images of the greatest renderers showcased in this book, I got the impression that they resembled one another, that they looked good one next to the other, that they allowed themselves to settle docilely in the format of the pages, as if they had been guided by a single mysterious editor, by a single master of elegance!

Let us try to give a critical order to our theme, setting three strategic questions to which we must respond, with three accompanying clarifying examples. The questions are:
– What can't we do without?
– What can be deduced?
– In what ways do we have less control?

What can't we do without?

The success of electronic representation is based on the speed, accuracy and perfection with which the project can be developed and replicated. From this point of view, its legitimacy is indisputable and comparable to the accuracy achieved by the applied sciences.

The great load of information which weighs on architectural design of the drawings for execution causes the computer to become the only, irreplaceable way to lead the project to the construction site. It is only thanks to computers that various professional offices in different European countries have been able to work together on one project in Berlin, the block on the corner of Unter den Linden and Friedrichstrasse, divided into five constituent buildings next to each other.[7]

7 The project, which has the curious English name "Upper East Side Berlin", brought together a group of architects that included von Gerkan, Marg und Partner, Paola and Romano Burelli, and Petra and Paul Kahlfeldt.

What can be deduced?

It is difficult to know if, while drawing on the computer, the architect follows a logical and analytical path at distinct moments; apparently he repeats a single procedure that is called "copy and paste". In electronic media "copying and pasting" reduces the time of conception and excludes the gradual approach to project execution. But this acceleration is compensated for by the great accuracy, the serial repetition, the speed of correction and sudden modifications to the design that the computer allows, which once were torture for manual drawing.

It has been a revolutionary transformation that touches a chord deep in an architect's soul: laziness, in the words of Nietzsche, combined with greed.[8]

In respect to the basic concept of the "copied in architecture" or "learning by replicating", let us ask ourselves what we can learn from designs that are being built today, studying them on the products of information technology. In the past, the system of manual drawing, with its slowness, with the industriousness of its axonometric projections and perspectives, with the laborious redrawing of its variants, meant that the drawn work was the only document of authenticity, so you could reconstruct the progression of the project through its drawings.

Whereas with electronic drawing we immediately reach the "true", albeit virtual, when we are still a long way from drawings for execution and the construction site. This "true", however, is not the original, it is one of many originals permitted by the rapid changes, amendments, tampering, and erasing that the computer allows.

It is the triumph of "varied copy" without an original to use as reference. One could say that the varied copy of the electronic drawing is a photographic copy altered several times, without the first shot, or where the first shot is lost.

We look back into the clear sequence of terms that define the work of Greek sculpture, replicated in Roman workshops. Lippold ordered them in the following sequence: *Kopie, Repliken, Variante, Umbildung, Neubildung, Neuschöpfung* (copy, replica, variant, adaptation, reworking, new creation). He described the evolution to which a "sculptural type" was subjected in its replicas, in its variations, until the birth of a "new type" emerged. The "type" in its sense of model, had an absolute value for the Greek and Roman workshops, the "type" was what allowed the replicas. All craftsmen have always lived reproducing "types" that have already been tested, and each introduced some correction, some small change in detail: their prestigious achievement was due to the long task of perfecting that the sculptural type underwent.

---

8 Friedrich Nietzsche, *Schopenhauer als Erzieher*, 1874, beginning of the text.

The real problem is that the art of great craftsmen could be preserved and handed down only inside the workshop; no other workshop was allowed to come into possession of his secrets, of his models. This system meant that so many of their skills are lost to us.

The computer can help us to save this wisdom. Maybe it is possible to use the computer to collect an art form and hand it down to people from different countries and different cultures.

The example that we will take is of something that was slowly refined in some Squeri in Venice (Italy):[9] the production of flat-bottomed boats of high manoeuvrability and an enhanced ability to move in shallow water. It is the process of constructing a lagoon boat called the "sampierota", redesigned and refined by Fiorenzo Bertan, who collected the secrets of one of the last shipwrights who still knew how to build, secrets that otherwise he would have taken to his grave.[10]

The success of this study is first measured by the building of a "sampierota" in any other shipyard, accurately describing the pieces and the method of construction. The cuts made by the shipwrights on different types of wood, the tolerances

used, the complex joinery, cannot be described except via their electronic representation.

What can be deduced?

Besides the fundamental principle of "copy and paste", there is a second principle, which we have already mentioned: that of "synecdoche binding" and the need to isolate a detail of the work as if it were separable from it.

The "synecdoche" in fact forces us to take over the screen with a single detail which demands to be the centre of our attention. Thus isolated, it can be subjected to a configuration before being copied and pasted on the façade of which it is but a small part. One might say that this process has always occurred in architecture. This would be true were it not that the detail, for instance the capital, had already been conceived as part of a whole: the order of architecture. The parts of the order were based on conventional dimensional relationships. Note that the order could, within certain limits, increase or decrease in size without any change in the relationship. This system of conventions should be also held true for our way of doing things on the computer keyboard. We draw the details without a precise scale. The accuracy is no longer determined by the scale that we use, as it once was. The same degree of accuracy

9   Small boatyards in Venice (Italy).

10   Fiorenzo Bertan researched the representation of architecture while professor at the IUAV University of Venice (Italy).

In what ways do we have less control?

will appear on all scales, blackening the design on larger scales, making it clear in smaller scales. I have never seen an architect designing a plan by computer, or a part, alongside a human figure, which would help him a lot, because set against the human figure we can immediately grasp the size of the detail. With the computer, we have entered into the world of "off the scale", drawings that seek their scale, their precise relationship with the place and the men who will inhabit them.

The absence of a precise reference scale makes the architectural design vulnerable, open to the paradox that Peter Eisenman suggested in an urban plan for Venice, on the site of the ex-Saffa in the late 1970s, when he designed the same pavilion building at the scale of 1 : 50, 1 : 100, 1 : 200, 1:500 in the same area, on the same table.

To illustrate the vices which the architect can get used to – failing to consider the relationship of scale to which he or she works – we can look at one example which has reverberated down the history of Italian architecture.

Canaletto, the great painter of Venetian views, used a dark room to draw his views of Venice, reversed but precise. On the drawings that resulted, he traced the shadows and wrote the names of colours that would be painted in by the students. He was a great reproducer of copies from his own workshop, which even so could not satisfy the demands of the British and northern European markets. He was also a great inventor of the "Capriccio", assembling in different locations ideal or un-built architecture. What was the likelihood of these "Capriccio" becoming reality?

Is it possible to determine if a design, such as Palladio's famous one for the Rialto Bridge in Venice, was really suitable for that site, designed for the precise spot of that place?[11] This is what Fiorenzo Bertan seeks to demonstrate using the electronic transcription of the place borrowed from Canaletto's dark room. Of course, Bertan was concerned only with the Rialto Bridge, investigating the dimensional relationship between the actual size of the canal and the size given by Palladio in his plan with its precise details. This study concluded that Canaletto was forced to shrink the size of the plan, adapting it to the Canal Grande; the size of the proposed bridge was such that it would have meant demolishing the system of buildings on both sides as well as considerably reducing the navigability of the canal due to the two pillars in the water.

The "off scale" Palladio's bridge has been so revealed by the precision of the computer. There is no doubt that the competition judges had many reasons for rejecting Palladio's design, preferring those developed and produced by Da Ponte.

11 Canaletto, "Capriccio con architetture di Palladio", now preserved in the Museum of Parma (Italy). The "Capriccio" is a montage of several buildings by Palladio: his bridge for the competition organized by the Venetian Republic, the Basilica and the Palazzo Chiericati in Vicenza (Italy).

In what ways do we have less control?

Reflecting on the possibilities offered by the computer, those of "replicating" the same plan, the same section, the same construction drawings, the same details, we can see that some architects have rebelled against this slavery and have taken another route enabled by the computer: that of deformation, torsion, expansion, compression of one or more Euclidean solids. Following this path, they thought to be rescued by the "eternal return of identity", because the design changed continuously throughout, and details became numerous.

Put more succinctly, "de-constructivism" is nothing other than the freedom to make a geometry complex to the point where only the computer can really manage it, remember it, transcribe it.[12] Thus, complexity is a new way for the architect to throw himself away in favour of technique. "Construction", which is the antidote of architecture, which is what prevents it from succumbing to the failings of other more "free" arts, has been sacrificed; Adorno's definition:

"Any successful work of architecture is also constructively successful" has been comprehensively negated.

The "virtual truth" of the "de-constructivist" renders, drawn while construction of the building was still a long way off, seems not to obey the force of gravity, because someone else will take care of gravity at a later date. Or the architect decides that the force of gravity will be taken care of by a first structure which is to be completely hidden behind the structure of the casing to which it is irresistibly attracted. The casing is not a façade, or rather, it is a façade only in the sense that it isolates the interior space from the outside. The indissoluble unity of structure and façade, of supporting parts and what they underpin, was broken. This phenomenon is not new, but computer graphics have made it very widespread, pushing architects increasingly further away from the location of their work, the construction site.

This has triggered a radical movement that, destroying the construction, the last characteristic of architecture as non-free art, had cast it into a state of "hubris": arrogance, excess, un-constructability, the thoughts which the architect should always keep at a safe distance. In architecture lack of interest in construction leads to "aesthetic hell" on a par with heresies in Christianity.

The impossibility of controlling these complicated shapes in manual drawing made me think about the way Canova,

---

12 The drawings for execution for the south elevation of Frank O. Gehry's DZ American Bank at Pariser Platz in Berlin (Germany), were made by Studio Neufert. The studio distorted and altered his plan so that it could actually be built. During the opening, however, the architect praised the fidelity with which they had built his façade. And he meant it because he could not remember his original plan.

Falling down into
a technically controlled world

the great neoclassical sculptor, prepared the replicas in marble of the plaster model of one of his works. He pierced it with hundreds of small nails, fastening them together with thin wire so that the plaster statue was wrapped like a web of triangles. The preparatory work on the block of marble followed this system of polygons and the students carried it out with diligence. The web of triangles fixed the stone which was to be cut, but the body of Niobe did not appear again, only the master would have uncovered her final form and rubbed her silky skin.

Architecture has always been tempted by the sin of "hubris". Putting a limit to this art and attempting to surpass it obey the same impulse.

The Greek temple had never to exceed a certain size; growing beyond it would have caused the human to outstrip the divine. Yet Greek man was tempted by "hubris" of the temple. The reasons are beyond us, probably rivalry between the Athenians and the Akragantini drove the latter to build a huge temple, massive enough to contain Goethe's shoulders in a single groove of one of its Doric columns.[13]

It is the temple of Zeus Olympico in Agrigento in Sicily (Italy), conceived in gigantic forms to which its stylobate, bases and column capitals bear witness to this day. Its telamoni, the giants at the centre of each inter-column that support the heavy architrave, do not seem to have been able to hold the weight and the temple collapsed while it was still under construction. The closed peristasis, the long naos lit from above, the column on an axis of longitudinal symmetry, are the technical flaws imposed on the architects by the enormous weight of the design. But obviously these design ploys were not enough to prevent it collapsing on the "hubris" of its designers. The Olympieion of Akragas is a more significant metaphor for architecture than the Tower of Babel. It was not a god who confused the languages of the builders, but the ambiguity of the Promethean technology: its ability to tie down and destroy the man while giving the illusion of freeing him.

The error of Prometheus is to have taught the technique to human beings, making them, from childhood, rational and masters of their own minds; they could obtain for themselves what they once sought from the gods. It was then that the sin of "hubris" was born and spread.[14]

What has been promised by the CAD systems as absolute freedom is the ability to control complex geometric figures, which the geometry of manual drawing did not easily allow. It is for this reason that so-called "avant-garde" of

---

13 Friedrich Schiller had just written the sentence "Da die Götter menschlicher noch waren, waren Menschen göttlicher" (when the Gods were still more human, men were more divine), in *Die Götter Griechenlandes*, 1785–1789.

14 Aeschylus: *Prometheus Bound*, verses 443–444.

our time has found refuge in the virtual representation of "complexity" a-dimensional, statically indeterminate, constructively non-programmable, physically non-constructible except with extremely lightweight materials with great ductility and low resistance to natural events.[15]

The design of some of the de-constructivist casings reminds us a little of the example of Canova's plaster casts surrounded by a web of triangles, but the architect does not even have an idea of the static structure his form will require. The great German engineer Jörg Schlaich, acclaimed by Frank O. Gehry, likes to say: "Do what you want architect, but I need the bars of the frame to be all the same for calculation!"

In the contemporary architecture of "hubris" – architectural arrogance – we promote the complete emancipation of the structure from the wall panelling or casing that surrounds it, thus creating conflict between these two aspects of the construction. A structure that follows its own rules may be purchased from among those pre-fabricated serial structures, while the casing becomes the only object of concern to the architect and investors.

The skin guides the architect, the skin distinguishes him from the others, the skin puts him in relation to the technologies which are not concerned about the durability of the building. It is a tectonically disintegrated architecture, which is preparing its end as constructive art, such as *Baukunst*.

The rift in architectural design is conceptual, methodological and practical, thus the same project may be entrusted to two different architects and two different construction companies. The dislocation that is produced in the architects is welcomed by the developer because the work is contracted out more easily: large prefabricated boxes in a casing that hides them!

It has thus become an "artistic style": the façade casing, which, as the most public part of the building, can now showcase advertising. This style, which I have called "prostituted art", seems to say to everyone: "I do not want to mean anything, nor represent anything except the message: 'come and buy!' If this message is aggressive enough, I have reached my goal."

Falling down into a technically controlled world

We are not alone in the technically influenced world for it contains the entire apparatus of architectural construction. The affirmation of "smart tools" in building production, of numerically controlled machines, coincided with the disappearance of carpenters and craftsmen from the construction sites.

15   This "architecture of extravagance" can be calculated in Gehry: "the unit of measurement of unnecessary complication."

The builders are gone, replaced by teams of assemblers, who arrive on site with their prefabricated pieces, disappear and are replaced by new assemblers, with new components to be built.

Behind all this there is a single constructive process: the "principle of studwork" that changes the project, puts the traditional company in the shade and allows the high-tech industry to expand.

Architectural design, besieged by the techniques, is experimenting on its own skin that is not only the gift of Prometheus, but also its curse.

In fact, when drawing a plan for execution, each technique requires you to comply with its security measures: the order that every technical breakthrough has in its specialist field is dispersed throughout, so we have greater accuracy in every order and ever greater disorder overall. Computer assisted design is entrusted with the task of reconstructing all these orders and extinguishing the conflict. This is the ratio of control over the sum of demands that architecture today requires, a sort of "machining" whose effects have not yet been carefully studied.

But architects are silent on this. At the last two Architecture Biennales in Venice there was an orgy of computer graphics and renders of virtual images. But architecture does not end here, it must necessarily deal with construction, with the construction site.

An art that is destroying its own foundations, the latest being construction, ends up killing itself or developing into another artistic genre. In spite of that, the "heretics of deconstruction" still call it "architecture".

Thus, this art, which cannot live without a foundation, without a shared set of goals, is privatized and so shatters what should be a common spirit in thousands of selfish directions. Attention is paid only to an "original superficiality". If someone wants to assert something, it must differentiate itself from its competitors.

Architecture will no longer feel obligated to a "higher truth" but only seek to improve in its own, lonely and selfish way.

**The "Hubris" of the
Olympieion in Akragas
A temple locked inside a temple**
*Drawings: A. R. Burelli, 2005–06
Techniques: Graphite, red pencil, red
ink and blood on Schoellershammer
paper*

HYBRIS

With the plunder of defeated Carthage in 480 BC the rich Sicilian city of Akragas decided to launch a challenge to the mother country by building the largest Doric temple in the Greek world. Some two millennia later two visitors with differing interests, interpreted the "big bones" of the surviving structure and its enormous basement: Johann Wolfgang Goethe showed his disapproval of what he felt was megalomania on the part of the architect by measuring the groove of a column with his shoulder; Albert Speer, in 1940, corroborated his misgivings: for Speer even the Greeks had overreached themselves and partaken on the "hubris" of the Titans. *(The word "hubris" is written in the ancient Greek characters of Akragas.)*

The sin of "hubris" is more clearly apparent in
this temple than in the Tower of Babylon. The
megalomania, the arrogance, the sheer excess of
the Akragantinians is materialized here, despite
the architects having exerted every ounce of their
skills. This image illustrates the section, the elevation
and a perspective, the details of the semi-column,
and two of the nine heads of Atlas discovered during
the excavations in 1930.

The dimensions of the peristasis (50.30 × 113.45 m) exceed those of the Temple of Apollo in Didim, while incorporating the central idea: that of a temple locked inside a temple.
In 1942–43 Fritz Krischen made a meticulous study of the Olympieion reconstructing its dimensions.

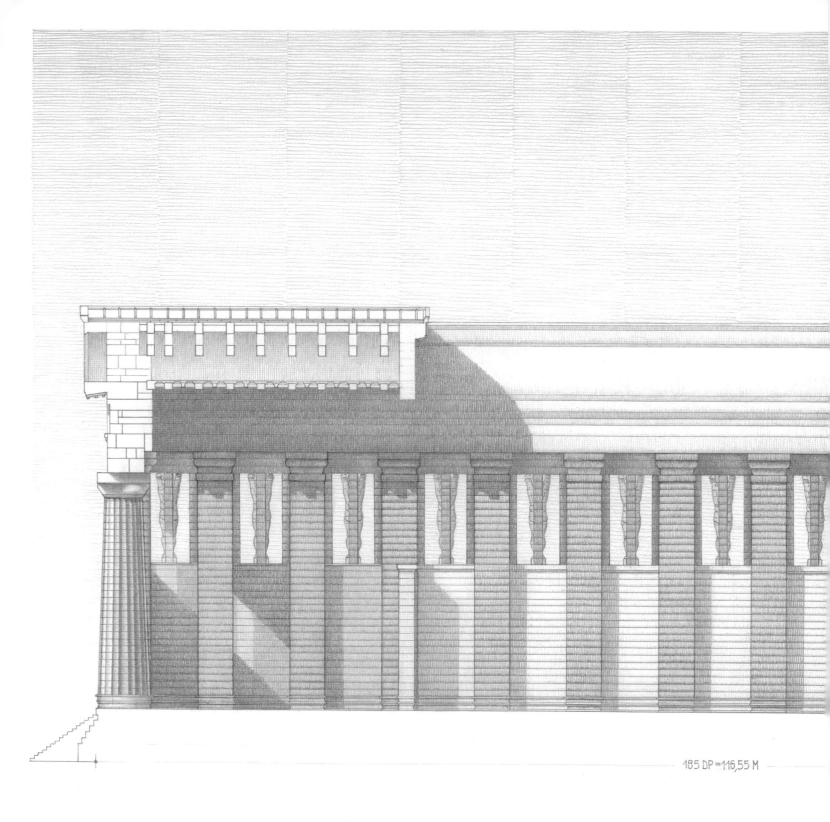

185 DP = 116,55 M

The height of the Olympieion from the base to the Kimmation is 34.65 m, while the diameter of the columns, almost all of which are semi-columns, is 4.20 m, which is, however, insufficient to support the architrave, which is 8.40 m high. To overcome this problem the temple's architects had to fit the column into a continuous wall that completely locked the temple in.

55 DP=34,65 M

The visual harmony of the temple is based on a series of measurements related to the golden section, which you easily detect in the repetition of the macro measurements: thirteen stones, with which the key elements of the temple are divided up. The thirteen stones anticipate the Fibonacci series: 2-3-5-8-13 (based on the height of a stone being equal to two Akragantinian feet: 2 × 31.5 cm).

ϷⱵBϷIϹ

DER GOLDENE SCHNITT LÄSST SICH DURCH UNGEBROCHENE ZAHLEN AUSBRUCKEN IN DER REIHE:

1	2	3	5	8	13	21	34	55	89	144	233	377	610	DOPPI MEDI
0,63	1,26	1,89	3,15	5,04	8,19	13,23	21,42	34,65	56,07	90,72	146,79	237,51	384,3	METRI

The semi-colonnade epistyle is opened only in the middle of the two pediments, putting a column on the axis of symmetry, perhaps a necessary contrivance to support the great weight of the tympanum.

The real temple is the naos formed by large square pillars and enclosed by a large ambulatory, a profound departure from the traditional closed cell. So the light needs to penetrate from the roof of the unbuilt naos, just in front of the statue of Zeus. This light also illuminates the covered ambulatory, which remains somewhat in darkness, once lit by the double opening that surrounds each 7 m tall Atlas.

Despite the skill involved and the precautions taken to reinforce the stability of the temple, archaeologists are convinced that it was never finished because it came crushing down on the heads of its builders.

Essay > Augusto Romano Burelli   The Olympieion of Akragas

**The Rialto Bridge by Andrea Palladio
in Venice (Italy)**
**Reconstruction of the project from a
"Capriccio" by Canaletto**
Text by Fiorenzo Bertan
Drawings by Diego Ersetig

The painting "Rialto con il progetto di Palladio ed altri edifici palladiani" (1742) by Antonio Canal (Canaletto) is now in the Galleria Nazionale di Parma. This work marked the birth of so-called "Virtual Architecture", the subject of an M. A. dissertation by Diego Ersetig at the IUAV University of Venice (Italy). "Virtual Architecture" is inextricably linked to Filippo Brunelleschi and the birth of perspective, but Canaletto, painter of the "vedute", of urban landscapes and the son of a theatre set designer, is probably the artist who best understood that perspective might describe architecture, even if only in an idealized form.

His use of perspective to realize "Capricci", architectural representations which represent not reality but figments of the imagination, reached its apotheosis with the reconstruction of the Rialto bridge project that Andrea Palladio has detailed in his "I Quattro Libri" of 1570.

The perspectival consistency of Canaletto's painting was analyzed by reconstructing the perspective of the three Palladian buildings which he depicted: the Rialto Bridge, the Basilica di Vicenza located on the right of the picture and the Palazzo Chiericati in the foreground on the left.

According to his artistic requirements, Canaletto used a single horizon, but distinct vanishing points for the buildings. The results of the analysis show that the architectural components were created by means of four different perspectives, one for each Palladian building and one for the Rialto setting. The perspective rendering allows us to verify that the proportions of the buildings are consistently painted faithfully to reproduce the originals, except for a small correction to the height of the Basilica to emphasize the central volume.

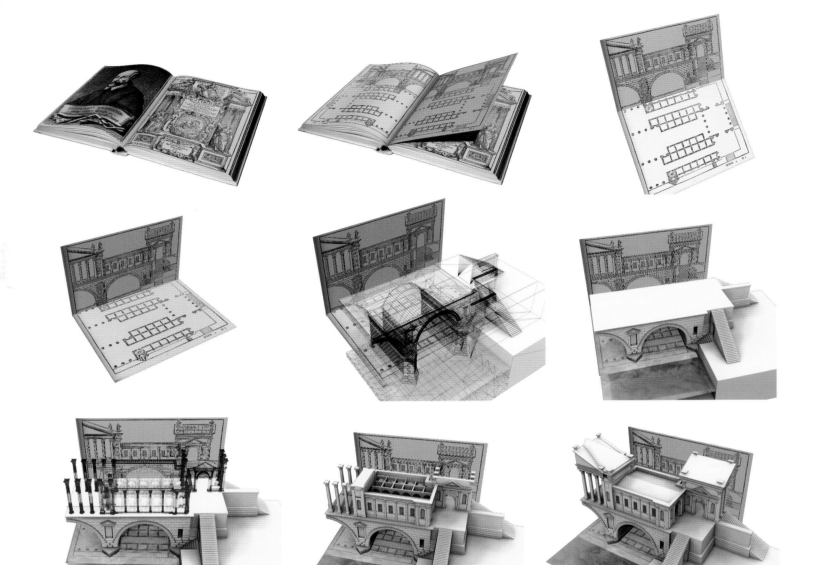

The investigation began with an analysis of Palladio's treatise and especially of the drawings on pages 26 and 27 of his "Terzo libro". These relate to the project he designed in 1569 for a competition organized by the Venetian Republic, but that project was never selected.

Also used were drawings by Francesco Muttoni (1740), which proved very helpful for reconstructing the project, as Canaletto had certainly done in order to paint his "Capriccio".

The more recent "Saggio storico sul ponte di Rialto in Venezia" (1841) by French architect Antoine Rondelet was also useful because he takes Palladio's drawings of the project and juxtaposes them with the plan of the Rialto.

The painting, probably commissioned in an antiquarian spirit by Consul Smith, may be regarded as one of the first ever "photomontages" of an architectural project. It is in fact an accurate representation, not so much of real buildings depicted in a different setting, but rather as a representation intended to give shape and context to a project that was never implemented.

In "I Quattro Libri" Palladio only gives a basic plan, a longitudinal elevation and a partial section in the centre. Furthermore there is no measurement or reference to buildings on the ground.

Having analyzed the project, we then turned to the drawing and the three-dimensional modelling of the bridge, considering the proportions of the parts and taking the stylistic information from the manual. The design of the bridge, as for all architecture by Palladio, was based on a unit that governs the entire building, the base measurement by which the single parts of the building relate to each other. The unit of measurement, used to control and proportionately scale drawings, was always the Vicentine foot (35.7 cm), to avoid approximations that would have been generated by working with the orthodox metric system. The Vicentine foot was divided into twelve ounces (one ounce is equal to 2.96 centimeters) and each ounce into four minutes (one minute is equal to 0.74 centimeters). Only at the end of the work, setting the CAD file parameters to generate the unit of measurement in meters, was it possible to measure the model with the decimal system and thus describe the drawings both in feet and meters.

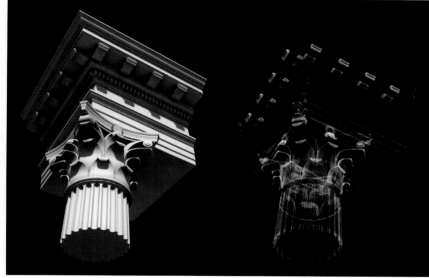

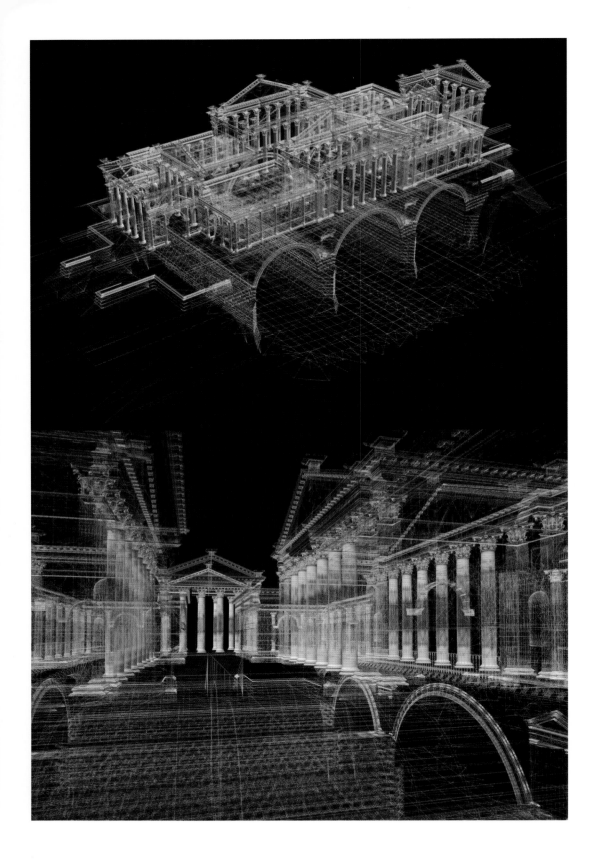

Essay > Augusto Romano Burelli

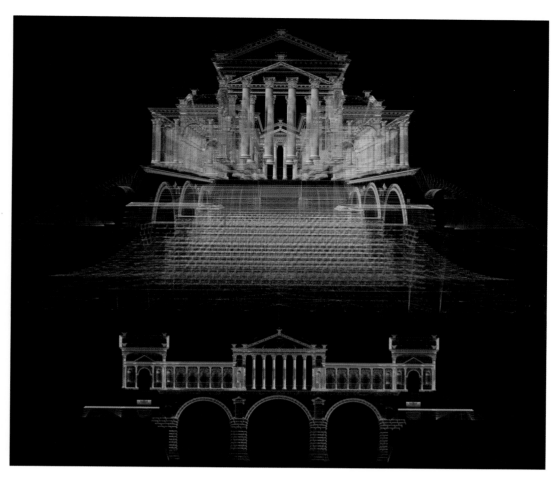

Palladio's first Rialto bridge for Venice was conceived in 1554, the second fifteen years later, in 1569. He also produced a drawing of a single-arch wooden bridge, which subsequently became the framework for building the current stone bridge. The construction material was what unites the two projects, as Palladio considered stone bridges were "more durable, thicker, and more glorious for the builders." The first project entailed building two symmetrical squares on the banks of the Canal Grande connected by a five-arched bridge. It was designed on a single sheet, now kept at the Museo Civico di Vicenza, depicting on one side the plan and on the other the elevation of the central section.

The second project, of 1569, modifies the ideas presented in the previous one. First, Palladio did not specify a location for the project, though there seems to be no doubt that the Rialto in Venice was intended, for he refers to "… the city, which is one of the greatest and most noble in Italy, and is a metropolis encompassing many smaller cities … the river is wide and the bridge was to be precisely the place where the merchants went to transact their business …".

In the second project Palladio reduces his structure from five to three arches by increasing their size to allow the passage of large vessels and also increases the number of workshops housed on the bridge to seventy-two to raise the amount of income derived from rents. He enlarges the loggia on the centre line so that in dimension it is equal to the width of the main central arch with the intention to earmarking the site for mercantile activity. The pedestrian circulation is here accommodated on three roads, the central one wider than the outer ones and each flanked by workshops. The bridge is built entirely on a platform 16 feet high (5.71 m) which is accessed via two secondary staircases placed laterally and a main staircase.

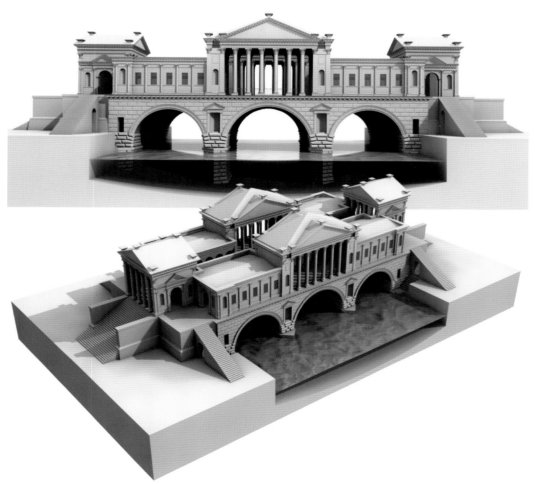

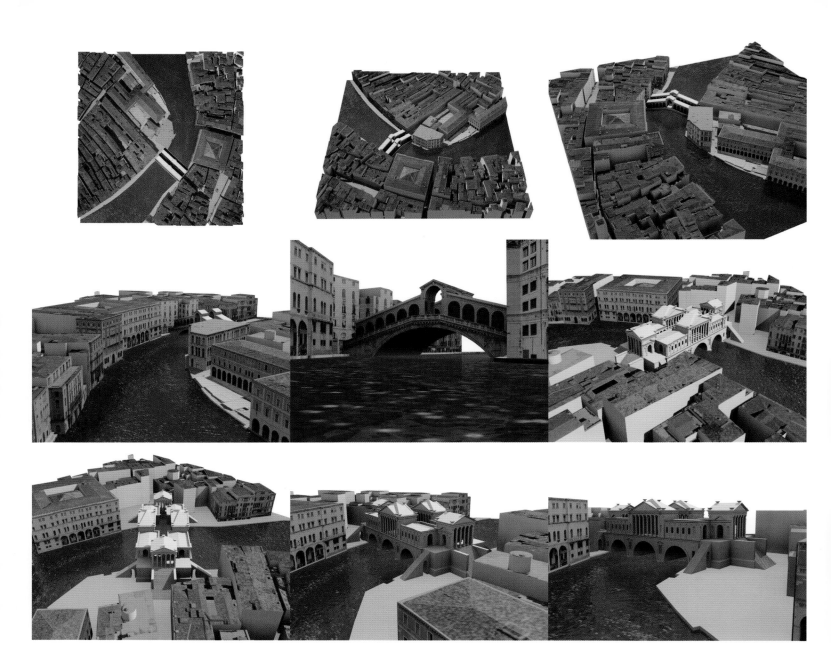

Essay > Augusto Romano Burelli

The considerable amount of reconstruction drawings and research are not only evidence of the work undertaken but can be used to gain an understanding of why Palladio's design was rejected.

The overlapping of the virtual model of the bridge with a film of the Rialto context clearly showed what the jury had only sensed when imagining the potential reality.

The reconstruction of Palladio's project reveals a nearly impenetrable wall, not a simple bridge. In addition, the height of the proposed buildings would have dwarfed their neighbours.

Moreover, the extraordinary size of the project would have made it necessary to demolish some buildings in the area, such as the Palazzo dei Camerlenghi which had only been completed a few years earlier. An unacceptable choice.

Antonio Da Ponte had to adapt the construction of his bridge to the existing one.

By means of this reconstruction we can appreciate the choice of the Commission from quite a different angle than the lengthy explanation produced by architectural historians. Some sought to interpret Venice's rejection of the project as a rejection of the classical language of Palladio, forgetting that this language had already been used in Piazza San Marco for the building of Sansovino's Zecca, as also by Vincenzo Scamozzi for the Procuratie Nuove.

Others have attributed this rejection to the difference between the simple round arch of Antonio da Ponte, easier to walk on even at high tide because of its considerable height, and the Palladian model based on three lower arches.

The precise reconstruction of the project and its insertion into urban context permit of a clearer critique. Probably everyone now endorses the Commission's choice, which rubber-stamped the construction of the rival design still visible today. So it was that a careful use of information technology enabled a verifiable and objective approach to the study of these disputes.

In the end we can also say that love for Palladio and his architecture forced Canaletto's hand. He decided to help the old master by imperceptibly correcting the "veduta" in favour of a more harmonious insertion of the project into its real context. Canaletto's "virtual" architecture is therefore not an accurate scientific reconstruction of the reality, but an instrument of subtle persuasion. Merely a "Capriccio"!

Survey of a Traditional Venetian Boat, the "Sampierota"

Text by Fiorenzo Bertan
Drawings by Fabrizio Viezzer

Once wood was abandoned as principal building material for ships in favour of steel, the knowledge of the ancient craft of boat building that had survived for centuries in the Arsenale of Venice, described by Dante in the Divine Comedy, was lost forever, after having been partially kept alive in small shipyards. This work, a dissertation by architect Fabrizio Viezzer at the IUAV University of Venice, made it possible to obtain a quantifiably reliable model of a traditional Venetian boat.

The first image shows the reconstruction of a scan of the Venetian "sampierota" made with a 3D laser-scanner. The "sampierota" is derived from Burano's "sandolo" and is the most popular Venetian boat.

It can be propelled by a single oarsman like the gondola, the most famous boat in Venice, but it can also be equipped with a lugsail.

The different images are linked to the "sampierota" which stays at the centre; the overlap is required for checking possible scanning errors.

To obtain a proper overlap of scans, it was necessary to place some metal balls around and above the boat. The balls, fixed during the survey, are the volumes that the scanner recognizes and that become common points of reference for the scans.

The use of a laser-scanner requires the subject to be fixed and not fluid. It was necessary to cover the parts of the boat coloured red because, in our case, these were not detectable by the laser beam.
Since it is a three-dimensional object with complex surfaces, the boat was turned over to get more overlapping views and to allow the laser-scanner to detect with precision the different surfaces even when the incidence angle was too low.
The image reproduced here is not a picture, but the result of the overlapping of different laser scans, after correcting for scanning errors, and highlights only the boat.
The laser scanned cluster of points then has to be dicretized, i. e. uniquely identifiable points are transferred and then the orthophotoplans can be created. This difficult post-production process allows us to generate a three-dimensional drawing of the boat, representing both the exterior and the internal components as well as those parts which are not easily accessible to the eye.
It is interesting how across the lagoon of Venice this boat is called "sampierota" while in Pellestrina and Chioggia it is called by its old name "sandolo". In fact the name derives from the village of San Pietro di Pellestrina where, in the nineteenth century, fishermen subtly modified their boats' shape in order to use them inside the lagoon with oares, or on the open sea with sails.

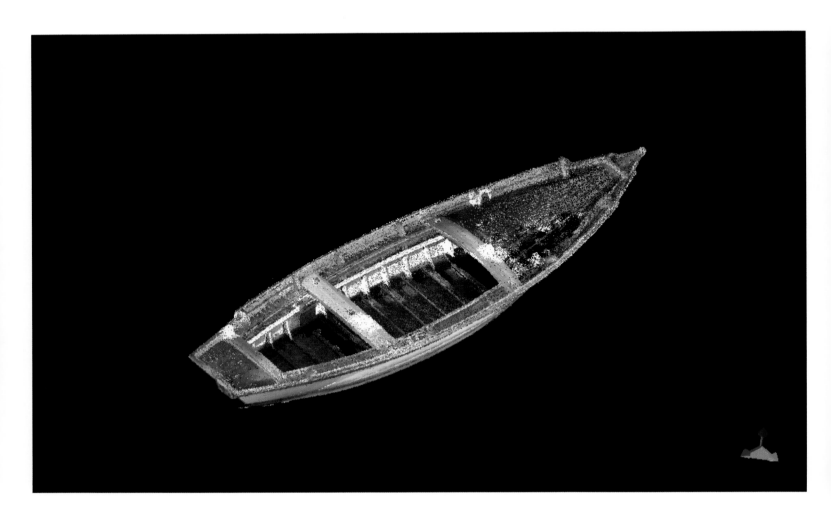

The structure of the "sampierota" is simple because it has straight inclined cross-sections and a flat bottom. You can see half the representation in "wire-frame", and thus discern the individual components from the laser scan survey. The second half on the right side is described by continuous surfaces, with shadows in monochrome, to capture the true sequence of volumes.

Unlike the "centinatura curva", which is a typical example of the traditional lagoon "tope" or utility barge, construction of the "sampierota" does not require the complex procedures of the ancient "Barche tonde" or round boats, of which the bow and stern of the gondola are examples of unsurpassed skill. In the case of a "sampierota", the only curvatures present are those related to planimetric sections of the craft, a form reminiscent of the almond. Nevertheless the bottom, although flat, has a slight curvature in the horizontal plane, that raises the prow and aft, called by shipwrights "cavallino" and set from the start by the central curvature of the "yard" (construction site) on which the entire construction of the boat is based.

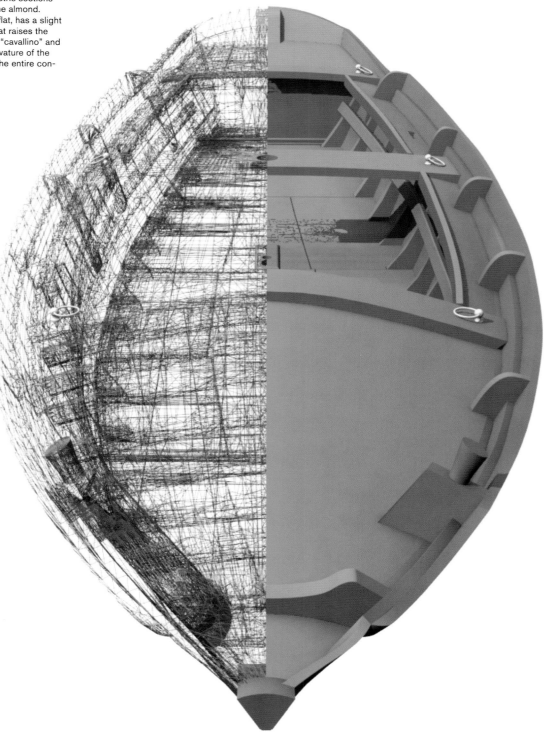

The mixed used of "wire-frame" and shaded surfaces in the render of the "sampierota" exemplifies the goals of boat surveying.

The first was accurately to determine the forms and traditional proportions. To do that a boat was chosen, which was built in the late 1960s by a "squerarolo" with a proven reputation in the Venetian lagoon: the shipwright Piero Menetto Pellestrina.

To obtain an accurate description of the boat, we compared the direct survey (made using a measuring tape and square protractor) with the one made by the three-dimensional laser-scanner.

The technique of direct survey is traditional and re-traces the way the shipwright designs the boat.

The laser-scanner is a tool that allows the scanning of the surface of an object by sending and receiv-ing laser beams that detect millions of points. The composition of surfaces through a network of fixed points determined during the direct survey, allows us to reconstruct three-dimensionally the entire sur-face of the object under scrutiny.

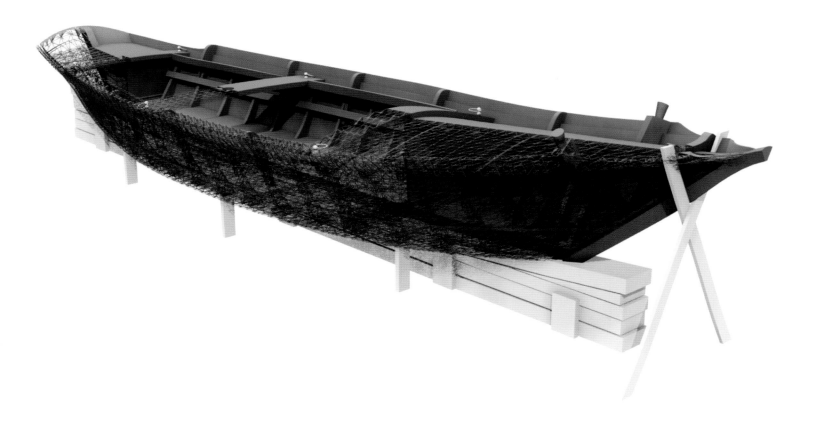

The three views of the boat retrace the work done through the direct survey, the one with the laser-scanner and the transfer of the significant points that allowed the conclusive identification of continuous surfaces of the boat. Direct survey and three-dimensional digitization have enabled the transition from real to virtual three-dimensional model.

The wooden boats are increasingly rare in the lagoon, replaced by fibreglass ones that are easy to mould and require little maintenance. The shipwrights cannot survive a transformation similar to that which replaced the horse-drawn carriage with the car.

To halt this unstoppable process and preserve that knowledge for all time, the work of the maestro Piero Menetto in his yard in Pellestrina was followed for about a year.

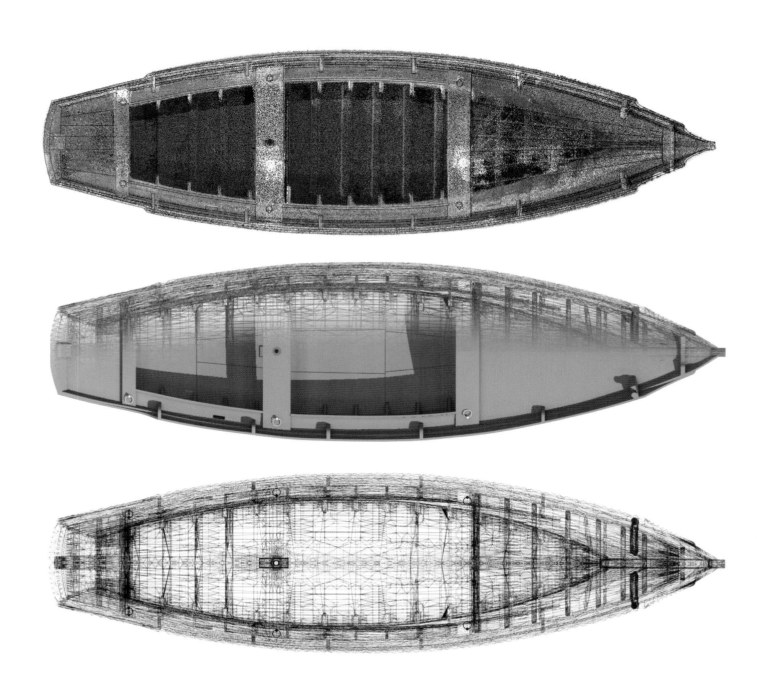

The second goal, and the more ambitious, was to define the shapes of individual pieces of the boat and record how long their assembly took. We therefore chose to use CAD software to trace all the construction stages of a "sampierota", just as in a yard. Together with master Menetto, photographs, practical examples and stories, all the phases of the construction of a "sampierota" were reviewed.

In the end, having collected sufficient information, we wanted to be able to preserve not only the drawings but the geometric-time line process of the physical construction of the boat itself.

To this end, a six-minute film was produced, which faithfully records each phase of boat construction and shows the sequence of assembly of 241 elements in wood or steel that are still required to build a "sampierota". The table details twelve significant moments from the film, describing the process of construction from the "yard" (construction site) to the launch.

Recently, Piero Menetto passed away. Without his wise help this work would never have been possible. Every time we show the film at a gathering of owners of traditional Venetian boats it is met with rapturous

applause. The final applause is the best testimony to the importance of the work.

The design of computer systems allows us to know not only the actual shape of a very special boat, but also to preserve for ever, and for everyone, the knowledge that few now possess in the lagoon of Venice.

Essay > Augusto Romano Burelli

Fabio Schillaci
To draw or not to draw?

Fabio Schillaci
To draw or not to draw?

To draw or not to draw?

Could the computer be an extension of our minds just like our hand? Actually, I don't think that is the right question. I think we would do better to discuss the relationship between architectural methods and thought, between thought and society, between image and culture. Rendering, like any form of art, is a mirror of the society: architectural images reveal the society, or at least its aspirations. But what is our society?

I'm sure that two or three centuries from now our descendants will remember us not only as the society of computers and digital technology but, most importantly, as that of the internet and global communication. But what does communication mean today? Communicating with whom? How? When rendering, communication is visual: obviously, since you are supposed to produce an image for someone to see. But who is it exactly who looks at our images?

During the opening ceremony of the Olympic Games in Beijing I was taken aback at how little attention was paid to the bird's nest stadium by Herzog & de Meuron. Incredible renders of the stadium were shown everywhere during the preparations. Everyone, architects or not, already recognized the Nest from the moment its images started turning up all over the world. I expected the stadium would be the major protagonist of the ceremony, but the TV cameras showed only fleetingly that China had succeeded in building it on time. Speaking to ArtefactoryLab, which rendered the images, I was very surprised to learn that the architects had involved the Lab from the beginning to use rendering techniques for developing the façade and appearance of the stadium. Later, I realized that in fact the building was supposed to showcase modern China to the world, so how its visual appearance was rendered was crucial for winning the competition.

To render, to represent. Representation was always used to communicate to the masses. Michelangelo's Sistine Chapel in Rome demonstrates God's greatness and tells the biblical Creation story to the world.

But today representation is growing more important and the rendering has become probably the most powerful tool for winning an architectural commission. This affects not only tangible drawings but also, more intellectually, the way people perceive things and architecture. Visual communication is a key factor in the internet and consequently in our culture. This is also what lies behind the recent explosion in the production of images, photos, diagrams and drawings during recent years: we mostly "look" at the world through the monitor. Thus, a render must "grab" your attention from among the sea of images we are daily deluged with.

Computer graphics, video and digital rendering are proliferating modern technologies due to the speed and ease with which they communicate information in a relatively short time, regardless of language barriers. This is probably – together with the internet – the most pragmatic reason for their contemporary diffusion.

Rendering is intimately connected to the internet. When drawings became digital, they were dematerialized and could thus easily move through the web. As a result, illustrators could access the global market, working for clients from many countries and moving their wares all over the world. This is already what happens for most of the offices whose work is shown in the gallery, for them the internet is effectively a mean to communicate with the client.

In future I foresee internet and rendering software slowly converging into software that runs online and can be used in parallel by different actors. Stack!Studios have already evolved software which can be used online directly by clients, who thus do not need powerful machines and can take advantage of their own computing power. This is an evolution of the concept of the renderfarm, which is bound to play an important role in the development of future software: webconnection to a main computing centre will reduce rendering time and infrastructural costs.

Our culture's emphasis on the visual forces illustrators to produce ever bigger, more breath-taking renderings in order to get viewers' attention. Yet digital technologies and software solutions are continuously evolving, allowing ever more special effects and features. So complex have they become that it is almost impossible to keep abreast of every possible setup of parameters or control exactly what they will produce.

Even if that might actually include potential for exploration and research, the trend is instead one of standardization towards realism. At the moment, illustrators are mostly asked to produce images which reproduce reality as far as possible. Such realism pushes illustrators to define the project very precisely in its materiality, illumination and form down to the smallest detail. This often happens even if the design is at a preliminary stage, where the task is only to show the concept, and as a result it is becoming increasingly common to see very detailed rendering of what is rather poor design. Moreover, the illustrator is asked to complete the design or to hide its weaknesses and turn something ugly into a thing of beauty. This problem is not with the tool, but how people use it. This has to do more with personal ethics than with technological issues. Instead of selling the design, we could use the potential of simulating reality to help architects double check designs and ideas before proceeding. This was the approach for the entry to the "Concorso internazionale per il Completamento del Museo Nivola" by Federico Pitzalis and Daniele Durante, who used lighting simulation to cut out the openings in the building, something that could well become a significant method of refining architectural design in the future.

As a matter of fact, hyper-realism leads to homogeneity of rendering and is what caused many illustrators to focus on technology. So the issue will be increasingly about technical skills, and the best actors will be those who are most familiar and in control of the software. As a result, differences between renderings will become marginal and images will be standardized.

On the other hand, digital technologies still have a great potential for including personalization. This does not depend on the digital tool we use, but on how we use it. Since the process of rendering is about reiterative actions, each personal style has to be researched in the variation and personalization of those reiterations. And it is in this interpretation of the process that the potential for human intervention lies. It is here, in this process of reiteration that the designer can best set his mark, evoking atmosphere and feeling just as when drawing by hand. This was clear to the first illustrators engaged in this process who were educated in hand drawing methodology. Their renderings were full of personality and told us a lot about their creators. This way of working created unique pieces even when they were later produced using digital tools, making them reproducible digital products.

This brings me to my final point, that digital technologies could include older techniques and traditions, enriching these technologies by opening them up to ever more heterogeneous expression.

Many people see a contradiction between hand and digital drawing. I definitely do not. Digital machines are the tool we need for exploration; they offer us huge potential to transcend the concept of industrial production line, which was based on standardized mass production. The computer is our industrial machine, software our tool and information the good we produce.

ArtefactoryLab, *Beijing Olympic Stadium (China) by Herzog & de Meuron*, perspective, 2003

Offices

Simon Jones & Associates Architectural Watercolours Ltd.

8 Clarence Rd., Llandeilo,
Carmarthenshire,
SA19 6HY, Wales
UK

www.simonjonesandassociates.co.uk

Simon Jones & Associates Architectural Watercolours is a "husband and wife team", composed of Simon and Caroline, who work from an office in their family house in rural Wales.

One half of the studio is very messy and devoted to painting; the other half is tidy and contains the computers.

The office has a number of long term contacts, most of which date back over 20 years, including practices like Arup, Fosters, HOK, McAslan to name a few.

The painting process, apart from rendering the materials accurately, basically adds everything that computer renders struggle with, i. e., atmosphere, liveliness, evocative light, a sense of the painting medium being alive (splashes, granulation, etc.) and, if possible, a sense of enjoyment.
Simon and Caroline Jones

Project:
Istanbul transport system, Istanbul (Turkey), 2003

Client:
Ove Arup, London (UK)

Software/Technique:
Hand ink drawing from client computer model onto
A3 tracing paper, transferred mechanically to A3
200 gsm NOT finish watercolour paper, Windsor
and Newton artist colour, scanning and image
manipulation

People involved:
Simon and Caroline Jones

Time needed:
To draw building and people 4 hours, for painting
and image manipulation 6 hours

Project:
Stanhope Hotel,
New York (USA), 2003

Client:
John Simpson & Partners, London (UK)

Software / Technique:
Computer modelling and hand ink drawing onto
A3 tracing paper, transferred mechanically to A3
200 gsm NOT finish watercolour paper, Windsor
and Newton artist colour, scanning and image
manipulation

People involved:
Simon and Caroline Jones

Time needed:
Computer modelling 4 hours, drawing building
and people 4 hours, painting and image manipulation
6 hours

www.simonjonesandassociates.co.uk

Project:
Dundrum shopping centre,
County Down (Northern Ireland)

Client:
B.K.D. Architects, Dublin (Ireland)

Software / Technique:
Computer modelling and hand ink drawing onto A3
tracing paper, transferred mechanically to A3 200 gsm
NOT finish watercolour paper, Windsor and Newton
artist colour, scanning and image manipulation

People involved:
Richard Lee, Simon and Caroline Jones

Time needed:
Computer model 4 hours, drawing building
and people 4 hours, painting and image manipulation
6 hours

125

Project:
Dundrum shopping centre,
County Down (Northern Ireland)

Client:
B.K.D. Architects, Dublin (Ireland)

Software / Technique:
Computer modelling and hand ink drawing onto A3
tracing paper, transferred mechanically to A3 200 gsm
NOT finish watercolour paper, Windsor and Newton
artist colour, scanning and image manipulation

People involved:
Richard Lee, Simon and Caroline Jones

Time needed:
Computer model 4 hours, drawing building
and people 4 hours, painting and image manipulation
6 hours

There are two images that I would see as an inspiration for our work: Turner's watercolour "Santa Maria della Salute from Grand Canal" (1840), and Hopper's Oil "Office in a small town" (1953).

I love these two paintings for different reasons.

The piece by Turner is full of vitality and is executed with great speed to capture the slanting light, probably from a boat bobbing in the Grand Canal; you sense that it was drawn purely for the artist's personal reference, as he was already thinking of his next four sketches.

Hopper probably took 4 months to complete his work, undergoing stages as rough sketch to large charcoal sketch. The model might be drawn from life, while the other elements might be inspired by photographs or sketchbooks.

Hopper's work is nostalgic and captures the mood of all those boring late afternoons that we have all experienced; the sunlight hitting the walls is somehow more timeless than Turner's light and while Turner's tiny people are transient and full of movement, Hopper's figure is buried in a timeless daydream.
Simon Jones

Project:
Great Court, British Museum,
London (UK), 2000

Client:
Foster & Partners, London (UK)

Software/Technique:
Hand pencil drawing from client computer model,
onto A1 600 gsm NOT finish watercolour paper,
Windsor and Newton artist colour, overwash of
FW liquid acrylic and Dr Ph Martins concentrated
watercolour

People involved:
Simon Jones

Time needed:
Drawing building and people 4 hours, painting
4 hours, client suggested modifications at their office
1 hour

Project 2:
Promotional calendar for Dutra B.V.,
Enschede (the Netherlands), 1994

Client:
Dutra B.V., Enschede (the Netherlands)

Software / Technique:
Hand ink drawing on A3 tracing paper, transferred
by hand to A1 600 gsm NOT finish watercolour
paper, Windsor and Newton artist colour, overwash
of FW liquid acrylic and Dr Ph Martins concentrated
watercolour

People involved:
Simon and Caroline Jones

Time needed:
Drawing 8 hours, painting 8 hours

Project 3:
Royal Crest House, Takasaki (Japan), 2002

Client:
Julian Bicknell & Associates, Surrey (UK)

Software / Technique:
Computer modelling and hand ink drawing onto
A3 tracing paper, transferred mechanically to A3
200 gsm NOT finish watercolour paper, Windsor
and Newton artist colour, scanning and image
manipulation

People involved:
Simon and Caroline Jones

Time needed:
Computer modelling 4 hours, drawing building
and people 4 hours, painting and image manipulation
6 hours

www.simonjonesandassociates.co.uk

Project 1:
Cheyne Row, Chelsea,
London (UK), 2005

Client:
Foster & Partners, London (UK)

Software / Technique:
Hand ink drawing from client computer model,
onto A3 tracing paper, transferred mechanically
to A3 200 gsm NOT finish watercolour paper,
Windsor and Newton artist colour

People involved:
Alan Marten and Simon Jones

Time needed:
Drawing building and people 2 hours,
painting 4 hours

131

Project:
Dining Room, Sir John Soane Museum,
London (UK), 1999

Client:
Self-commissioned

Software/Technique:
Hand pencil drawing onto A3 tracing paper,
transferred by hand to 600 gsm NOT finish
watercolour A2 paper, Windsor and Newton
artist colour

People involved:
Simon Jones

Time needed:
Drawing 4 hours, painting 6 hours

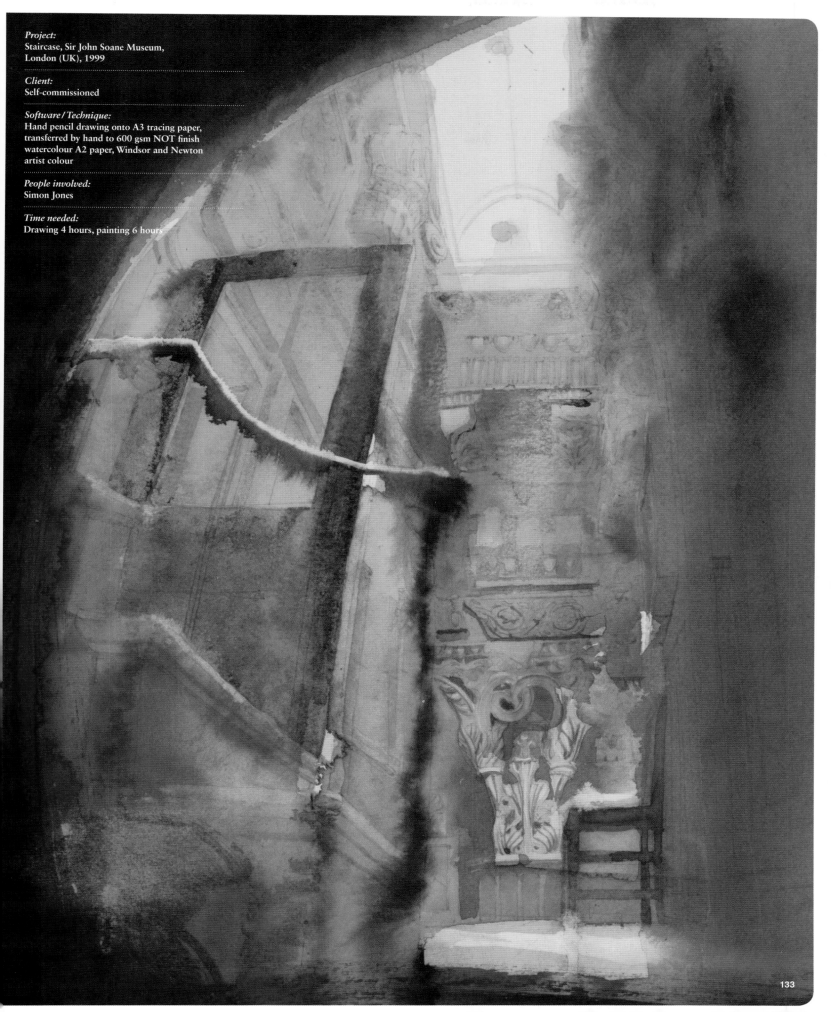

Project:
Staircase, Sir John Soane Museum,
London (UK), 1999

Client:
Self-commissioned

Software / Technique:
Hand pencil drawing onto A3 tracing paper,
transferred by hand to 600 gsm NOT finish
watercolour A2 paper, Windsor and Newton
artist colour

People involved:
Simon Jones

Time needed:
Drawing 4 hours, painting 6 hours

Process

The working process generally starts by choosing the view
to be rendered with the client.

For that, sometimes we use a photo of the existing site
(fig. 1), while other times we prefer a computer model
(fig. 2), either made by client or ourselves.

We do 3D modelling in Superscape, a very old and very
fast program. Generally we quickly portray buildings as
cubes with windows, applying doors and detail as textures.
If necessary, we also employ up to three subcontractors for
computer modelling and line drawing.

We prefer to proceed with image manipulation in Ipix,
again a very old and very fast program, and occasionally
in Photoshop.

Sometimes, as in this case, we work up the computer
render to establish the degree of transparency and the
direction of the sun light (fig. 3).

We then use the render and site context photos to produce
a line drawing (fig. 4).

Sometimes we add people, cars etc., mostly derived from
our hand-produced library, to animate the drawing.
After the client has agreed to the project, we print the
image onto watercolour paper, produce a tonal sketch to
aid composition and light, paint it and continue later
on with some post scanning work done on computer to
add reflections, etc. (fig. 5).

1. Existing site

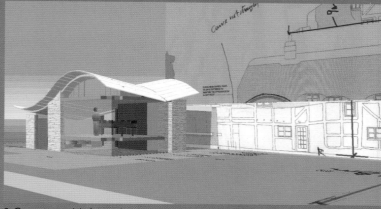

2. Computer model of extension

3. Colour computer render

4. Line drawing

5. The final watercolour

Process

This painting was one of three illustrating an "eco town" just outside London for the green developer Blue Living. The design was at its master planning phase and the precise architecture details of the development had not been fully determined. To reflect this stage in the development of the site, the building forms are non-committal, simply showing large south-facing glazing, shared street surfaces, some green rooves and ecological use of rainwater. As this is our third rendering of the kind, we think there must be a trend for eco towns as a solution to the growing housing shortage in the UK.

1. The first illustration, a "tonal sketch", is a reduced photocopy of the original drawing, sketched over with soft pencil to indicate areas of highlight, midtone, darks and shadows. The original drawing produced on tracing paper at A3 is a trace of the clients SketchUp model with details the implementation on some details.

2. The line drawing is photocopied onto 300 gsm water-colour paper (Waterford NOT). The white tops of clouds are drawn with a white candle.

3. The whole sky area is wetted so the watercolour flows like air. I use artists quality Windsor and Newton watercolours, partly because they produce a good texture and brilliant colours, but also because I like working with this particular brand of colours. Raw Sienna by Rowney, for example, is quite different from the Windsor and Newton version of the same colour.

4. Cobalt blue was applied onto wet paper for the higher, darker areas of the sky.

5. Cerelleum was applied for the lower, lighter areas of the sky near to the horizon, then the darker parts of the clouds were rendered with a mixture of cobalt blue and raw sienna, by working into the wet background.

6. Raw sienna was used to cover all the areas except the white highlighted walls of the buildings where the paper was left bare.

7. Tree: still working while the background is damp, a sap green and raw sienna mix is applied quite thickly to stop spreading.

8. Hairdryer: we chose to let the first wash dry naturally for about 10 minutes to allow the paint form a good granulated texture, before finishing off the work with a hairdryer.

9. A warm colour, a mix of raw sienna and cadmium red, is applied with a small brush to people, shadows and dark interior areas.

10. A local colour is applied with a small brush to cover clothes, road colour, etc.

11. The use of shadow wash of cadmium red and cobalt blue models the forms and unifies the composition.

12. White mullions are obtained with fine "rigger" brush, T-square and set square, liquid acrylic paint with touch of cadmium yellow, so that the window forms are carefully drawn in.

13. Some further highlights and a few more spots of colour are added to complete the painting. Probably some further work in Photoshop will be needed to aid composition.

Work setup

1. Tonal sketch

2. Wax resist on clouds

3. Water on sky

4. Cobalt blue on sky

5. Cerelleum blue on sky

6. Raw sienna

7. Tree

8. Hairdryer

9. Warm colour

10. Local colour

11. Shadow wash

12. White mullions

13. Final image

Detail

Lee Dunnette AIA

3568 Byrd Ave
Allentown, PA 18103
USA

www.leedunnette.com

Lee Dunnette is the sole proprietor and only employee of his architectural rendering office: think of it as a "hermit in the basement" business model.

Lee is 58 years old and has worked with eminent architects such as I. M. Pei, Aldo Rossi, Rafael Viñoly, and renowned firms such as HOK, Beyer Blinder Belle, Ehrenkrantz Eckstut, to name but a few.

He defines himself as an "unabashed romantic, always focused on the play of light in his renderings".

The emotional effect caused by light is a fascinating subject that has been mined by artists for centuries. The season, time of the day, and weather vary in every rendering, and are closely related to the design and context of the building being portrayed. Dusk is a favourite time of the day, affording a dramatic stage set, but there are any number of other ways to spotlight a given design.
Lee Dunnette

Project:
Tank Theatre, New Orleans, Louisiana (USA), 2004

Client:
Self-commissioned

Software / Technique:
Computer layout, AccuRender rendered, pastel

People involved:
Lee Dunnette

Time needed:
About 2 weeks

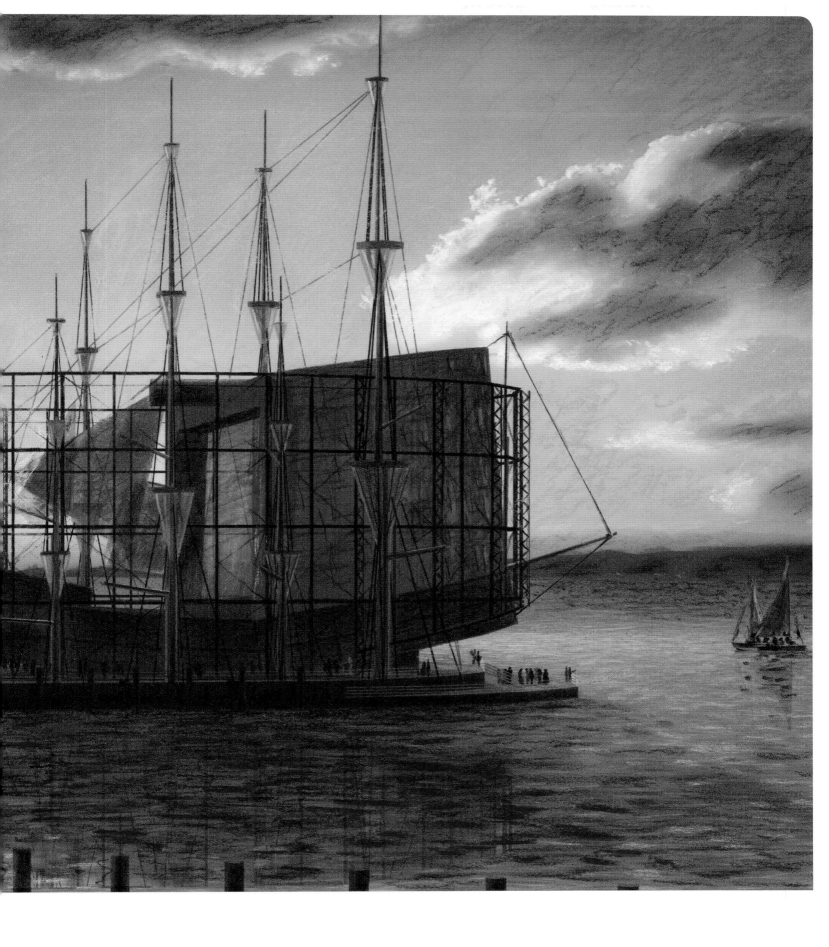

Project:
Pyramid at the Grand Louvre, Paris (France), 1994

Client:
Pei Cobb Freed & Partners, New York (USA)
Michel Macary Architects, Paris (France)

Software / Technique:
Hand and computer layout, acrylic

People involved:
Lee Dunnette

Time needed:
About 3 weeks

A successful rendering has three actors and must satisfy three requirements: the Architect wants accurate modelling of the design, the Salesman wants a natural rendering of the design in context, and the Artist wants to evoke an emotional response from the viewer.

With the advent of computer aided rendering, the first two requirements are easily achieved by any talented technician. The third requirement is not so easy, but it is the stage when rendering becomes art …
Lee Dunnette

Project:
Worth Square Building, New York (USA), 1985

Client:
Self-commissioned

Software/Technique:
Hand layout, airbrush, watercolour, pencil

People involved:
Lee Dunnette

Time needed:
About 3 weeks

WORTH SQUARE
BUILDING

Project:
St Vincent Church, New York (USA), 1990

Client:
Self-commissioned

Software / Technique:
Hand layout, freehand ink, transparent ink

People involved:
Lee Dunnette

Time needed:
About 2 weeks

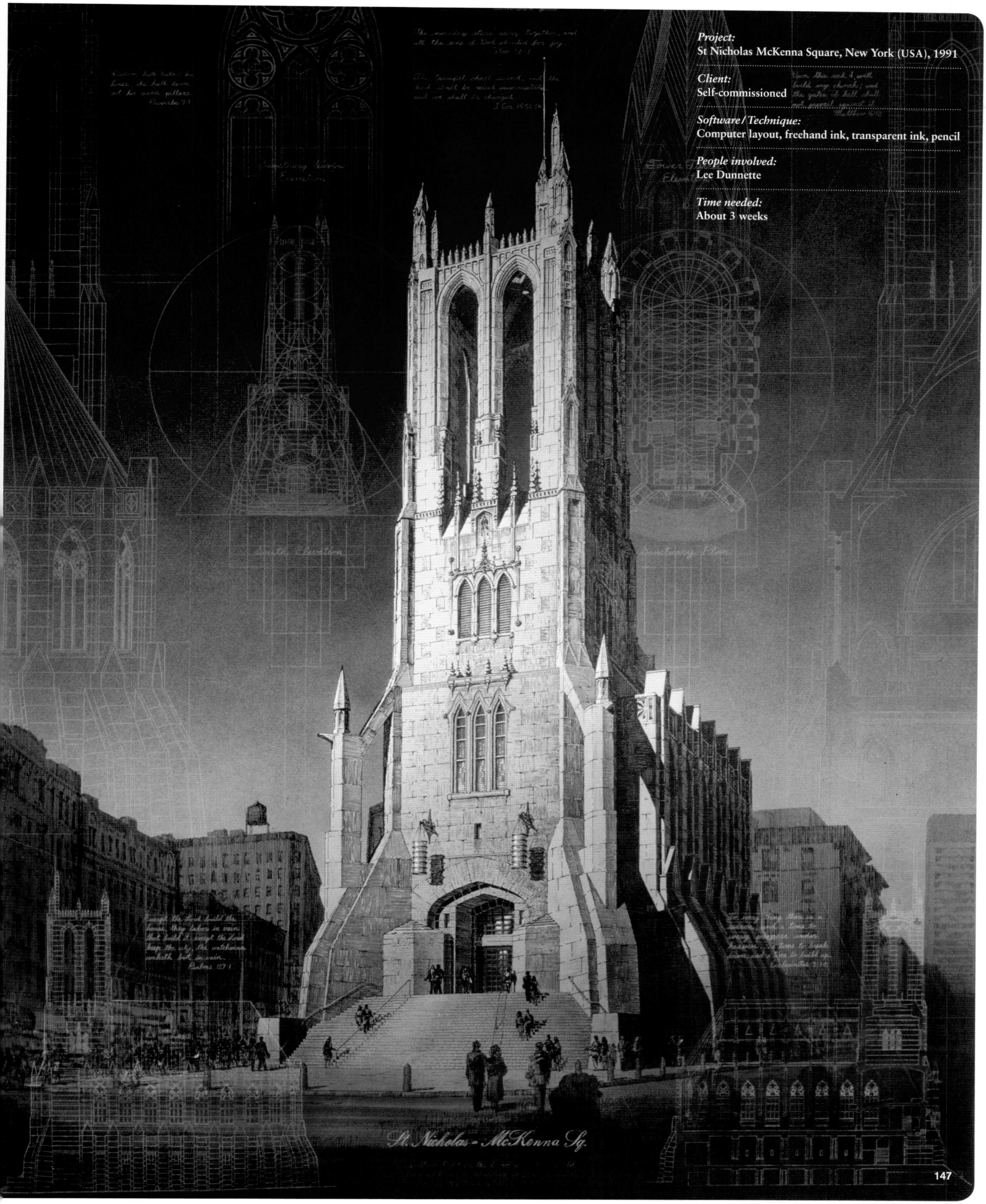

St. Nicholas – McKenna Sq.

Project:
St Nicholas McKenna Square, New York (USA), 1991

Client:
Self-commissioned

Software / Technique:
Computer layout, freehand ink, transparent ink, pencil

People involved:
Lee Dunnette

Time needed:
About 3 weeks

... I do not propose to tell you how to solve this conundrum, but rather to note that this is the ultimate problem that all renderers must confront and solve. There are many paths to the solution, but none is either easy or obvious.

Lee Dunnette

Project:
Tower, Des Moines (USA), 1994

Client:
Brooks Borg & Skiles, Des Moines, Iowa (USA)

Software/Technique:
Computer layout, acrylic

People involved:
Lee Dunnette

Time needed:
About 2 weeks

Project:
Vancouver Library, Vancouver (Canada), 1990

Client:
Hardy Holzman Pfeiffer Architects, New York (USA)

Software/Technique:
Computer layout, acrylic

People involved:
Lee Dunnette

Time needed:
About 2 weeks

Process

I prefer to build the base computer model myself, so to become completely familiar with the design form and materials.

By proceeding as far as possible with the model I clarify the design, moving from AutoCad to Accurender to Photoshop on a Wacom pen tablet. If the work looks stale when I use digital techniques, I switch to hand sketching in pencil, pen or pastel, before returning to digital.

The process can be simply stated as: first establish the facts, then do whatever it takes to get a unique, dramatic, emotional image.

Having been both a "client" and a renderer, I try to communicate regularly to avoid surprises. I always require at least approval of viewpoint and colour sketch, and always allow the client a final review of the finished work.

Contact is maintained via phone and email, depending on the client's preference.

Although regular contact is essential to a smooth relationship and a satisfied client, micro management of the process can destroy the "soul" of a rendering, and an experienced renderer needs to know when to concentrate and work independently.

1

2

3

4

5

Project 1:
Catskill Studio, New York (USA), 1991

Client:
Self-commissioned

Software / Technique:
Hand layout, watercolour

People involved:
Lee Dunnette

Time needed:
About 2 weeks

Project 2:
St Cyril Church, Alexandria (USA), 2008

Client:
Self-commissioned

Software / Technique:
Computer layout, AccuRender rendered, Photoshop, pastel

People involved:
Lee Dunnette

Time needed:
About 2 weeks

Project 3:
Astronauts Memorial (USA), 1989

Client:
Self-commissioned

Software / Technique:
Hand layout, pastel

People involved:
Lee Dunnette

Time needed:
About 2 weeks

Project 4:
St Nicholas Sanctuary, New York (USA), 1991

Client:
Self-commissioned

Software / Technique:
Computer layout, freehand ink, transparent ink

People involved:
Lee Dunnette

Time needed:
About 2 weeks

Project 5:
Spiral Stair, Tampa Bay (USA), 1993

Client:
Self-commissioned

Software / Technique:
Computer layout, AccuRender rendered

People involved:
Lee Dunnette

Time needed:
About 2 weeks

Dennis Allain AIA

50 Fairview Road
Lynnfield Massachusetts 01940
USA

www.dennisallain.com

Dennis Allain founded his own studio in 2004, having worked fifteen years as a designer/architect with several Boston based firms.

Dennis was awarded several prizes, like the Hugh Ferriss Memorial Prize 2006, the highest award in the field of architectural illustration.

Dennis Allain personally creates all the work. The studio offers design services as well as final illustrative products, and can count on several specialized consultants who provide financial, accounting, computer, and colour calibration expertise when required.

If I were to employ more people to work on each project I would probably spend more time directing the process and less time producing the artwork that attracted the client in the first place. My approach could change in the future but, at the moment, the key to our production's philosophy rests in this notion of a "single hand".
Dennis Allain

Project:
Saint George Cathedral, winter 2007

Client:
Self-commissioned

Software / Technique:
Digital, Cinema 4D, Photoshop

People involved:
Dennis Allain AIA

Time needed:
Design, 3D model + illustration = 40 hours

Over time, it was the flexibility to create various subject matter in 3D and the desire to maintain a "traditional" look and feel at the same time, that compelled me to explore the artistic possibilities with the use of both 3D and 2D software.
Dennis Allain

Project:
Air Conditioner, fall 2003

Client:
Self-commissioned

Software/Technique:
Digital, Cinema 4D, Photoshop

People involved:
Dennis Allain AIA

Time needed:
Illustration = 32 hours

I moved to working in 3D in late 2000. I tested several 3D programs and eventually adopted Cinema 4D.
I found that C4D had a very logical layout and a material system easy to understand. Furthermore, the render engine had, and still maintains, a quality to speed ratio that is second to none.
Dennis Allain

Project:
Arthur V. McCarthy Memorial, 2006

Client:
Self-commissioned

Software / Technique:
Digital, Cinema 4D, Photoshop

People involved:
Dennis Allain AIA

Time needed:
Design, 3D model + illustration = 40 hours

I started playing with Photoshop in 1995. As an architect and designer, it became apparent that I needed to continue to nurture and develop my Photoshop skills. It was a program that I could use to manipulate and edit "hand drawn" artwork and to create original images.
Dennis Allain

Project:
Plaza View, China, 2007

Client:
Callison, Seattle (USA)

Software / Technique:
Digital, Cinema 4D, Photoshop

People involved:
Dennis Allain AIA

Time needed:
Design, 3D model + illustration = 22 hours

Project:
City Aerial, 2007

Architect:
Gensler, Los Angeles (USA)

Software / Technique:
Digital, Cinema 4D, Photoshop

People involved:
Dennis Allain AIA

Time needed:
3D model + illustration = 20 hours

DENNIS
ALLAN 07

165

Project:
Exostra IV, summer 2006

Client:
Self-commissioned

Software / Technique:
Digital, Cinema 4D, Photoshop

People involved:
Dennis Allain AIA

Time needed:
Design, 3D model + illustration = 40 hours

Project:
The Station, spring 2004

Client:
Self-commissioned

Software / Technique:
Digital, Cinema 4D, Photoshop

People involved:
Dennis Allain AIA

Time needed:
Design, 3D model + illustration = 34 hours

Project:
Neptune, India, 2008

Client:
Forrec, Toronto (Canada)

Software/Technique:
Digital, Cinema 4D, Photoshop

People involved:
Dennis Allain AIA

Time needed:
Illustration = 20 hours

Project:
River view, Kingdom of Saudi Arabia, 2007

Clients:
Callison, Seattle (USA)

Software / Technique:
Digital, Cinema 4D, Photoshop

People involved:
Dennis Allain AIA

Time needed:
Design, 3D model + illustration = 34 hours

Process

Today I create all my illustrations in two environments: 3D and 2D respectively.

At the onset, a client will present a verbal description of the project along with any relevant visual material to include: architectural drawings, 3D models, sketches and/or photographic references.

Sometimes the clients have prepared a 3D massing model that can be imported into Cinema 4D before further design "testing" is applied right in the 3D model.

A day or two is spent sketching by hand and modelling: design detail, lighting schemes, camera viewpoint(s) and general material selections are the key stages of this process. Once these elements are finished, the first preview is submitted to the client for review and approval.

Once approved, the 3D model undergoes a final revision and is rendered out to be imported into Photoshop. The 3D base image has very little texture information. Most materials are represented as base colours with more complex conditions i.e. glass, ocean, special patterning, etc. being textured by procedural shaders accordingly. The base Cinema 4D rendering is typically 3000 pixels in width and is imported into Photoshop for final painting.

Once in Photoshop, the second and final phase is started.

There I apply colour in a multitude of layers, each being of low opacity. It is this "build up" of colour (similar to a watercolour process) that helps achieve the look and feel of a hand-painted image.

Project 3:
Courtyard, USA, 2007

Architects:
Confidential

Software / Technique:
Digital, Cinema 4D, Photoshop

People involved:
Dennis Allain AIA

Time needed:
3D model + illustration = 20 hours

1. The 3D base image

2. Reflections and materials

3. Plants and details

4. Final image

171

Kirk Fromm, design + illustration

2000 Hamilton Street, #864
Philadelphia, PA 19130
USA

www.kirkfromm.com

Kirk Fromm began his illustration career in 1998, ten years after graduating from Kansas State University with a degree in Interior Architecture.

The core business of the studio is the production of 2D architectural illustrations, typically at the early, conceptual stage of the project.

Initially, Kirk worked in watercolour and coloured pencil, and generated perspectives entirely by hand. Today, his illustrations are still drawn by hand over computer generated models, and for the last few years colour has been applied in Photoshop in a digital-analog-digital process.

As with photography and graphic design, digital technology is forcing architectural illustration into a similar period of "democratization" where many more people can join in the process and produce work of high quality. This has altered the task for those of us wishing to continue as professional illustrators. I've had to move beyond just depicting a building with reasonable accuracy. Now I try to tell a story around the subject I'm rendering, add personality and life, and create something that hopefully continues to stand out in an increasingly crowded field.

Kirk Fromm

Project:
Landscape redevelopment proposal for St Joseph's
University, Philadelphia (USA), 2007

Client:
Metro Architects, Narberth (USA)

Software/Technique:
Pencil drawing over photographic base, digitally
painted in Photoshop

People involved:
Kirk Fromm

Time needed:
4 days

Project:
Landscape redevelopment proposal for St Josephs
University, Philadelphia (USA), 2007

Client:
Metro Architects, Narberth (USA)

Software / Technique:
Pencil drawing over SketchUp model base,
watercolour and digital paint in Photoshop

People involved:
Kirk Fromm

Time needed:
1.5 weeks

When I started my activity in this field in 1998, most leading renderers were using watercolour, and my early work grew from their influence …

… today, I still draw from that experience, achieving something resembling a watercolour, while pushing the limits beyond what could be expected from traditional methods, consciously building up texture and brushwork, and looking for ways to introduce the irregularities typical of the more traditional medium. *Kirk Fromm*

Project:
Proposed residential community,
view of rooftop "living room", Denver (USA), 2007

Client:
Hive Communities, Denver (USA)

Software / Technique:
Pencil drawing over client-provided 3D model base,
painted in Photoshop

People involved:
Kirk Fromm

Time needed:
3 days

Project:
Blankley Hall renovation study, Glenside (USA), 2006

Client:
GLP Architects, Wyncote (USA)

Software/Technique:
Pencil drawing over photo montage, digitally painted
in Photoshop

People involved:
Kirk Fromm

Time needed:
3 days

Project:
Resort development, Sylt (Germany), 2007

Client:
Hapimag, Baar (Switzerland)

Software / Technique:
Pencil drawing over SketchUp model base, painted in
Photoshop with photo-based entourage

People involved:
Kirk Fromm

Time needed:
1 week

Project:
Casino lounge, Miami (USA), 2008

Client:
EwingCole Architects, Philadelphia (USA)

Software / Technique:
Pencil drawing over SketchUp model base, painted in
Photoshop

People involved:
Kirk Fromm

Time needed:
4 days

Project:
Redevelopment proposal for downtown Millburn,
Millburn (USA), 2008

Client:
WRT, Philadelphia (USA)

Software / Technique:
Pencil drawing over SketchUp model base, painted in
Photoshop with photo-based entourage

People involved:
Kirk Fromm

Time needed:
1 week

1

Project 1:
Prova, 2008

Client:
Self-commissioned

Software / Technique:
Created from photos, SketchUp models, digitally
assembled and painted in Photoshop

People involved:
Kirk Fromm

Time needed:
Many hours

Project 2:
Proposed "Downtown" development,
Miami (USA), 2009

Client:
Beame Architectural Partnership, Coral Gables (USA)
with RMGA, developer

Software / Technique:
Pencil drawing over SketchUp model base, digitally
painted in Photoshop

People involved:
Kirk Fromm

Time needed:
1.5 weeks

Project 3:
Proposed "Uptown" development,
Miami (USA), 2009

Client:
Beame Architectural Partnership, Coral Gables (USA)
with RMGA, developer

Software / Technique:
Pencil drawing over SketchUp model base, digitally
painted in Photoshop with photo-based entourage

People involved:
Kirk Fromm

Time needed:
1 week

2

3

Process

I use a wide variety of data to create a rendering – plans, sketches, photos, 3D models, etc. – provided by the client, pulled from personal photo collections or from the many sources available on the web. These resources are then used directly in the image or as a base for my drawing.

What's available for a given project will often direct the approach I use to create my renderings. If the client has a high-quality 3D model, then I'll use an image from that and concentrate on adding the surrounding entourage. If photos are available for the view, and entourage elements can be sourced photographically, then the final illustration might have a more realistic quality. If I draw the entourage and architecture from scratch, then the final rendering typically heads in the opposite direction, and have a softer, more obviously "hand-drawn" look.

For a 3D model, I usually only build a "stage set", so to establish the view angle and scale. I print out a view from the model and draw over it, adding details and background, often switching several times between my drawing board and the 3D model as an image is worked out. The final linework is drawn in pencil on trace, then scanned and brought into Photoshop for colour.

I build my colour up in many layers, constantly pushing the overall image away from the "natural" colour of the initial photos or model into something with a more "lush" and impressionistic feel. As each element is introduced, painted and adjusted, the surrounding elements follow suit until the desired colour and saturation is achieved. As with traditional media, I start with the larger elements to establish the overall tone, adding the smaller details at the end.

The digital revolution has definitely made my job easier in many ways. I can keep my clients updated throughout the process, and final renderings can be sent via email the moment they're done. A certain type of tree, or style of furniture, or the dimensions of a playing field, any information I might need for a rendering is only a quick web-search away. On the other hand, clients have also adjusted to the available technology and now expect more choices, changes and adjustments. As a result, I try to build in as much flexibility into my final renderings as possible in anticipation of their needs.

Project:
Landscape redevelopment proposal for St Josephs University, Philadelphia (USA), 2007

Client:
Metro Architects, Narberth (USA)

Software / Technique:
Pencil drawing over SketchUp model base, watercolour and digital paint in Photoshop

People involved:
Kirk Fromm

Time needed:
1.5 weeks

Step 1: The rough SketchUp model built over the architect's landscape plan.

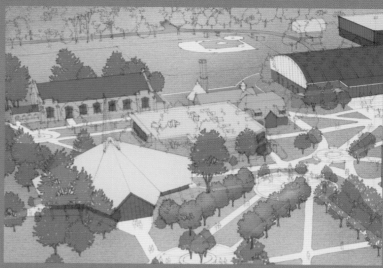

Step 2: The rough SketchUp model was used as the basis for a pencil drawing. The grass colour was built up with a combination of scanned watercolour as well as colour applied in Photoshop.

Step 3: The addition of shadows along with fine-tuning of the other colours.

Step 4: Further details are addressed and the overall tone is closer to the final result.

Step 5: The trees and buildings nearly complete.

Step 6: The final image, with subtle embellishments throughout, along with colour on people and cars to complete the rendering.

ArtandDesign-Studios.com

884 N. 23rd St.
Philadelphia, PA 19130
USA

www.artanddesignstudio.com

ArtandDesignStudios.com is the artist-architect team of Anna Loseva and Sergei Losev.

Anna and Sergei acquired a mastery of hand media before the advent of computers, and remain committed to the aesthetics of hand-drawn imagery.

The studio produces images for architectural practices with an emphasis on the human component of the architectural environment.

The introduction of computers and software into our practice made the rendering process significantly more efficient and responsive to the client's requests. The digital tools make it possible to adjust the rendering in ways that were not feasible in the past. Today, our images would not be possible without the use of modern digital tools.
Anna Loseva

Project:
PIM-MD Hospital Aerial, Jeju (South Korea), 2008

Client:
Ballinger, Philadelphia (USA)

Software / Technique:
SketchUp, Google Earth, pencil, watercolour,
Photoshop

People involved:
Anna Loseva and Sergei Losev

Time needed:
5 days

Project:
JFK Plaza, (diptix image), Philadelphia (USA), 2007

Client:
Wallace Roberts & Todd, Philadelphia (USA)

Software/Technique:
SketchUp, watercolour, Photoshop

People involved:
Anna Loseva and Sergei Losev

Time needed:
5 days

Project:
Chestnut Hill College, Philadelphia (USA), 2007

Client:
SaylorGregg Architects, Philadelphia (USA)

Software/Technique:
Pencil, watercolour, Photoshop

People involved:
Anna Loseva and Sergei Losev

Time needed:
7 days

We usually draw people, objects, and architectural perspectives on separate pieces of paper, and scan and fit them together on the computer screen.

We store the digital files of people, trees, and cars and create a library of images, making subsequent projects more cost-effective.

The digital file, rather than a watercolour on paper, is now our final product.
Anna Loseva

Project:
W Las Vegas Hotel & Casino, Las Vegas (USA), 2006

Client:
Lacina Heitler Architects, New York (USA)

Software / Technique:
Architectural Desktop, watercolour, Photoshop

People involved:
Anna Loseva and Sergei Losev

Time needed:
4 days

Project:
Ocean Park Mall, Moscow (Russia), 2008

Client:
Forrec Ltd., Toronto (Canada)

Software / Technique:
SketchUp, watercolour, PhotoShop

People involved:
Anna Loseva and Sergei Losev

Time needed:
7 days

Project:
Lansdowne Theatre Restoration,
Lansdowne (USA), 2007

Clients:
John Millner Architects Inc, Chadds Ford (USA)

Software/Technique:
PhotoStitch, pencil, watercolour, Photoshop

People involved:
Anna Loseva and Sergei Losev

Time needed:
7 days

Project:
La Salle University Cafeteria, Philadelphia (USA),
2006

Client:
DLR Group, Philadelphia (USA)

Software / Technique:
SketchUp, pencil, watercolour, Photoshop

People involved:
Anna Loseva and Sergei Losev

Time needed:
6 days

Project:
The Franklin Institute Earth Sciences Exhibit,
Philadelphia (USA), 2007

Client:
The Franklin Institute, Philadelphia (USA)

Software / Technique:
Pencil, watercolour, Photoshop

People involved:
Anna Loseva and Sergei Losev

Time needed:
6 days

Process

The first step of the process is the client's agreement on the perspectival point of view.

Sometimes this happens through a review of the client's digital model and the choice of the view to be rendered is made on the computer screen. At other times, we either hand sketch or create a SketchUp model, depending on the project. Upon the client's approval, the illustration moves into the drawing stage.

The development of the Private School Garden image illustrates this process.

The work began with a hand sketch. A rectangular frame could not accommodate the story of the Garden within the confines of conventional perspective. Capitalizing on the school's philosophical emphasis on process, we came up with an idea of multiple frames, incorporating intermediate stages into the final image.

Once the client approved the composition, we began to work on the drawing: while one of us developed the perspective, the other drew people, plants and trees. All elements were assembled in Photoshop and underwent multiple adjustments, travelling from the computer screen through the printer to the drawing tables, and back, numerous times.

The finished drawing was emailed to the client and, again, adjusted according to the client's requests. The adjustment was facilitated by the fact that each element existed in its own Photoshop layer.

Finally, the central piece was rendered in watercolour over a digital line print, then scanned and inserted into the larger drawing. In many cases, the final watercolour is also subject to digital adjustments.

1. Hand sketch with the concept of multiple frames

Project:
Private School Garden, Philadelphia (USA), 2009

Client:
Purdy O'Gwynn Architects Inc., Philadelphia (USA)

Software / Technique:
Pencil, pen, watercolour, Photoshop

People involved:
Anna Loseva and Sergei Losev

Time needed:
4 days

2. Development of the perspective

3. Insertion of people, plants and trees

4. Rendered final image with multiple frames incorporating intermediate stages

Andy Hickes
Digital
Architectural
Illustration

303 West 29th Street #B
New York, NY 10001
USA

www.rendering.net

Andy Hickes started his career in the 1970s. The office has evolved over the years from one person to many and back again.

Andy founded his first office in his brother's basement in Washington DC. Four years later he moved to New York City and founded a new office consisting of eight airbrush stations. During the last twenty years he has switched completely to computer and reduced the office to a single room with one assistant.

Andy Hickes's work spans thirty-five years during which the profession has been revolutionized many times. His portfolio encompasses a significant period of time, one that has seen an era of big changes in the methodology as well.

With the digital revolution, the personality of each renderer's style in the 1970s was replaced with greater visual conformity in the 1990s. This, however, was later on compensated by a perfected technique made possible by ever-advancing software, resulting in deeply saturated colour, more subtle variations in light, richer surface texture and an overall level of realism never seen before.
Andy Hickes

Project:
Motown Café, Las Vegas, Nevada (USA), 1998

Client:
Haverson Architecture and Design,
New York City (USA)

Software/Technique:
Photoshop

Time needed:
3 weeks

Project:
Multi-use complex Times Square,
Hong Kong (China), 1996

Client:
Brennan Beer Gorman architects,
New York City (USA)

Software/Technique:
3ds Max, Photoshop

Time needed:
6 weeks

Like all renderers, in the 1970s I worked exclusively by hand, building the drawing piece by piece with components that were separately rendered, individually perfected and then merged in the final product.
Andy Hickes

Project:
Honolulu, Hawaii (USA), 1983

Client:
Brennan Beer Gorman Architects,
New York City (USA)

Software/Technique:
Airbrush

Time needed:
2 weeks

Project:
Trump World Tower at United Nations Plaza,
New York City (USA), 2002

Client:
Costas Kondylis Architects, New York City (USA)

Software / Technique:
3ds Max, Photoshop

Time needed:
3 weeks

As the 1990s dawned, the impact of increasingly powerful computers running ever more sophisticated software gradually reshaped not only the way renderings were made, but the way they looked.
Andy Hickes

Project:
Lobby of the Trump World Tower at United Nations
Plaza, New York City (USA), 2002

Client:
Costas Kondylis Architects, New York City (USA)

Software / Technique:
3ds Max, Photoshop

Time needed:
3 weeks

Project:
Honolulu, Hawaii (USA), 1983

Client:
Brennan Beer Gorman Architects,
New York City (USA)

Software/Technique:
Airbrush

Time needed:
2 weeks

Project:
Estée Lauder installation, Las Vegas (USA), 2004

Client:
Estée Lauder Design, New York City (USA)

Software / Technique:
Photoshop

Time needed:
2 weeks

Project:
Studio 54, Club, New York City (USA), 1980

Client:
Tony Walton, New York City (USA)

Software / Technique:
Paint on back of acetate

Time needed:
10 days

Project:
Canal Centre Multi-use complex,
Alexandria (USA), 1982

Client:
Brennan Beer Gorman Architects,
New York City (USA)

Software / Technique:
Airbrush

Time needed:
2 weeks

Process

The overall sequence of rendering begins with choosing what is fixed and has to be illustrated as specified by the architect/designer. These are usually the architectural materials that create the form and substance of the building. The client is most concerned about these and they must be accurate. Specified planting comes next because, although its location is determined, I have some flexibility when choosing size and season.

Once the basic forms are in place, I select preliminary views. Good compositional skills are vital for this stage of the process because the view can transform a rendering into a haphazard snapshot or a professional photograph, depending on its quality. It determines if the work will be marred with perspectival distortion that sacrifice a realist look and disorient the viewer. Perspectival distortions can ruin the most sophisticated entourage.

The entourage "people" are next. Of course they provide scale, but actual placement of people is an important compositional element and can also be used to direct the viewer's eye. The intended viewers of the rendering are the non-professionals, because my work is used mostly for publication, advertising, and fund-raising rather than as a basis for design approval. These viewers focus their attention on the people present in the rendering and are unforgiving if they are badly done or awkwardly placed.

Cars elicit less volatile emotions but have the disadvantage of being visually dated within a few years. The life span of renderings can be five or ten years. You do not want your rendering of the Grand Hotel spoilt by a glamorous couple getting out of what looks like a used car in front.

Lastly I add the sky and glass reflections. These are two of the least fixed aspects of the rendering and where drama can be added if appropriate. All the rest of the rendering is then adjusted in colour and contrast to match the sky.

Project 1:
Madison Square Garden West,
New York City (USA), 2000

Client:
Andy Hickes, New York City (USA)

Software / Technique:
3ds Max, Photoshop

Time needed:
6 weeks

Project 2:
Plaza Hotel Ballroom Restoration,
New York City (USA), 2008

Client:
Andy Hickes, New York City (USA)

Software / Technique:
Photoshop

Time needed:
3 weeks

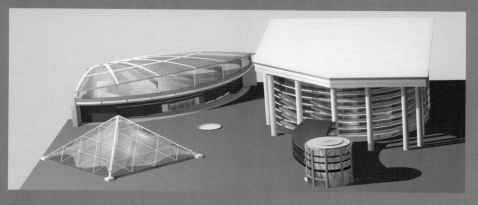

1
Once I have gathered all the data I create a rough computer model and I send the client a few preliminary views.

2a
Once I have received the client's approval, I proceed with rendering the chosen view.

2b
When the rendering is complete I present it once again to the client and then insert all the changes and additional details he has specified.

The Plaza

LABTOP
RENDERING

63 rue rambuteau
75004 Paris
France

www.labtop-rendering.com

Labtop rendering is composed of its director, Thomas Sériès, and seven freelance collaborators – all architects. The Paris-based studio is opening a second office in Los Angeles.

Thomas Sériès is Professor of architectural project communication tools at the École Spéciale d'Architecture of Paris.

Labtop Rendering is a multidisciplinary office that focuses on architecture as a system of signs. The studio mostly works for architects and is involved in architectural competitions.

… so we're not that much into the real appearance of things. We consider the projects with an emotional edge, searching for the potential rather than the reality. As a matter of fact, our whole crew is mostly made by young architects at the start of a promising architectural career. Wannabe architects and not 3D engineers.
Thomas Sériès

Office > LABTOP RENDERING

Project:
Bawadi, Dubai (United Arab Emirates), 2007

Client:
BIG, Copenhagen (Denmark)

Software / Technique:
Cinema 4D, Photoshop

People involved:
1

Time needed:
1 day

225

Project:
Deichmanske Library, Oslo (Norway), 2009

Client:
Schmidt Hammer Lassen Architects, Aarhus
(Denmark)

Software / Technique:
Cinema 4D, Photoshop

People involved:
3

Time needed:
1 week

In traditional 3D rendering, the software is designed to achieve renderings ever closer to reality. At some point we grew skeptical of this idea and we had to question this temptation in light of what's really at stake.
Thomas Sériès

Project:
Tour signale, La Défense (France), 2008
.....
Client:
Libeskind, New York (USA) and AUC, Paris (France)
.....
Software / Technique:
Cinema 4D, Photoshop
.....
People involved:
3
.....
Time needed:
2 days

Project:
Apraskin, St Petersburg (Russia), 2007

Client:
MVRDV, Rotterdam (the Netherlands)

Software / Technique:
Cinema 4D, Photoshop

People involved:
3

Time needed:
5 days

Somehow, the spectacular edge is something we use carefully.

Having said that, we try to brighten the project with an emotional edge rather than simply apply specific technical notions: we intend to be noticeable but explicit. This means that we like to control our features and try to achieve a spectacular view but not at all costs, never systematically.

As in all things, it is always a matter of proportion between the explicit and the emotional: we like to spice up our images but refrain from burning the whole thing.
Thomas Sériès

Project:
Museum, Wrocław (Poland), 2008

Client:
Odile Deck, Paris (France)

Software / Technique:
Cinema 4D, Photoshop

People involved:
3

Time needed:
2 days

Project:
Zorlu, Istanbul (Turkey), 2007

Client:
Odile Deck, Paris (France)

Software / Technique:
Cinema 4D, Photoshop

People involved:
3

Time needed:
2 days

While making an image, we never lose sight of the overall project and the purpose of the image, which is essentially to give a clear explanation of the strongest architectural intentions.

A beautiful image might not always be a clever one. We are constantly adjusting our work, fine tuning the image so that it can be easily understood. A clever image is a useful one. Its quality and effect is not determined by the software and the hardware favoured, rather by the successful combination of well-aimed shots.
Thomas Sériès

Project:
Restaurant, Opéra Garnier, Paris (France), 2008

Client:
Odile Deck, Paris (France)

Software / Technique:
Cinema 4D, Photoshop

People involved:
3

Time needed:
5 days

Project:
Bombay, Bombay (India), 2007

Client:
Skidmore Owings & Merrill LLP, Chicago (USA)

Software / Technique:
Zoom, Cinema 4D, Photoshop

People involved:
2

Time needed:
1 week

Our motto is that you need to give the public the kind of visible signals necessary to a clear understanding of what is happening. Anybody can be cool, but to achieve awesome it takes practice.
Thomas Sériès

Project:
Deichmanske Library, Oslo (Norway), 2009

Client:
Schmidt Hammer Lassen Architects,
Aarhus (Denmark)

Software / Technique:
Cinema 4D, Photoshop

People involved:
3

Time needed:
1 week

Process

I have to clarify that we have never been involved in any drawing contest of any kind. Most of the time we are commissioned for architectural competitions. Because we sell our work for architecture competitions, we get involved in the project at its first stage.

We use 3D software as a research tool with constant feedback from the commissioning architect. The project is subject to many many updates in a very short time. The design keeps changing until the very last minute.

What is important in our process is to be very responsive at that time, so we need to be super efficient and very clear in our approach. Experience has shown that a wise and clever architect often dislikes neat and accurate renderings because a realistic image does not show the unfinished project in its best light.

In any case our job negotiates between time, budget, and optimal result.

The 3D rendering process is cumbersome and costly, and therefore not flexible enough for our commissions. So we develop other techniques, collage and such like, which are less sophisticated, a lot quicker, and produce a convincing result: explicit, cheap and efficient.

A clear example of our method of working is the BIG – Shanghai renderings. There's this first image which is like a preview, a rough view where we've positioned all the elements to compose the scene. The second image is the final rendering. Interestingly, BIG chose to show the first image on its website while the second one, smoothed up for the jury, was presented in the competition entry. The preview has a fresher appeal compared to the better tuned final rendering, a result that seems to corroborate our theory that well-done is not always what one would expect.

Project 1:
Danish pavilion, Shanghai (China), 2008

Client:
BIG, Copenhagen (Denmark)

Software / Technique:
Cinema 4D, Photoshop

People involved:
2

Time needed:
3 days

Project 2:
Tour, Paris (France), 2006

Client:
Fra Loci Anima, Paris (France)

Software / Technique:
Cinema 4D, Photoshop

People involved:
2

Time needed:
3 days

1 Preview

1 Final rendering

2 Colours and atmosphere proposals

Rendertaxi GbR

Rendertaxi GbR
Königstrasse 31
52064 Aachen
Germany

www.rendertaxi.de

Rendertaxi was founded in Aachen in 2004 by Alexander Pfeiffer and Felix Volland. Today the company is composed of eight persons – mostly architects and students of architecture – working together at one table in a renovated old building in the city of Aachen.

The core business of the studio consists in the digital production of images and animation for European architects.

The images produced are intended for visual communication and examination of the design concept as well as for marketing and promotion.

Successful collaboration with our clients is based on architectural understanding and the ability to quickly read the design concept, and to interpret it to the full satisfaction of all involved following a constant, in-progress communication. Our goal is to elaborate and visualize the essence, aesthetics and function of the product and the concept to perfection.
Alexander Pfeiffer and Felix Volland

Project:
Wisniowy Garden Project (Poland), 2008

Client:
Massimiliano Fuksas Architetto,
Frankfurt (Germany)

Software / Technique:
Cinema 4D, VRay, Rhino, Photoshop

People involved:
Alexander Pfeiffer, Stefan Amann

Project:
Central Station, Bologna (Italy), 2008

Client:
UN Studio, Amsterdam (the Netherlands)

Software / Technique:
Cinema 4D, VRay, Rhino, Photoshop

People involved:
Felix Volland, Stefan Amann, Jens Kampermann,
Moritz Krogmann, Davit Mulugeta

Many factors lead us to the genesis of a vivid and meaningful image: our persistent and genuine passion for our job, our ambition to create something special and discover something new, as well as the pleasant, serene and professional atmosphere that surrounds our team.
Felix Volland

Project:
Savska, Zagreb (Croatia), 2008

Client:
Anin Jeromin Fitilidis, Düsseldorf (Germany)

Software / Technique:
Cinema 4D, VRay, Rhino, Photoshop

People involved:
Alexander Pfeiffer, Stefan Amann, Davit Mulugeta, Michael Padberg

Project:
Headquarter Patrizia, Augsburg (Germany), 2007

Client:
Kadawittfeldarchitektur, Aachen (Germany)

Software / Technique:
Cinema 4D, VRay, Rhino, Photoshop

People involved:
Alexander Pfeiffer

There are many different styles for a rendering, from an abstract and concept-oriented representation to a perfect simulation of space and light in a photo-realistic image. It is an ever changing reality, since the continuously growing capacity and technical possibilities raise our ambitions and our clients' expectations at the same time. In all this our main concern remains the same as it concentrates on visualization as a mean for transmitting an architectural concept: we focus on the stylization and abstraction of the design as well as on the use of graphic components, to achieve the essence and concept of the building.
Felix Volland

Project:
Gateway Competition, Birmingham (UK), 2008

Client:
UN Studio, Amsterdam (the Netherlands)

Software / Technique:
Cinema 4D, VRay, Rhino, Photoshop

People involved:
Felix Volland, Alexander Pfeiffer, Stefan Amann, Moritz Krogmann

Project:
Post office, Rotterdam (the Netherlands), 2008

Client:
UN Studio, Amsterdam (the Netherlands)

Software/Technique:
Cinema 4D, VRay, Rhino, Photoshop

People involved:
Felix Volland, Stefan Amann, Gülsüm Dizdar,
Andreas Horsky, Moritz Krogmann, Michael Padberg,
Alexander Pfeiffer

Project:
Visans Hus, Västervik (Sweden), 2007

Client:
Visans Hus Arkitekter, Stockholm (Sweden)

Software / Technique:
Cinema 4D, Maxwell Render, Photoshop

People involved:
Felix Volland, Christoph Wasserhoven

The daily observation of the environment provides our main source of inspiration, together with the work of many very talented colleagues in the field of computer graphics, architectural visualization and photography, especially the work of the photographer Walter Niedermayr.
Felix Volland

Project:
Central Station, Bologna (Italy), 2008
....

Client:
UN Studio, Amsterdam (the Netherlands)
....

Software / Technique:
Cinema 4D, VRay, Rhino, Photoshop
....

People involved:
Stefan Amann, Jens Kampermann, Moritz Krogmann, Davit Mulugeta, Felix Volland

Project:
Beachroad, Singapore, 2007

Client:
UN Studio, Amsterdam (the Netherlands)

Software / Technique:
Cinema 4D, Maxwell Render, Rhino, Photoshop

People involved:
Felix Volland, Alexander Pfeiffer

Project:
Waterfront, Dubai (United Arab Emirates), 2007

Client:
UN Studio, Amsterdam (the Netherlands)

Software/Technique:
Cinema 4D, VRay, Rhino, Photoshop

People involved:
Alexander Pfeiffer, Stefan Amann, Daniele del Grande,
Felix Volland, Claude Wantz

Project 1:
Study, 2006

Client:
Self-commissioned

Software / Technique:
Cinema 4D, Maxwell Render, Photoshop

People involved:
Alexander Pfeiffer

Project 2:
Study, 2006

Client:
Self-commissioned

Software / Technique:
Cinema 4D, Maxwell Render, Photoshop

People involved:
Alexander Pfeiffer

Project 3:
Asian Games, Guangzhou (China), 2008

Client:
gmp, von Gerkan, Marg und Partner, Aachen
(Germany)

Software / Technique:
Cinema 4D, VRay, Rhino, Photoshop

People involved:
Alexander Pfeiffer, Stefan Amann, Daniele del Grande,
Moritz Krogmann, Michael Padberg, Felix Volland

Project 4:
Augustinerhöfe, Nuremberg (Germany), 2008

Client:
Allmann Sattler Wappner, Munich (Germany)

Software / Technique:
Cinema 4D, VRay, Rhino, Photoshop

People involved:
Stefan Amann

1

2

3

4

Process

An image is produced in several steps: Commission – Idea – Preparation – Production – Postwork.

Early integration in the process allows us to bring into the project our own experience in visualization and in successfully completed projects.

We tend to appoint a project manager responsible for the creation of the image concept, structuring and observation of the agenda, as well as communication with the client. The project manager guides the team, distributes the tasks and ensures the final quality of the images. He also constantly communicates with the client, updating him during the whole course of the project.

Since one of the most important parts of our creative activity is concept visualization for architectural contests, where we work under strong time pressure – and often with unfinished data for concept and construction – we built up a procedure that allow us to work with great flexibility and to react rapidly to changes and corrections from the client until completion.

Flexibility is the key factor for a successful project when we are working on a short-term project.

A large part of our image composition, as well as its final look, is created in two-dimensional post-processing. Parallel to the 3D work, the team starts the 2D post-production as soon as the first preview rendering is ready.

Depending on the project and its specifications, the different compositional elements for the image – i.e. sky, background, people, cars, trees, etc. – are either added during the 2D post-production or inserted during the rendering process as 3D elements and rendered with the model.
The creation of images and animations is organized in several passes and channels that allow us great freedom for composing and correcting during post-production.

3D modelling in Cinema 4D
We work with complex "instanced" structures because this allows us to
rapidly adapt the geometry and helps manage the details.

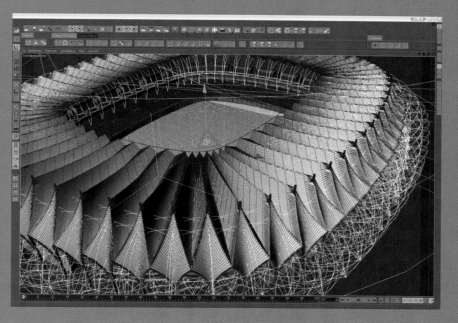

Interface in Cinema 4D
The object manager is crucial when working on extensive models,
because it allows a hierarchical array of single objects.

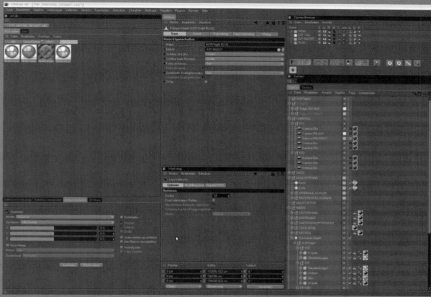

Post-production in Photoshop
Layers and masks allow non-destructive work. In this way you can then
save and re-use your setting for a new rendering.

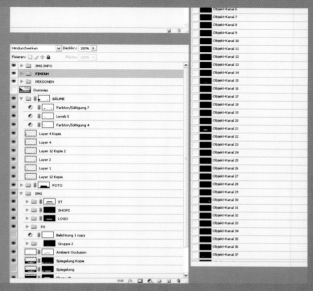

studio amd, painting + motion

333 Westminster Street
Studio 200
Providence RI 02903
USA

www.studioamd.com

Jon Kletzien and Richard Dubrow founded studio amd in 1992. Today, the company comprises seventeen persons and three studios: the Providence headquarters (Rhode Island) and branches in Tampa (Florida) and New York City.

The studio's core business is the production of images and animation for architects and developers around the world.

studio amd was the first digital studio to win the Hugh Ferriss Memorial Prize for illustration and in 2008 was also awarded a Siggraph Technical Achievement prize and a CINE Golden Eagle for animation.

… the operative word here at studio amd is "life". Many firms are able to reproduce with accuracy the design of important architectural projects. However, only a few can actually show the individual character and personality of each project, so obvious to both the architect and the client when they first expressed their design concept. The art of studio amd moves hearts, as well as minds. And, in so doing, that art moves the deal … whether in winning a commission, building public consensus, convincing funding partners, or attracting buyers and tenants …
Richard Dubrow

Project:
2014 Winter Olympics, Sochi (Russia), 2007

Client:
HOK Event | MASS Studio

Software / Technique:
3ds Max, VRay, Photoshop

People involved:
4

Time needed:
2 weeks

Project:
Swede Hill House, Block Island,
Rhode Island (USA), 2008

Client:
Aquidneck Fine Properties, Rhode Island (USA)

Software / Technique:
3ds Max, VRay, Photoshop

People involved:
3

Time needed:
2 weeks

1

2

Project 1:
Sherwood Equities Tower, New York (USA), 2006

Client:
Kohn Pedersen Fox Architects, New York (USA)

Software / Technique:
3ds Max, VRay, Photoshop

People involved:
2

Time needed:
1.5 weeks

Project 2:
Hermitage Guggenheim Museum,
Vilnius (Lithuania), 2008

Client:
Studio Daniel Libeskind, New York (USA)

Software / Technique:
3ds Max, VRay, Photoshop

People involved:
3

Time needed:
2 weeks

Project 3:
40 Mercer Residences, New York (USA), 2006

Client:
André Balazs, New York (USA), and Jean Nouvel,
Paris (France)

Software / Technique:
3ds Max, Brazil, Photoshop

People involved:
3

Time needed:
2 months

Project 4:
Los Angeles Federal Courthouse,
Los Angeles (USA), 2007

Client:
Perkins & Will, Chicago (USA)

Software / Technique:
3ds Max, VRay, Photoshop

People involved:
2

Time needed:
2 weeks

3

4

Project:
Proposed Lounge, Boston (USA), 2006

Client:
3SIX0 Architects, Providence (USA)

Software / Technique:
3ds Max, VRay, Photoshop

People involved:
3

Time needed:
2 weeks

Project:
Kowloon Tower, Kowloon (Hong Kong), 2008

Client:
Kohn Pedersen Fox Architects, New York (USA)

Software / Technique:
3ds Max, Hi Res QFX, Photoshop

People involved:
3

Time needed:
1 week

Project:
New York City Centre, New York (USA), 2008

Client:
Polshek, New York (USA)

Software / Technique:
3ds Max, VRay, Photoshop

People involved:
4

Time needed:
2 weeks

Project:
456 West 19th Street, New York (USA), 2007

Client:
Tamarkin Co., New York (USA)

Software/Technique:
3ds Max, VRay, Photoshop, print with coloured
pencil (illustration done in conjunction with Paul
Stevenson Oles, FAIA)

People involved:
3

Time needed:
2.5 weeks

Project:
Los Angeles Federal Courthouse,
Los Angeles (USA), 2007

Client:
Perkins & Will, Chicago (USA)

Software / Technique:
3ds Max, VRay, Photoshop

People involved:
2

Time needed:
1.5 weeks

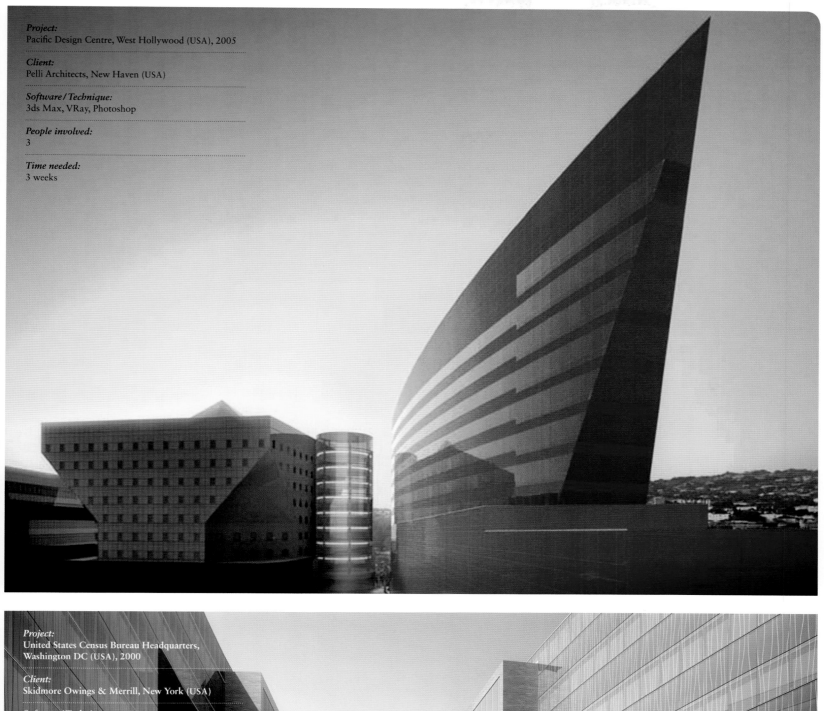

Project:
Pacific Design Centre, West Hollywood (USA), 2005

Client:
Pelli Architects, New Haven (USA)

Software / Technique:
3ds Max, VRay, Photoshop

People involved:
3

Time needed:
3 weeks

Project:
United States Census Bureau Headquarters,
Washington DC (USA), 2000

Client:
Skidmore Owings & Merrill, New York (USA)

Software / Technique:
AutoCAD, 3ds Max, Hi-Res QFX

People involved:
3

Time needed:
2 weeks

Process

Our drawing process starts with listening and understanding where the building is going to be positioned geographically and in its creator's mind.

This type of information helps us place the sun, suggest the right light and setting for the site and enrich the environment to further the architect's message.

Once the point of view and the intensity/location of the primary light source have been determined, the 3D work can be triaged, and the most efficient means to accomplish it are set forth and executed. Models are assembled from a variety of sources, created in Z Brush, AutoCAD, Revit, Onyx Tree, Rhino or most likely 3ds Max.

At this stage of the rendering process wireframe images are submitted to the client in order to confirm the geometry/detailing of the architecture, and fine-tune the view's composition.

Now that all the information has been logged in Max (we use the VRay render engine) we can add the lighting and materials.

During this process we share low res preview images with the client a couple of times to make sure we are moving in the right direction and to receive further direction on material specifications.

About three days before the deadline, we start rendering the final elements and masks. Finally we bring them together in Photoshop piece by piece to composite them, add entourage, and transform basic computer rendering into a handcrafted piece of digital art.

Finally the client receives one last update and then we finalize all details before delivering a flattened image file.

Federico Pitzalis

via Andrea Busiri Vici 36/38
00152 Rome
Italy

www.bv38.com

Federico Pitzalis's studio is a small office comprising the owner, one employee and a varying number of freelance collaborators.

The studio concerns itself with the production of renderings for regular clients between Rome and Munich, and Pitzalis's philosophy is far removed from a "puristic rendering approach", where the images result from precise settings of the rendering engine.

Every phase of the construction of an image is essential to us and there isn't one more prominent than the others as they all contribute to the all important final result. Post-production, for example, can be very light, or on the contrary, fundamental for structuring an image. It sometimes happens that we need to compute the same image many times with small "ad-hoc" variations and combine them during the post-production to achieve the final result. In other cases, post-production is almost absent and it is the cut, the framing, the light that compose the image.
Federico Pitzalis

Project:
Concorso internazionale per il Completamento del
Museo Nivola, Orani (Italy), 2007

Client:
Federico Pitzalis and Daniele Durante, Rome (Italy)

Software / Technique:
Rhinoceros, 3ds Max, VRay, Photoshop

People involved:
Federico Pitzalis

Time needed:
1 day

Project (double page):
Nuova sede dell'Istituto Postelegrafonici,
Rome (Italy), 2007

Client:
Daniele Durante with AI Engineering,
Rome (Italy)

Software / Technique:
Rhinoceros, 3ds Max, VRay, Photoshop

People involved:
Federico Pitzalis

Time needed:
2 days

Project (double page):
Institut des cultures d'Islam, Paris (France), 2008

Client:
Nemesi Studio, Rome (Italy)

Software / Technique:
AutoCAD, 3ds Max, VRay, Photoshop

People involved:
Federico Pitzalis, Claudio Cortese

Time needed:
2 days

Project:
Residence Eurodomus Z27Z31,
Rome (Italy), 2001

Client:
Nemesi Studio, Rome (Italy)

Software / Technique:
AutoCAD, Artlantis, Photoshop

Time needed:
2 days

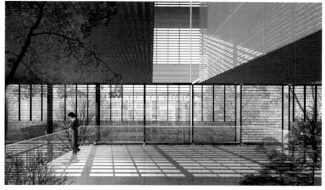

Project (double page):
Atasehir Residential Project, Rome (Italy), 2008

Client:
Nemesi Studio, Rome (Italy)

Software / Technique:
AutoCAD, 3ds Max, VRay, Photoshop

People involved:
Federico Pitzalis

Time needed:
2 days

Project:
Concorso internazionale per il Completamento del
Museo Nivola, Orani (Italy), 2007

Client:
Federico Pitzalis and Daniele Durante, Rome (Italy)

Software / Technique:
Rhinoceros, 3ds Max, VRay, Photoshop

People involved:
Federico Pitzalis

Time needed:
3 days

Process

The process starts by gathering and analysing information from the client, mostly 2D drawings and sketches.

The material received is used to build a rough 3D model in Rhinoceros, where we fix some points of view to submit to the client.

After his approval we export the model to 3D studio Max where we start setting the lights, materials, environment and vegetation.

After computation with the VRay rendering engine, the resulting image is imported in Photoshop and there animated with extra elements like people, furniture, etc.

Case-by-case communication with the client is very important for the process.

Sometimes it is very fast, essentially a kick-off briefing and a final review. In other cases we need to communicate several times and build the image step-by-step with the client.

The most important meeting is the first one, where we identify – together with the client – the goals to be achieved and the "flavour" of the image.

Project:
Commercial, Apartment and Office Tower, Hanoi (Vietnam), 2008

Client:
Nickl & Partner Architekten AG, Munich (Germany)

Software / Technique:
Rhinoceros, 3ds Max, VRay, Photoshop

People involved:
Federico Pitzalis, Marco De Angelis

Time needed:
4 days

Marco Giovanni De Angelis/ Studio Vision Srl

Via Annibale de Gasparis 61
00143 Roma
Italy

www.omology.com

Marco Giovanni De Angelis joined Studio Vision srl in 2008. He graduated at the Università La Sapienza di Roma with a degree in architecture.

The studio works for regular clients based in Rome and has its core business at the digital intersection between cinema, architecture and advertising.

Marco Giovanni De Angelis regularly contributes articles, essays and interviews on computer graphics to il Giornale dell'Architettura and his expertise as digital specialist is often called upon for researching architectural visualization at the Università La Sapienza di Roma.

For us the most important elements of our renderings are the atmosphere, the feeling behind our images which could express elegance, harmony, melancholy, etc. … To visualize these feelings, we resort to a clever use of the light and to the investigation of the link between the project and the site. Sometimes we use iconographic references relevant to the situation in which we work. The careful and balanced use of all these elements afford us success in our communication with the clients and the viewers.

Marco Giovanni De Angelis

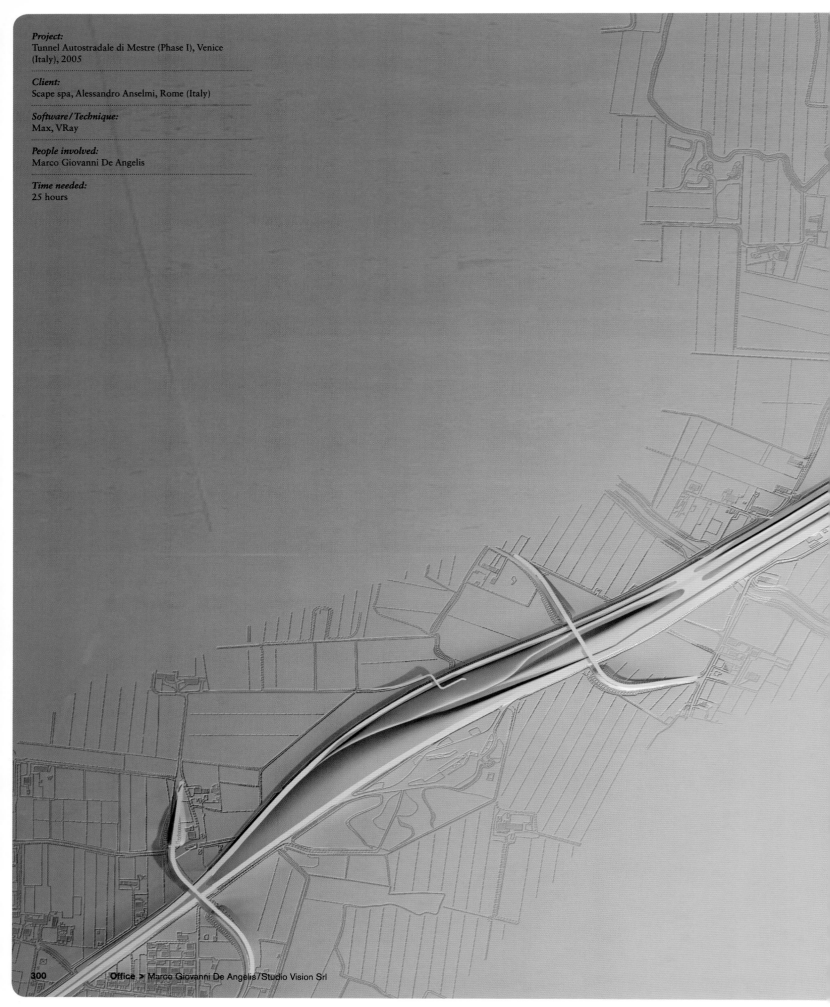

Project:
Tunnel Autostradale di Mestre (Phase I), Venice
(Italy), 2005

Client:
Scape spa, Alessandro Anselmi, Rome (Italy)

Software/Technique:
Max, VRay

People involved:
Marco Giovanni De Angelis

Time needed:
25 hours

Office > Marco Giovanni De Angelis/Studio Vision Srl

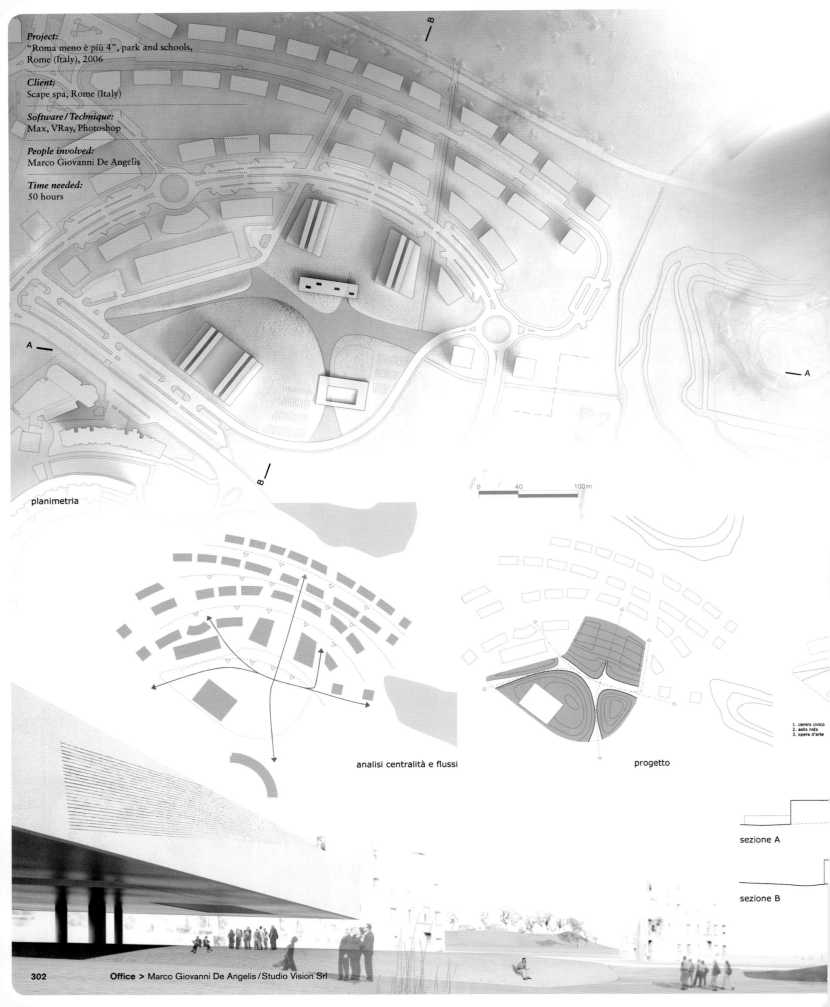

Project:
"Roma meno è più 4", park and schools,
Rome (Italy), 2006

Client:
Scape spa, Rome (Italy)

Software / Technique:
Max, VRay, Photoshop

People involved:
Marco Giovanni De Angelis

Time needed:
50 hours

planimetria

0   40   100 m

analisi centralità e flussi

progetto

1. centro civico
2. asilo nido
3. opera d'arte

sezione A

sezione B

edifici e opere d'arte

1. vento sud-ovest
2. vasca d'aqua
3. impianto geotermico
4. impianto di fitodepurazione
5. luce da schermare
6. parete schermata

bioclimatico

1. colline verdi
2. colline artificiali
3. macchia
4. filari

vegetale

0   40   100 m

Communication with the client is crucial. We express our creativity specifically in relation to the client: he is the first person we need to convince that one solution is better than one other. It is a mutual process: as he verifies his project through us, we verify our ideas with him …
Marco Giovanni De Angelis

Project:
Urban planning for residential houses, hotels and offices, Naples (Italy), 2008

Client:
Scape spa, Rome (Italy), and Francis Soler, Paris (France)

Software / Technique:
Max, VRay, Photoshop

People involved:
Marco Giovanni De Angelis, Massimo Marinelli

Time needed:
35 hours

Project:
Urban planning for residential houses, hotels and offices, Naples (Italy), 2008

Client:
Scape spa, Rome (Italy), and Francis Soler, Paris (France)

Software / Technique:
Max, VRay, Photoshop

People involved:
Marco Giovanni De Angelis, Massimo Marinelli

Time needed:
15 hours

Project:
Lamezia Terme Airport, Catanzaro (Italy), 2008

Client:
Scape spa, Rome (Italy)

Software / Technique:
Max, VRay, Photoshop

People involved:
Marco Giovanni De Angelis, Massimo Marinelli

Time needed:
25 hours

… it is essential to start the discussion on the basis of the drawing, even if it is provisional, as it provides a good reference point. The drawing itself is both the mean and the content of the exchange that happens between the person who sends it and the one who receives it …
Marco Giovanni De Angelis

Project:
Forlanini residential houses, Milan (Italy), 2008

Client:
Scape spa, Rome (Italy)

Software / Technique:
Max, VRay, Photoshop

People involved:
Marco Giovanni De Angelis, Massimo Marinelli

Time needed:
25 hours

Office > Marco Giovanni De Angelis / Studio Vision Srl

Project:
Villa in Is Molas, Cagliari (Italy), 2007

Client:
Massimiliano Fuksas, Rome (Italy)

Software / Technique:
Max, VRay, Photoshop

People involved:
Marco Giovanni De Angelis, Rodolfo Migliari,
Nicola Sganga, Fabio Barretta, Giuseppe Salino

Time needed:
70 hours

Project:
Villa in Is Molas, Cagliari (Italy), 2007

Client:
Massimiliano Fuksas, Rome (Italy)

Software/Technique:
Max, VRay, Photoshop

People involved:
Marco Giovanni De Angelis, Rodolfo Migliari,
Nicola Sganga, Fabio Barretta, Giuseppe Salino

Time needed:
70 hours

... we often try to determine a clear hierarchy in our images. This allows us to carry out our work in a more efficient manner, as well as helping clarify the client's understanding and promote the project.
Marco Giovanni De Angelis

Project 1:
Private house, Rome (Italy) 2008

.....

Client:
Scape spa, Rome (Italy)

.....

Software / Technique:
Max, VRay, Photoshop

.....

People involved:
Marco Giovanni De Angelis

.....

Time needed:
25 hours

Project 2:
Four interventions in Arsenale di Venezia (tesa 113), Venice (Italy), 2006

.....

Client:
Scape spa, Rome (Italy)

.....

Software / Technique:
Max, VRay, Photoshop

.....

People involved:
Marco Giovanni De Angelis

.....

Time needed:
30 hours

Project 3:
Palais de Justice à Tolbiac, Paris (France), 2006

.....

Client:
Scape spa, Rome (Italy)

.....

Software / Technique:
Max, VRay, Photoshop

.....

People involved:
Marco Giovanni De Angelis

.....

Time needed:
30 hours

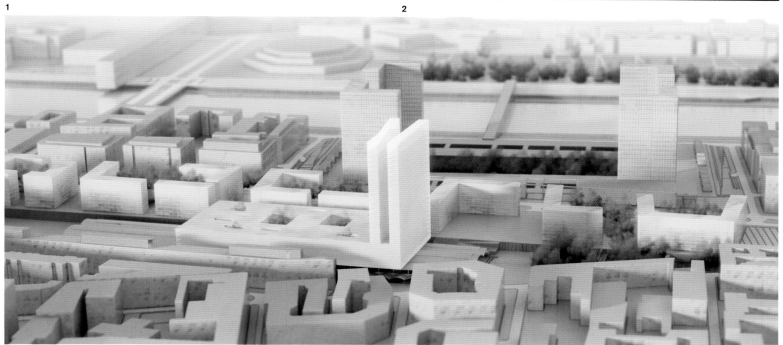

Process

The first step of our process consists in the meeting with the client, where we grasp what the images need to communicate: elements, atmosphere, relations, sensations.

Subsequently, we start working on the image. We build a rough 3D model and quickly brainstorm on it with the client, choosing the most interesting and communicative framings. At the same time we also try to establish which source elements are still missing and might need to be considered at a later stage: light, site, materials, fittings, vegetation and people.

Once the points of view have been chosen, we work on the drafts, adding all the elements. This step of the process is crucial and communication with the client is vital for its success. We prepare the setup for the light and contextually deepen the atmosphere, the site characteristic and the iconographic references. We normally add two or three key materials, as well as a bit of vegetation.

Once the draft is approved by the client, we work on the high-resolution image, which means modifying the 3D model, defining the materials and the site.

While the work on the site is not yet critical in this phase of the process, work on the project still demands flexibility and a lot of communication with the client, who actually starts now to verify his ideas of the design geometry, space, details, materials, etc.

After computing the image in high resolution, we proceed with the post-production, which helps us complete the image by correcting the colours, adding some light sources, vegetation and some visual effects.

As it is very useful to calibrate light and atmosphere, post-production is actually becoming more and more important in our process.

Sometimes, because of special project conditions, the aforesaid process can lose linearity and became very complex.

This was the case with the competition for the highway near Mestre, where we faced a double challenge: a delivery in two phases, and the landscape on a very large scale, in a very flat top view.

After researching the shape with the architects (images 1 and 2), we needed to perform some tests before concluding that the best way to portray the project was to reproduce the image as a bas-relief, to highlight the plasticity of the terrain movements which, on a large scale, seem to be very light. Our reference was a muscle bundle, as if drawn by Leonardo da Vinci.

Then, for the second phase of the competition (image 7 and following), we were asked to refine this interpretation, adding the terrain. The result was a representation where the bas-relief and the reference to Leonardo are still present but the emphasis is on the landscape, highlighting the continuity of land and the green as well as the wet atmosphere of the plane of the River Po.

Project:
Tunnel Autostradale di Mestre (Phase II), Venice (Italy), 2006

Client:
Scape spa, Alessandro Anselmi, Rome (Italy)

Software / Technique:
Max, VRay, Photoshop

People involved:
Marco Giovanni De Angelis, Justyna Morawska

Time needed:
50 hours

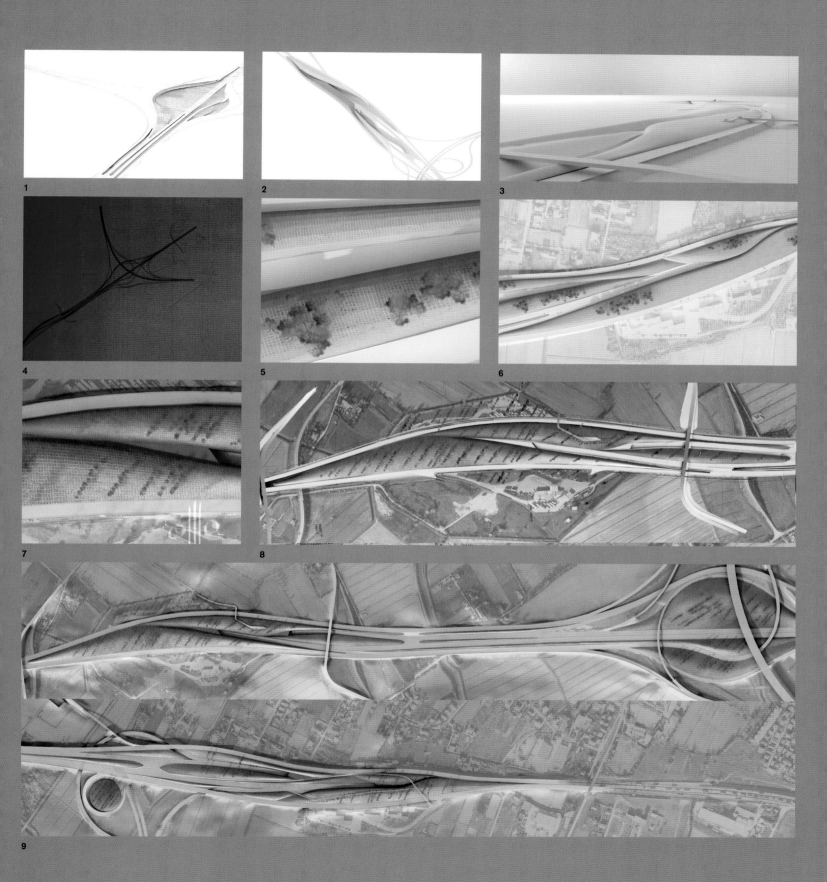

1

2

3

4

5

6

7

8

9

ArtefactoryLab

99 rue du Faubourg du Temple
75010 Paris
France

www.arte-factory.com

Artefactory was founded in 1999 in Paris by three friends.

Today the office has grown to seven partners and twenty freelance artists, and changed its name to ArtefactoryLab.

The studio produces images and animations for architects, property developers and artists. Its portfolio reveals many significant names and works, including the images of the Beijing Olympic Stadium for Herzog & de Meuron and Yi Zhou's video "One of these days".

… even if it's not obvious – and it should not be – the spectator feels that there are multiple subjects at stake, a certain complexity that lets him discover things in the image that are not limited to the representation of a building. We try out new things in every project, by avoiding a "copy and paste" scheme from our previous projects. Every project is individual and has its own inherent potential and possibilities that we try to understand and then possibly reveal.
ArtefactoryLab

Project:
Louvre Abu Dhabi (United Arab Emirates), 2007

Client:
Ateliers Jean Nouvel, Paris (France)

Software / Technique:
3ds Max, VRay, Photoshop

People involved:
3

Time needed:
3 weeks

Often the idea for the image itself starts with imagining the building in its context and function in an abstract way.

We try to conceptualize an image by asking ourselves a few key questions. What is the project about? What is its context? …
ArtefactoryLab

Project:
Guggenheim Museum Guadalajara (Mexico), 2005

Client:
Ateliers Jean Nouvel, Paris (France)

Software / Technique:
3ds Max, VRay, Photoshop

People involved:
4

Time needed:
2 weeks

… What is the client's desire and the scope of the image?

Can we describe a certain atmosphere, can we tell a "story", can we highlight a specific detail or atmosphere in the project or underline a feature? …
ArtefactoryLab

Project:
Beekman Tower, housing and office,
New York (USA), 2008

Client:
Gehry Partners, Los Angeles (USA)

Software / Technique:
3ds Max, VRay, Photoshop

Time needed:
1 week

Project:
Jeddah Airport, Jeddah (Kingdom of Saudi Arabia)

Client:
OMA, Rotterdam (the Netherlands)

Software / Technique:
3ds Max, VRay, Photoshop, Combustion

People involved:
5

Time needed:
3 weeks

… Is it possible to create something that adds to the project within the frame set up by its own limits?
Can we explore a new solution or just experiment with something new: a technique, a process, a composition?
ArtefactoryLab

Project:
Shanghai Hotel, 2008

Client:
Patrick Jouin, Paris (France)

Software/Technique:
3ds Max, VRay, Photoshop, Combustion

People involved:
3

Time needed:
2 weeks

We believe in creating subject matter within each project: this could be a still life or the perfect rock. It is a way of adding density to an image.
ArtefactoryLab

Project:
Paris Hotel, Paris (France), 2008

Client:
Patrick Jouin, Paris (France)

Software / Technique:
3ds Max, VRay, Photoshop, Combustion

People involved:
2

Time needed:
2 weeks

Project:
Las Vegas Casino, Las Vegas (USA), 2008

Client:
Herzog & de Meuron Architekten AG,
Basel (Switzerland)

Software / Technique:
3ds Max, VRay, Photoshop, Combustion

People involved:
5

Time needed:
2 weeks

Project:
Las Vegas Casino, Las Vegas (USA), 2008

Client:
Herzog & de Meuron Architekten AG,
Basel (Switzerland)

Software / Technique:
3ds Max, VRay, Photoshop, Combustion

People involved:
5

Time needed:
2 weeks

Project:
Philharmonie de Paris, Paris (France), 2008

Client:
Ateliers Jean Nouvel, Paris (France)

Software / Technique:
3ds Max, VRay, Photoshop

People involved:
2

Time needed:
1 week

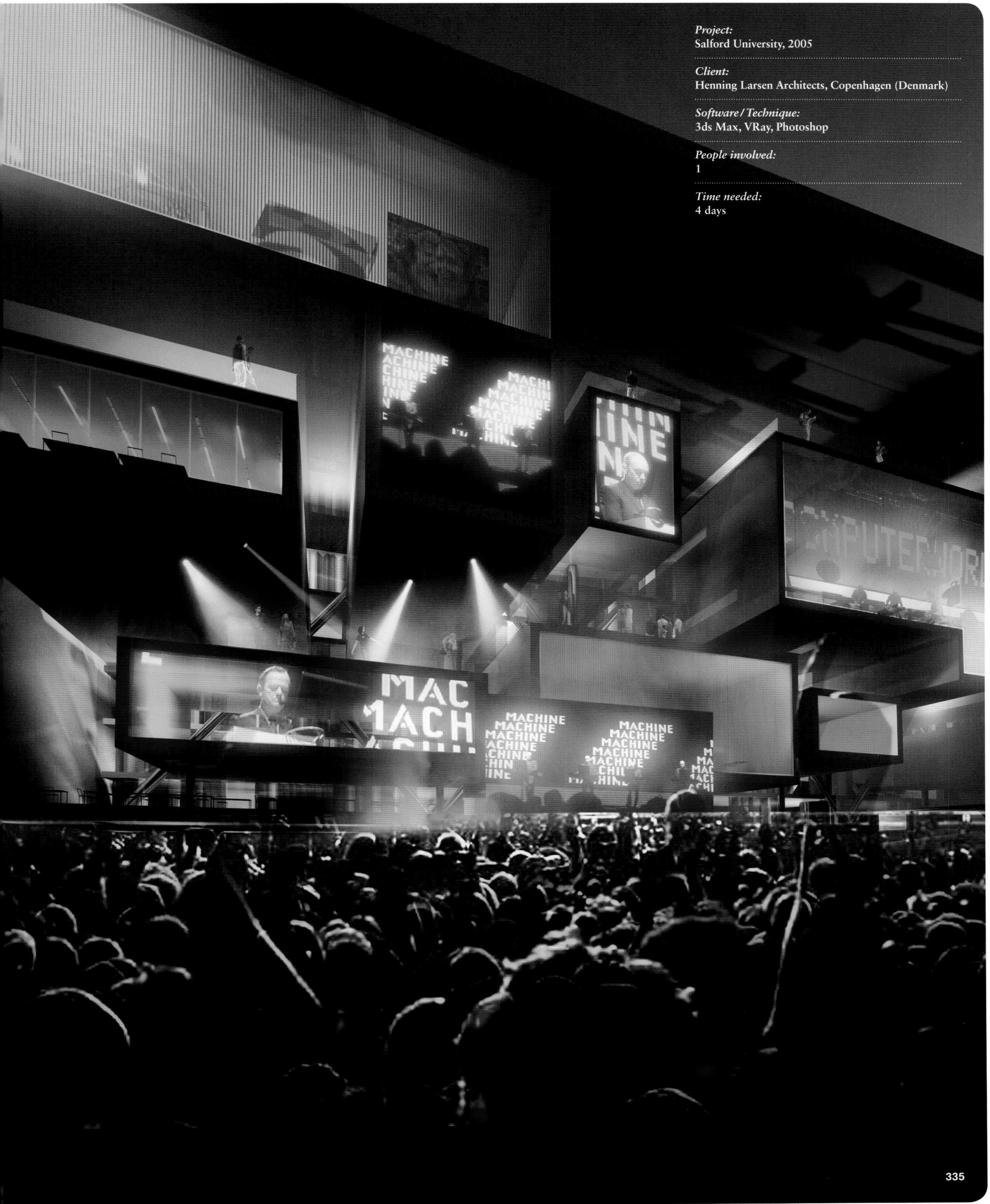

Project:
Salford University, 2005

Client:
Henning Larsen Architects, Copenhagen (Denmark)

Software / Technique:
3ds Max, VRay, Photoshop

People involved:
1

Time needed:
4 days

Project:
Paradise (3D animation), 2004

Client:
Studio Yi Zhou, Paris (France)

Software / Technique:
3ds Max, VRay, Photoshop, Combustion

People involved:
6

Time needed:
3 months

Project:
One of these days (3D animation), 2004

Client:
Studio Yi Zhou, Paris (France)

Software / Technique:
3ds Max, VRay, Photoshop, Combustion

People involved:
6

Time needed:
3 months

Process

Our process starts with the preliminary review and careful examination of all the information and specifications given by the client.

The material given to us differs from project to project. Sometimes we have to work from simple sketches, while on other occasions we are supplied with very detailed information about the project (drawings, site photographs, materials, precise ideas concerning the final image).

We try to ask ourselves (and of course the client) many questions: how to represent the building, which source of light is the most suitable, which materials, colours and general atmosphere better define the project …

At this stage reference images are of great importance. These images are often photographs, sometimes paintings or movies. They don't necessarily have to be relevant to the topic of the rendering and often do not concern architecture: they are artistic photographs like paintings and sculptures, or could be natural elements. Any additional detail can be interesting: the shadow of a tree on the office wall; a Paris scene with people walking in the street and creating a special dynamic effect or a concrete wall with holes in it.

It's a simple and free exercise that responds to the question: "what does this project make me think of?" It can concern any aspect of the project, an atmosphere, a special situation, a way to frame a subject, a point of view.

We also do sketches of the images we want to build, trying to construct a composition and imagine the result.

Communication with the client starts at the very beginning of the project and ends with the final rendering. This means we constantly send out sketches, then the first previews, then material test renderings and then the first high resolution images. The image gets built by this close exchange, shared comments, discussions, criticism and corrections.

Larger architectural firms will respond differently than smaller firms where less people are involved in the design process. This is another element that needs to be taken in account at the beginning of the project.

Project:
Beijing Olympic Stadium, Beijing (China), 2003

Client:
Herzog & de Meuron Architekten AG,
Basel (Switzerland)

Software / Technique:
3ds Max, VRay, Photoshop

People involved:
4

Time needed:
3 weeks

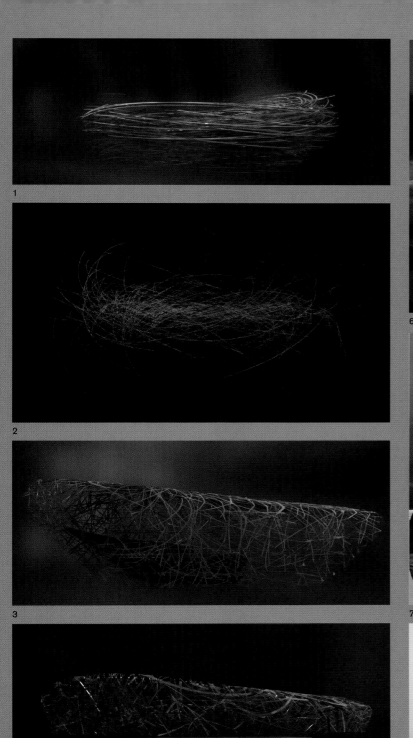

1

2

3

4

5

6

7

8

pure

Belziger Strasse 69/71
10823 Berlin
Germany

www.purerender.com

pure is a team of architects, designers and 3D artists based in Berlin. There is also a production office in Montreal as well as sales offices in Miami and Dubai. pure was founded in 2006 by Marc Gruber-Laux, Jonathan Brosseau and Marc Lamoureux. The company consists of seventy employees and fifteen freelancers and is directed by Marc Gruber-Laux.

pure uses cutting edge technology to create strikingly realistic images.

The core business is the production of renderings and animation for architects, designers, real estate developers, advertising agencies and brand name companies.

We never lose sight of the each project's unique marketing message and translate our client's vision into digital (art) masterpieces, which possess a quality and sophistication never seen before. The difference is in the details and the atmosphere.
Marc Gruber-Laux

Project:
Renaissance, New York (USA), 2008

Client:
Self-commissioned

Software / Technique:
3ds Max, VRay

People involved:
Benjamin Brosdau, Klemens Neumann, Marc Gruber-Laux, Markus Dallmann, Benny Herudeck

Time needed:
3 weeks

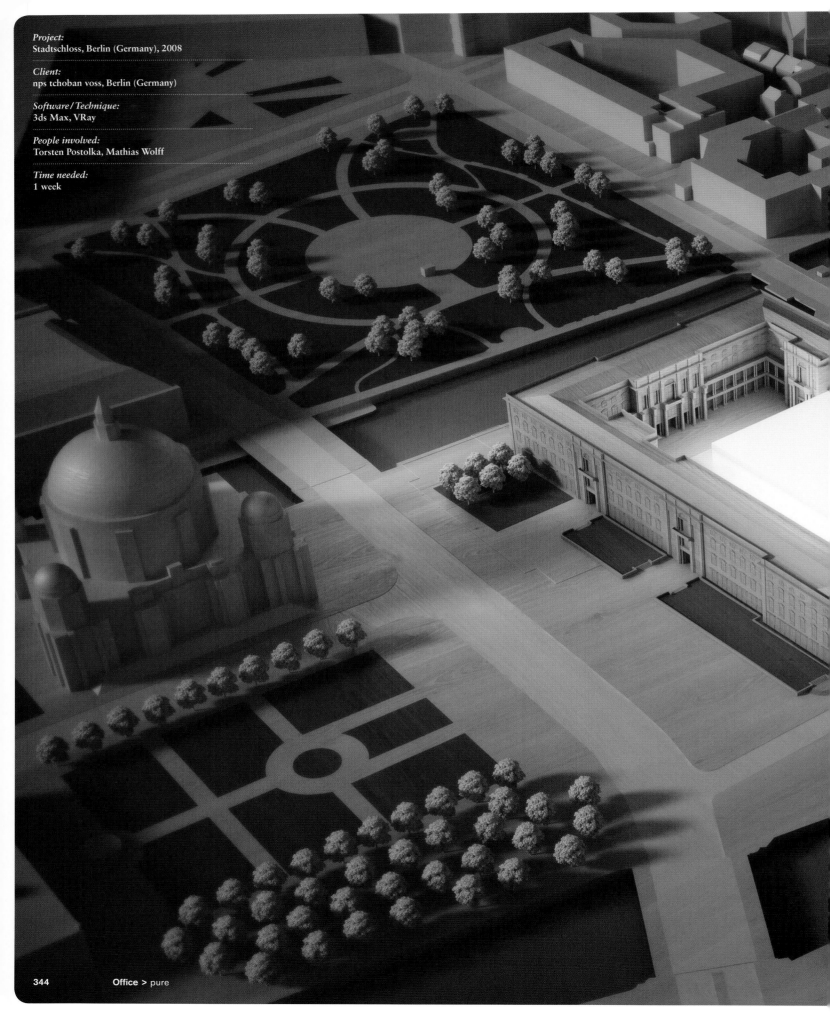

Project:
Stadtschloss, Berlin (Germany), 2008

Client:
nps tchoban voss, Berlin (Germany)

Software / Technique:
3ds Max, VRay

People involved:
Torsten Postolka, Mathias Wolff

Time needed:
1 week

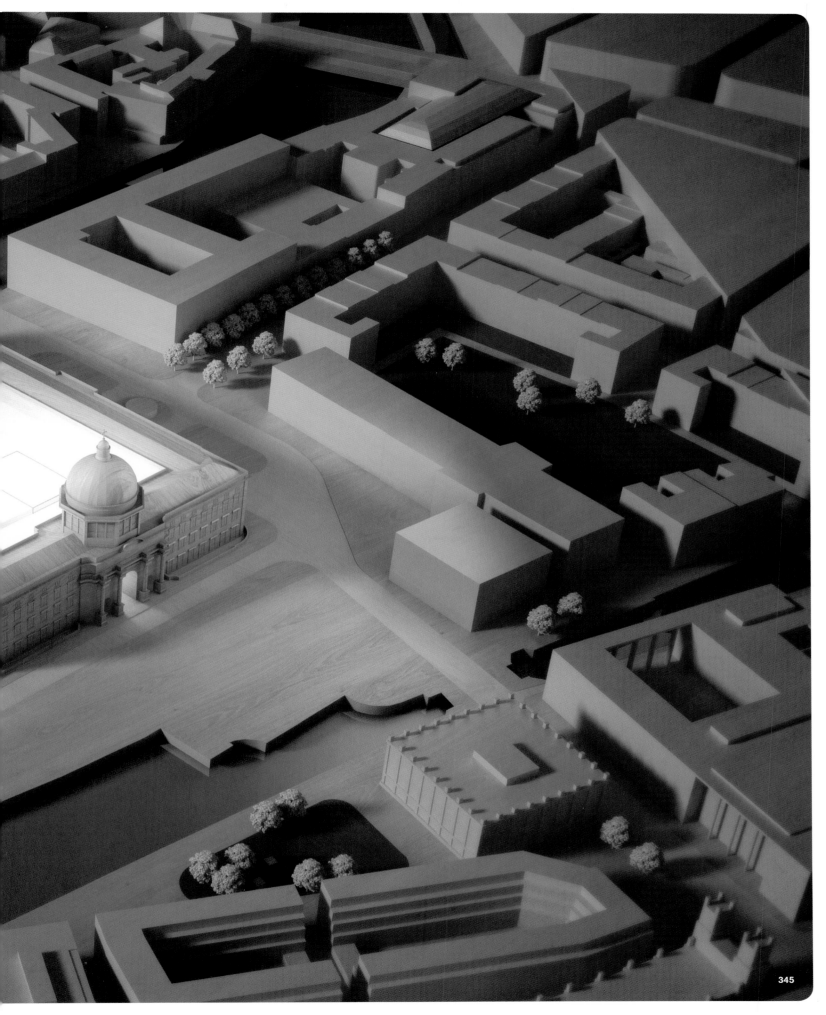

It is our passion for every aspect of architecture and design that drives us to create these striking digital images.
Marc Gruber-Laux

Project:
Astoria on the 10th, Calgary (Canada), 2008

Client:
Arcus Development, Calgary (Canada)

Software/Technique:
3ds Max, VRay

People involved:
Klemens Neumann, Benjamin Brosdau, Oliver Köpcke

Time needed:
2 weeks

Project:
Bedroom, Hong Kong (China), 2008

Client:
Self-commissioned

Software/Technique:
3ds Max, Maxwell

People involved:
Benjamin Brosdau

Time needed:
1 week

Digital renderings and 3D visualization have become essential tools of communication in every aspect of the designing and marketing process. We bring visions to life. Our renderings are filled with emotion, which is a vital asset to every client's campaign.
Marc Gruber-Laux

Project:
Baccarat, Dubai (United Arab Emirates), 2008

Client:
Dubai Pearl (United Arab Emirates)

Software/Technique:
3ds Max, Maxwell

People involved:
Benjamin Brosdau, Markus Hund, Mathias Wolff, Oliver Köpcke

Time needed:
2 weeks

Project:
Luise Townhouses, Berlin (Germany), 2008

Client:
TPA & Vivacon, Berlin (Germany)

Software / Technique:
3ds Max, VRay

People involved:
Tom Freitag, Torsten Postolka, Guido Trappen

Time needed:
2 weeks

Project:
Interior, 2007

Client:
AYA Global, Montreal (Canada)

Software / Technique:
3ds Max, VRay

People involved:
Benjamin Brosdau, Mathias Wolff, Markus Dallmann,
Svetlana Pett

Time needed:
2 weeks

Project:
YOO, Berlin (Germany), 2008

Client:
TPA & Vivacon, Berlin (Germany)

Software / Technique:
3ds Max, VRay

People involved:
Anke Fuchs, Markus Dallmann, Ben Schmidt

Time needed:
2 weeks

Project:
YOO, Berlin (Germany), 2008

Client:
TPA & YOO, Berlin (Germany)

Software / Technique:
3ds Max, VRay

People involved:
Oliver Köpcke

Time needed:
1 week

Project:
Loft, London (UK), 2008

Client:
Self-commissioned

Software / Technique:
3ds Max, Maxwell

People involved:
Benjamin Brosdau

Time needed:
1 week

Project:
Bathroom Showroom, 2007

Client:
Bathroom provider

Software/Technique:
3ds Max, VRay

People involved:
Benjamin Brosdau, Marc Gruber-Laux

Time needed:
1 week

Project:
Kitchen Showroom, 2008

Client:
Kitchen provider

Software / Technique:
3ds Max, Maxwell

People involved:
Benjamin Brosdau, Vasilii Maslak

Time needed:
1 week

Process

At the beginning of each project an art director and a project manager are appointed. Together they oversee the entire process from start to finish, managing the various stages, addressing the workflow and the artists, plus communicating with the client on all aspects of the project.

The first meeting with the client is crucial in determining the content and the artistic direction. We prefer a meeting face to face, although we often communicate via e-mail and telephone as many of our clients are located in different countries.

In the on-going chain of communication we strive to constantly review the images in process. To be as efficient as possible, we developed a highly specialized, yet simple, on-line tool (IAS), which allows clients to conveniently log into their specific project and post comments directly onto the images themselves, providing a centralized place of reference which is constantly supervised by the project manager and thus enabling a detailed history of the images in progress at all stages.

At the start of each image a design board is created, containing very specific suggestions concerning the interior design, furniture and so on, customized to each project's needs. Once this is approved by the client, the modelling can start.

The first model is fairly basic, without textures and ligthing, used solely for the purpose of selecting the point of view for the frames, which is the next step. Once approved, a coloured preview is produced, containing textures and lighting.

After two or three rounds of these previews, the image has improved so much that we can now proceed with computing the final high-resolution image.

The final stage of rendering is the post-production with Photoshop, which completes the process.

1 The set for rendering in 3D Studio Max

2 Post-production with Photoshop

Stack! Studios Srl

Piazza S. Marcellino 6 int 11
16124 Genova
Italy

www.stack-studios.com

Stack! Studios was founded at the end of 1998 in Siena, Italy, by David Rossman and Massimo Ciani. Today the company is composed of ten or eleven people and a two-hundred-node renderfarm.

The core business consists in the production of competition renderings and animations for several clients in Europe, Asia and America. The final images are the result of a profound technical knowledge and of the extensive use of a software developed in-house. The most important of these software packages is *Felix*.

Felix is our on-line visualization software; it is permanently connected, through a secure web connection, to a two-hundred-node renderfarm. Its first version, released in 2002, went through four development stages and has been tested repeatedly during the past six years. Now the software is ready and will be commercialized in the near future. For me, developing the software was the most enjoyable experience in my fifteen years of computer graphics.
David Rossman

Project:
CityLife Project, Milan (Italy), 2004

Client:
Arata Isozaki, Tokyo (Japan)
Daniel Libeskind, New York (USA)
Zaha Hadid Architects, London (UK)
Pier Paolo Maggiora, Turin (Italy)

Software / Technique:
Lightwave, Matador

People involved:
4 people

Project:
YAS Marina Hotel, Abu Dhabi
(United Arab Emirates), 2008

Client:
Asymptote Architecture, New York (USA)

Software / Technique:
Felix

People involved:
2 people

Thanks to its huge computing centre, Felix has great rendering power compared to all existing solutions and can be executed on one thousand computers (eight thousand cores), thus improving productivity hundredfold.
David Rossman

Project:
Strata Tower Dubai
(United Arab Emirates), 2006

Client:
Asymptote Architecture,
New York (USA)

Software/Technique:
Lightwave, Matador

People involved:
1 person

Project:
Penang Global City Centre,
Penang (Malaysia), 2008

Client:
Asymptote Architecture,
New York (USA)

Software / Technique:
Lightwave, Matador

People involved:
4 people

Each project inspires us in a different way. Sometimes we capture the correct mood for a project only in the last few hours, however usually the first rendering is the right one.
David Rossman

Project:
Central Library, Seattle (USA), 2008

Client:
Rem Koolhaas, Rotterdam (the Netherlands)

Software/Technique:
Felix

People involved:
1 person

We do not have a specific "style"; to the contrary, we try to avoid everything that could easily be defined as a style. Our only references are good architectural photos (never renderings), films and our own everyday experiences.
David Rossman

Project:
Casa Levene, Madrid (Spain), 2007

Client:
No.Mad architects, Madrid (Spain)

Software / Technique:
Felix

People involved:
1 person

1

2

Project 1:
Pierres Vives Building, Montpellier (France), 2005

Client:
Zaha Hadid Architects, London (UK)

Software / Technique:
Felix

People involved:
1 person

Project 2:
Pierres Vives Building, Montpellier (France), 2005

Client:
Zaha Hadid Architects, London (UK)

Software / Technique:
Felix

People involved:
1 person

Project 3:
Caja Granada, Granada (Spain), 2008

Client:
Campo Baeza, Madrid (Spain)

Software / Technique:
Felix

People involved:
1 person

Project 4:
Business Bay, Dubai (United Arab Emirates), 2007

Client:
Zaha Hadid Architects, London (UK)

Software / Technique:
Felix

People involved:
2 people

1

2

3

4

Project 1:
Guggenheim Museum, Vilnius (Lithuania), 2008

Client:
Zaha Hadid Architects, London (UK)

Software / Technique:
Lightwave, Matador

People involved:
4 people

Project 3:
Spiralling Tower, Barcelona (Spain), 2008

Client:
Zaha Hadid Architects, London (UK)

Software / Technique:
Felix

People involved:
2 people

Project 2:
Dancing Towers, Dubai (United Arab Emirates), 2007

Client:
Zaha Hadid Architects, London (UK)

Software / Technique:
Lightwave, Matador

People involved:
2 people

Project 4:
Palahockey, Turin (Italy), 2004

Client:
Arata Isozaki, Tokyo (Japan)

Software / Technique:
Lightwave, Matador

People involved:
1 person

Felix

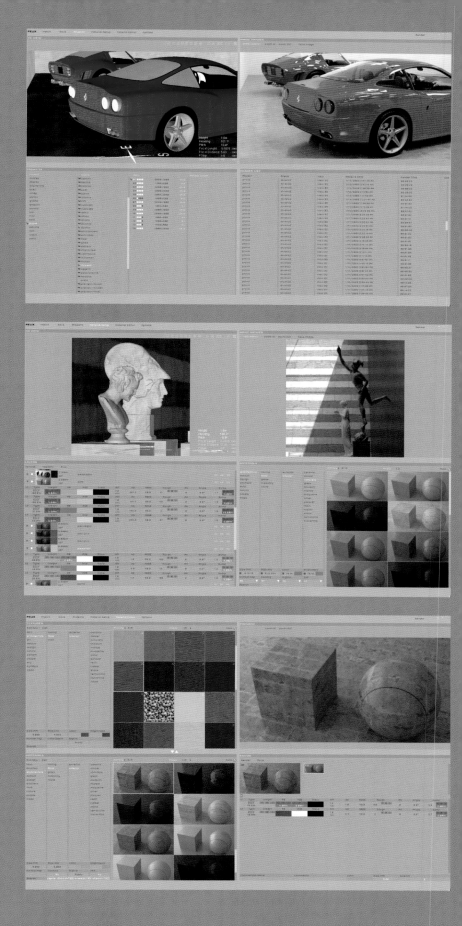

Graphical user interface (GUI):
Here you can navigate between projects, set-up your cameras, and build render queues containing up to 100 renderings at the same time. Felix can render 10 to 20 renderings at the same speed as a single one.

Material set-up:
The material assignment tab. At the bottom right you see the online material library.

Material editor:
Once you have created a material with Felix, it is possible to share it worldwide in real-time, retaining the copyright of the material.

Fabio Schillaci
The making of a render

As a matter of fact, there are several software solutions for rendering available on the market. Each package presents a different interface and logic and all have good and bad features, so it is impossible to pinpoint the best software for rendering. Instead, you should try a few out and then choose the most convenient for your way of working.

Therefore, instead of offering detailed instructions on how to use a specific software, I prefer to give you an explanation of the most common and crucial steps across different techniques and software solutions.

Whatever software you adopt, the most important thing is to understand the process.

A school in Cheboksary

This section shows the making of a render through one case study.

The project refers to a pre-fab panel building system: a school project in Cheboksary (Russia) managed by Jennifer Tobolla for the Berlin-based studio Meuser Architekten GmbH.

The images were commissioned during the preliminary stages of the design with the intent to render the pre-fab panel system in the area of the main entrance, while also offering an aerial view of the entire building.

A render is the result of an algorithm based on four steps:

1. Data collection and organization
2. Three-dimensional modelling
3. Mapping, illumination and computing
4. Post-production

Project:
High school, Cheboksary (Russia), 2008

Client:
Meuser Architekten GmbH, Berlin (Germany)

Software / Technique:
Rhinoceros, 3ds Max, VRay, Photoshop

People involved:
Fabio Schillaci

Time needed:
10 days

1. Data collection and organization

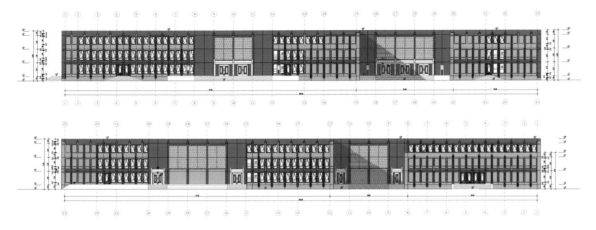

Original elevation drawings

Exactly the same as for a physical model, the first step for a renderer is to gather all the information needed to understand the design and build the model. This is often technical drawings, sketches, photos and it can differ – depending on the case – in format, quantity and quality. Sometimes, the material is unclear or unfinished and requires interpretation by the renderer. Other times, the material is very poor and the design must be interpreted. In any case, in order to work properly, it is a good idea to "clean" and select the material, so to prepare it for working. Concerning photos, sketches and other materials, this simply means cataloguing them in order to easily recall information when needed.

Concerning the drawings, this means actually eliminating from them all the superfluous information which would clutter the file and make three-dimensional working less easy.

In the case study, for example, the material gathered was mostly made up of technical drawings for execution, which were reduced by eliminating notations, furnitures, hatches, quotations and axes before importing them to the three-dimensional modelling software.

Plans, elevations and sections after reducing
information. Bottom right: material gathered with
façade specification of materials and colours

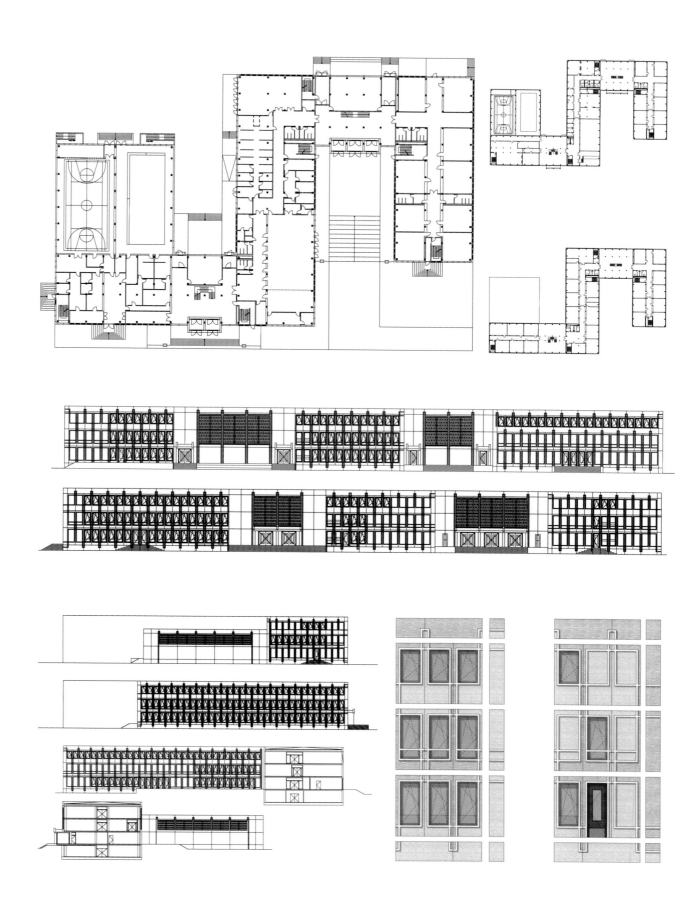

2. Three-dimensional modelling

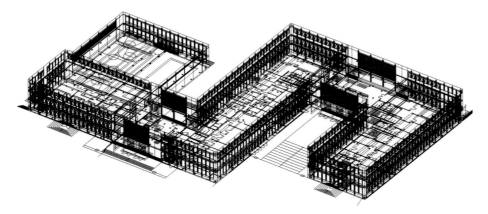

Axonometric projection of the model made out of lines

The "reduced" drawings were imported in a software for modelling before being grouped and placed on separate layers, that could be turned off and on depending on the situation.

Later on, the drawings were placed and orientated in the three-dimensional space, coherently with the geometry of the building. Thus, sections and elevations must correspond to their place on the plan, and floor plans must be positioned at their actual height on the section. The resulting model – which is still a technical drawing – is very precise and acts as guideline for the three-dimensional building as well as first preview: it is indeed useful to verify the view to be rendered and the geometry of the building.

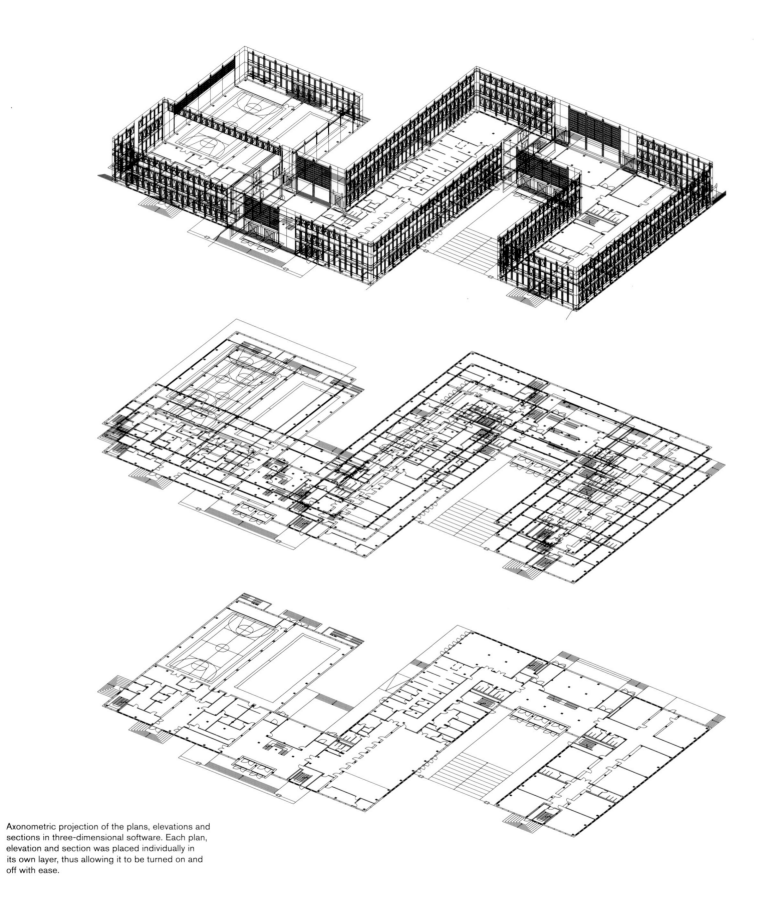

Axonometric projection of the plans, elevations and sections in three-dimensional software. Each plan, elevation and section was placed individually in its own layer, thus allowing it to be turned on and off with ease.

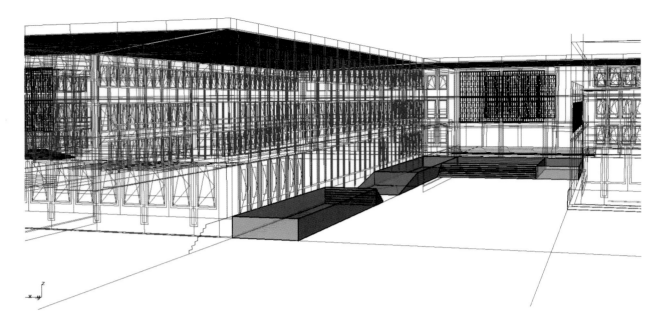

Screenshot of the area close to the gymnasium and
the secondary entrance of the building

Duplicating, moving, rotating, extruding, stretching and
subtracting are the most important and common actions
you will ever perform when working with professional
modelling software.

Extruding means creating a solid starting from a planar
figure, a rectangle, a circle or a more complex figure.
Stretching means deforming an existing solid in one
direction. Subtracting means making holes in, engraving
or cutting an existing solid by intersecting it with one or
more other solids.

Generally, every type of building is achievable through
these few tools, except for those presenting double-
curved geometries which require other actions specific
to non-Euclidean geometry. The whole modelling
process is iterative and meticulous, and it is very important to organize it well, always keeping the next step
clearly in mind.

It needs a bit of experience to understand what is worth
modelling and what not: a very realistic render, for
example, needs the model to be as detailed as possible,
defining every detail you want to be visible in the final
scene; on the contrary, a rough model without details is
the best tool to highlight a concept.

As a principle, it is always good to model every piece
of information that might be important to understand
the design.

1

Extrusion of a box starting from a rectangular figure

 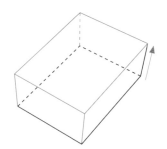 

2

Stretching an existing box in one direction

3

Duplication of an existing box

4

Subtraction of two solids (in red) from a bigger one and resulting holes

5

Subtraction of solids (in red) from a bigger one to create window holes

 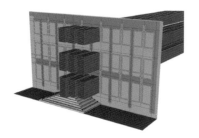 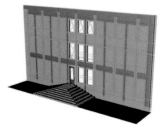

Extruding, moving and subtracting

(action sequence for the modelling of a façade
made up of three different materials)

1

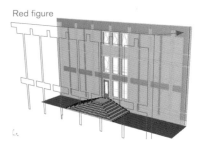

Starting point for building the façade (note the red figure)

2

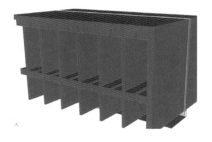

Extrusion of the red figure and boolean subtraction

3

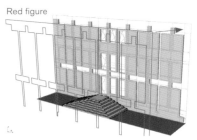

Resulting volume after subtraction

4

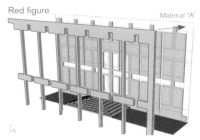

Secondary extrusion of the red figure and material "A"

5

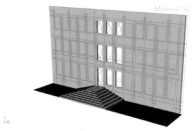

Placing material "A"

6

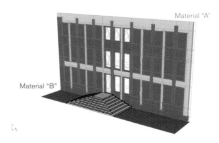

Changing the colour for material "B" (dark)

7

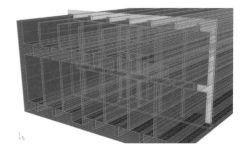

Extrusion of a new figure

8

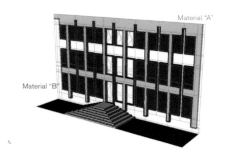

Subtraction of the new red volume from material "B"

9

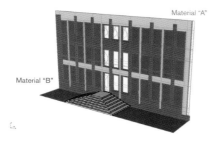

Material "A"

Material "B"

Secondary extrusion and final shape for material "B" (in red)

10

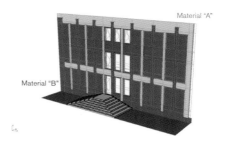

Material "A"

Material "B"

Changing colour and layer to material "B"

11

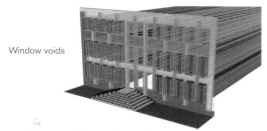

Window voids

Extrusion of the window voids

12

Subtraction for creating the window voids

13

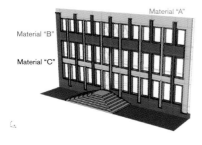

Material "A"

Material "B"

Material "C"

Changing colour and new layer for material "C"

14

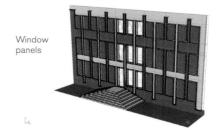

Window panels

Extrusion of the window panels

15

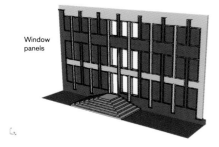

Window panels

Changing colour and layer for the window volume (the same as "B")

16

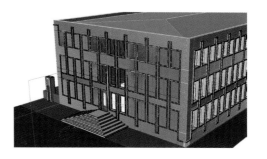

Final model of the façades

Stretching, moving, rotating and duplicating

(action sequence for modelling a stairway in the school secondary entry)

1

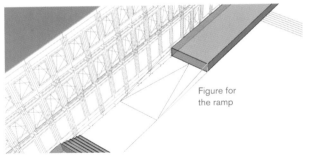

Tracing and placing the figure for the ramp (in yellow)

2

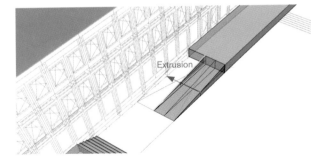

Extrusion of the ramp figure (in yellow)

3

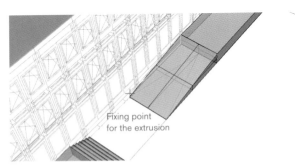

Completion of the ramp (fixing the end of the extrusion)

4

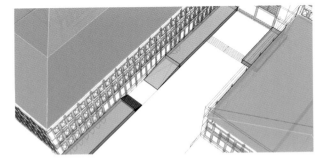

Zoom out on the secondary entry

5

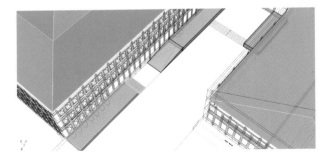

Selection of existing volumes (in yellow) to use for the entry stair

6

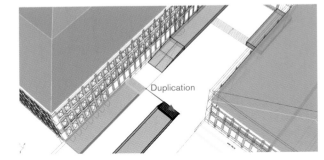

Duplication of the original volumes (in yellow)

7

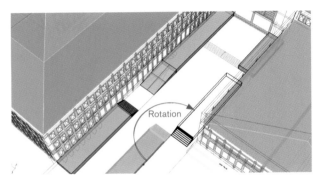

Rotation of the new volumes according to fit the entry

8

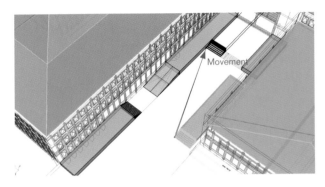

Moving the new volumes to the entrance

9

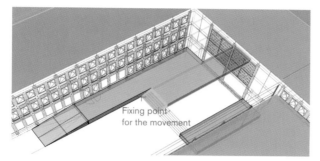

Tracing and placing the figure for the ramp (in yellow)

10

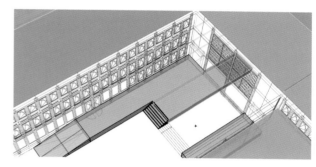

Extrusion of the ramp figure (in yellow)

11

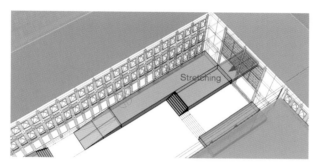

Completion of the ramp (fixing the end of the extrusion)

12

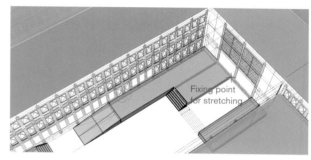

Zoom out on the secondary entry

13

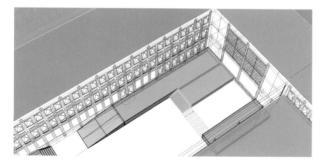

Selection of existing volumes (in yellow) to use for the entry stair

14

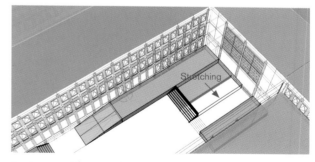

Duplication of the original volumes (in yellow)

15

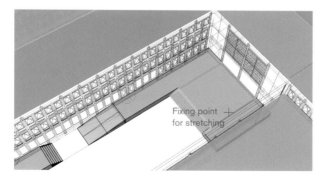

Rotation of the new volumes according to fit the entry

16

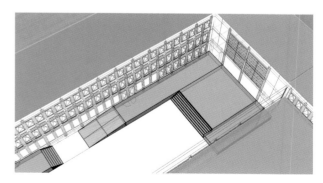

Moving the new volumes to the entrance

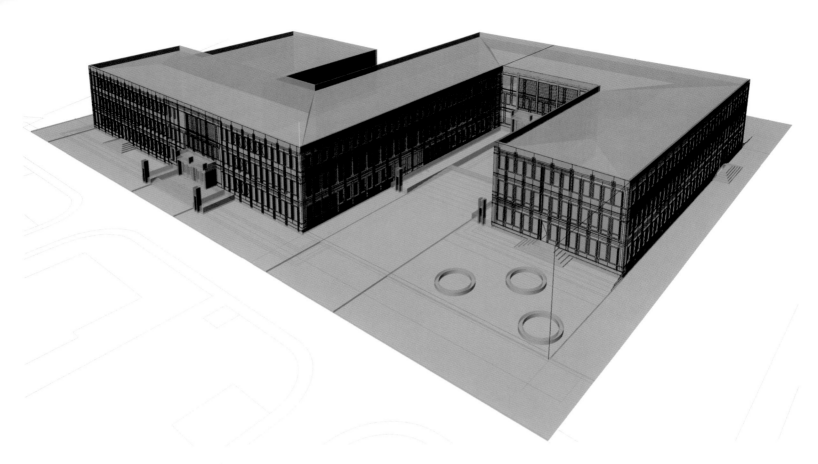

Preview of the three-dimensional model rendered
without textures

Once the model is completed and all the volumes are organized in layers by material, it is possible to move on to the next step which is the mapping.

As you will note in the case study, the model is lacking textures and accessories (i.e. trees, peoples, cars, etc.). This actually depends on the resources and libraries of three-dimensional objects available to you. Three-dimensional libraries are becoming ever more important, and they can make the crucial difference in the final result. It is not always necessary for you to personally model accessories, as this task is very time consuming, since many websites allow you to download them from the internet.

As a matter of fact, many product retailers are now offering free three-dimensional models of their products, and the number and quality of specialized websites offering downloadable 3D accessory models is growing. Choose your three-dimensional accessories carefully and save them in your personal library, so that they will always be available when you need them. The quality of your library will affect the quality of your work. Just remember that the three-dimensional model is the basis for rendering, and even if you lack some accessories and are forced to drop them, you will have the chance to add them at a later stage, during the post-production.

Preview render without texture of the main
entrance area

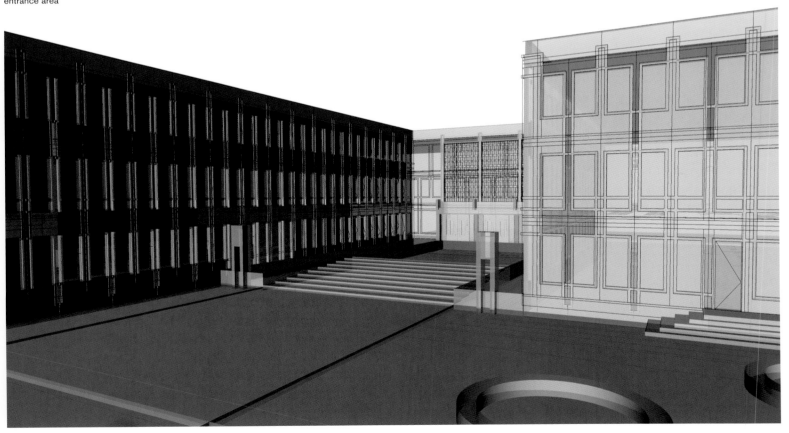

3. Mapping, illumination and computing

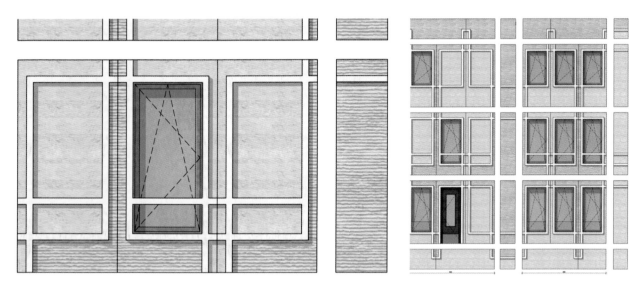

Façade detail with materials

Before starting this section, is worth remembering that the rendering engine is a software that can process and display the image data required for rendering. In computer graphics, a rendering engine is needed to render a three-dimensional scene as either an image or a video. There are several engines available on the market, and the choice of one or the other can very strongly influence the final result. Mostly, 3D modelling software already includes one or more rendering engine, but others are available on the web as plug-ins which you simply need to install on your computer and which run once the software starts. Each engine has its own characteristic and peculiarities, thus is advisable to choose it according to the result you want to achieve. The next important step is mapping. Mapping means creating and assigning a material to your model, by placing a texture on each three-dimensional element.

A texture can basically be any image made out of pixels. It can have different formats (the most common is jpg) and it does not need to be high-res. The images have to be planar and, if possible, without light effects, otherwise this will clash with the overall light scene once rendered (this is one of the most common problems, together with repetition of the texture pattern). The use of textures depends on the libraries you own, and a lot of material is already available on the internet. If needed, you can directly take a photo of the material. In that case it is very important that you shoot the photo so that the image is flat (without perspective) and with a diffuse light without any shadows or shines.

Set of textures used for the case study

Professional software programs have a specific section – often called the material editor – where you can load, manage and combine textures for material. The material editor gives you the opportunity to reproduce almost any material, and to recall material reproduced in the past. Every material can be created simply by loading a texture in its diffuse slot. This is the case with brick walls, concrete, wood, textiles, etc. Special materials like glass, mirror and water are a basic shaded material with a high percentage of transparency, reflection and fractal bump map respectively. The bump map is a very important tool to give three-dimensionality to a flat surface or when visualizing a rough material like stone or concrete. A bump map is basically a black/white image you need to load on the bump slot of the material. This will give the textures three-dimensionality according to the black/white fields (black represents depth and white height).

If you need to produce the bump of a natural material (i.e. stone), the best way to proceed is to convert the original photo of the stone into grayscale, then to invert it and finally to give it more contrast, thus to avoid gray zones. As for the bump map, black/white images can be applied to produce complex textures with different levels of reflection across the texture: the black will make less reflection and the white will produce more. The same applies to refractions, transparency, translucency, etc.

1 *Texture for material "A" and material preview on the editor*

2 *Texture for material "B" and material preview on the editor without bump map*

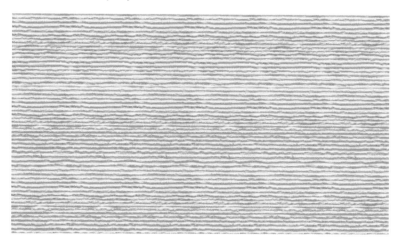 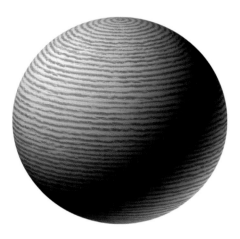

3 *The bump map for material "B" and the material preview (after addition of the bump map)*

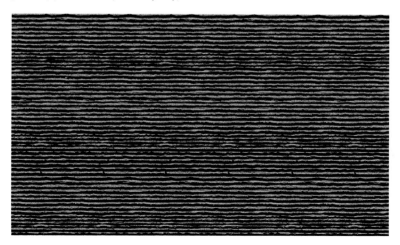 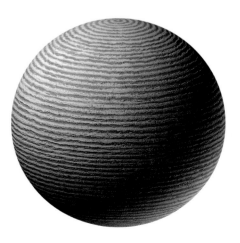

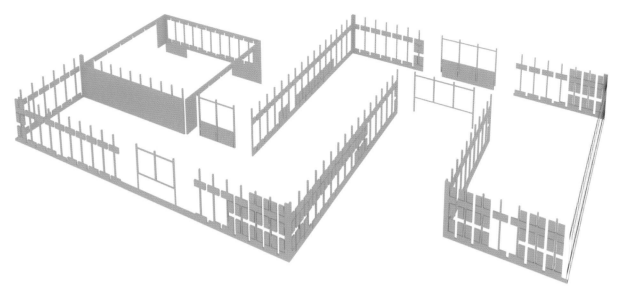

Overview of one group of elements which will receive
the same material

If you have grouped all the elements requiring the same material, you just need to select each group and to assign the relevant material by clicking on the "assign material" command or simply by dragging the icon of the texture from the texture editor directly to the groups on the scene. The software will place the texture on the elements by default and you might want to adjust this slightly to improve on the final result. To adjust the placing and its ration to the elements you need to enter the property of the elements, search for "UVW mapping" and then scale, rotate and move the texture until the ratio is correct. Professional softwares allow you also to place the texture on a cylinder or a sphere. That will affect the way the texture is projected on the elements. The way to map the elements has to be decided according to their geometry (i.e. spherical mapping if you want to map a sphere).

1

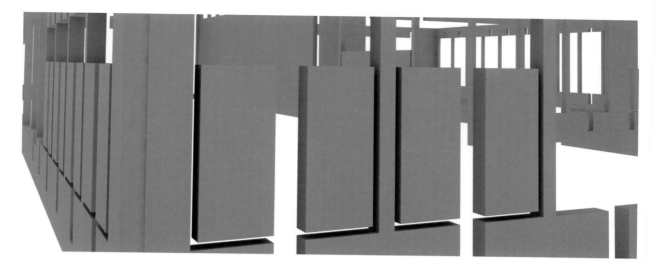

Group without texture

2

The texture is placed by default

3

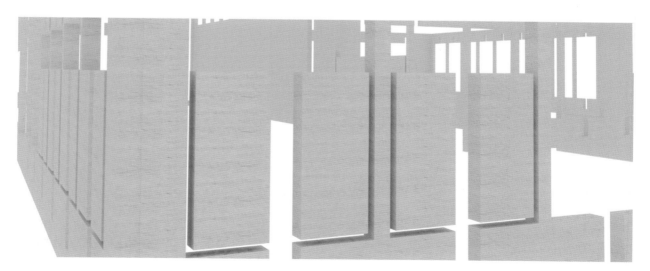

The texture is scaled and moved to achieve the correct ratio

How to place and adjust the textures

(action sequence for mapping groups of elements)

1

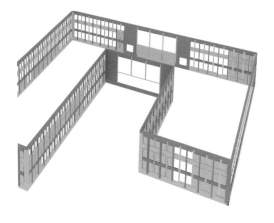

Starting points with the two main groups of elements (dark and light blue)

2

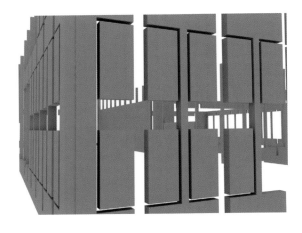

The light blue group is hidden to allow work on the dark blue group

3

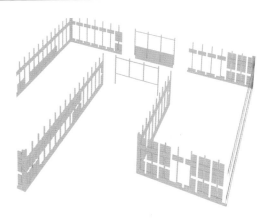

Material assigned to the dark blue group as box mapping

4

Detail of the material placed by default

5

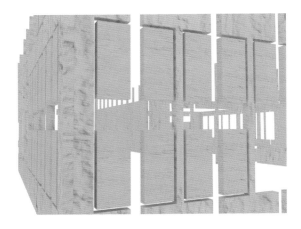

Detail of the material placed by default showing a conflict between two elements of the same group in the corner of the building

6

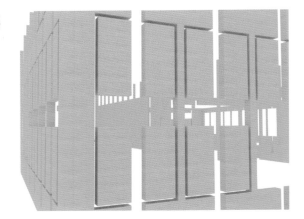

The texture is scaled and moved to achieve the correct ratio

7

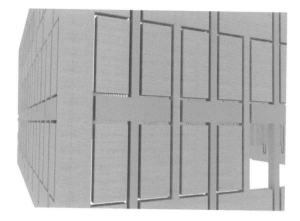

The light blue group is turned on

8

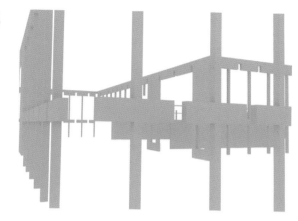

The dark blue group is turned off

9

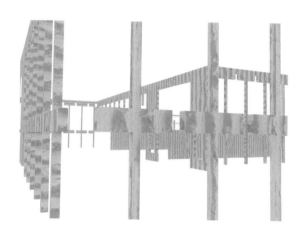

The second material is assigned to the light blue group as box mapping

10

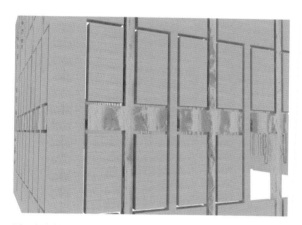

The dark blue group is turned on as reference for scaling

11

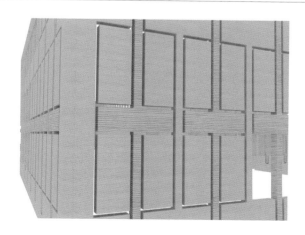

The texture is scaled and moved to achieve the correct ratio

12

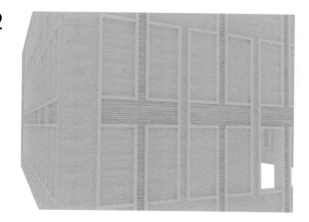

A third group (pilaster strip) is turned on, and mapped with a matt beige

Material used for tiling the floor with bumped borders
to simulate the joints between the tiles

Once again, the making and placing of the textures is a meticulous job, which must be done well to avoid problems after computing the image. The better the textures and their placing, the better the final image will be. Sometimes problems arise, as in the case of the brown tiled floor next to the main entrance steps in the case study. The tiling pattern made out of big brown slabs did not exactly fit within its area and some cutting of the pattern occurs. Since the tiling was achieved by "bumping" the borders of the image and not by modelling the tiles in 3D, it was decided to scale and to move the texture until an optimal situation was found.

Since the camera for the final image was positioned at the bottom of the steps, the placing of the texture there needed special attention. In the end, the full tiles were placed in the foreground area, while the cut tiles remained in the background area. This did not really affect the final image, since the cut tiles were almost invisible to the camera.

1

Detail of the main entrance situation
(work in progress)

2

Material assigned by default

3

Material placement and tiling layout

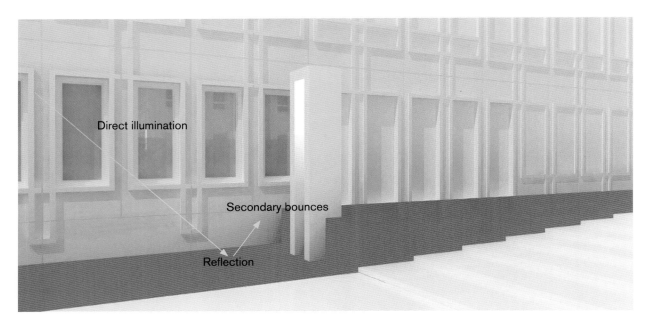

Direct illumination

Secondary bounces

Reflection

Global illumination with secondary bounces of light
reflecting the red from the floor onto the walls

Once the mapping is finished, the next step is to set up
the illumination of the scene. Before doing that, it could
be useful to review the concept of global illumination.
Global illumination is an algorithm that allows to
calculate a quite realistic illumination for the scene. As
well as calculating the primary bounces of light coming
from a light source, it also calculates the secondary
bounces reflecting from and between the elements,
thus creating indirect illumination and simulating the
conditions of illumination quite realistically.
Global illumination requires the precise definition of
several numerical parameters and the final illumination is
the result of the combination of all these parameters.

Different parameters can produce completely different
conditions of light (i. e. at night, sunrise, indoor and
outdoor), ranging from the simulation of natural and
artificial lights to a completely abstract illumination.
Because of the number of parameters you need to set, the
set up of global illumination is a slow process which
needs experience. In order to control what happens to the
scene when changing one or more parameter, it is advisable to calculate intermediate low resolution previews.
The global illumination can be exported from one scene
to another, thus optimizing the process, or you can
set standard basic scenes to be customized according to
the situation.

1

Light setup without global illumination

2

Light setup with global illumination but without secondary bounces (value 0.1)

3

Light setup with global illumination and secondary Bounces (value 1.0)

Photo used as Environment Skylight to produce realistic illumination and reflection on the windows

Global illumination allows you to project the illumination of an image all over your scene, which is a very important feature you can use to simulate the skylight.

Real skylight is quite complex to simulate because of its wide range of light intensity, but if you assign a photo of the real site to the Environment Skylight slot, the software will project the illumination of the photo on the scene, and, furthermore, all reflective objects (glass, mirror, etc.) will reflect the photo. An even more precise technique uses an HDRI (High Dynamic Range Image) instead of the photo. An HDRI is basically an image with a wider range of light intensity than the common textures and closer to real skylight. HDRI skylights can be found on the web.

The correct setup of the light sources is essential for the illumination. Light sources project light rays and shadows on your building, so their position and intensity will deeply affect the scene and its atmosphere.

A light source can be assimilated to a vector – or a combination of vectors – projecting particles of light: imagine an arrow projecting light like a "torch". Like global illumination, light sources require the specification of several numerical parameters to control size, intensity and shadow sharpness.

Light sources can be placed in four main groups, according to the direction of the light rays and the way the particles propagate in space:

– Omni light: 360° centrifugal vectors, all perpendicular to a spherical surface
– Spot light: a directional vector which propagates like a cone
– Planar light: several vectors perpendicular to a surface
– Direct light: a cylindrical bunch of parallel vectors

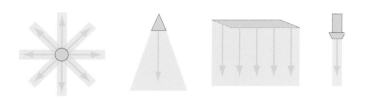

Different types of light source (simplification). From the left: omni, spot, planar and direct light

When choosing the correct type of light source for the project, consider the features of the light you want to simulate. The sun, for example, is an omni-directional light source, which is so far away that all its rays can be treated as parallel vectors: this is the case of direct light.

1

Direct light: note the shadows and the highlighted parts of the building

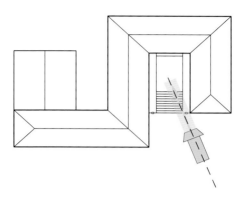

2

Rotating the light source on the plan changes shadows and highlights, creating a completely different atmosphere

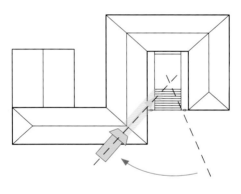

3

This situation is the opposite of the first one, where the right part of building was highlighted and the left was in shadow

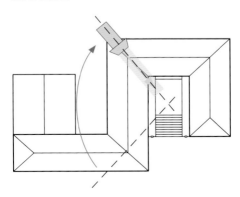

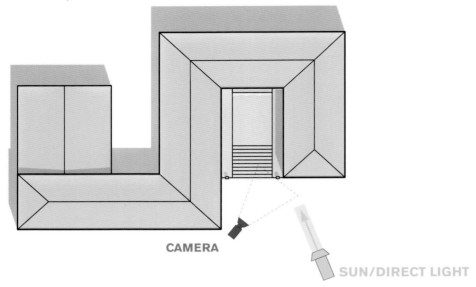

CAMERA

SUN/DIRECT LIGHT

Camera and sun position on the plan

In reality, most of the light we experience during the day comes from the sun, thus we usually do not need further light sources to create a realistic scene. One direct light source suffices as the global illumination and the skylight will have an additional effect. As mentioned above, the position and inclination of the direct light affects the overall atmosphere of the rendering: use them to your advantage, to highlight some parts of the design and create some movement in the least interesting areas.

Sunlight and shadows are important tools to create a dramatic atmosphere and to highlight the building. When rendering a scene by night, once again you can play with the soft moon rays (i.e. a very gentle direct light) or with different sources of artificial light (i.e. lamps simulating omni lights). You could adopt a soft yellow tone to render the summer sunlight; use red, blue and pink lights to create a dramatic atmosphere or introduce special effects like fog, light volume, fire to achieve a level of realism.

1

Note the relationship between the shadows and the angle of the direct light

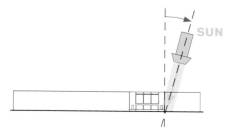

2

When the angle of direct light increases, the shadows become longer

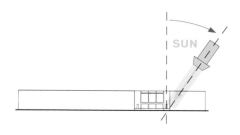

3

When the direct light inclination increases further, very long shadows will appear

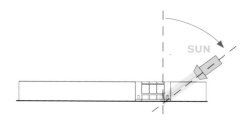

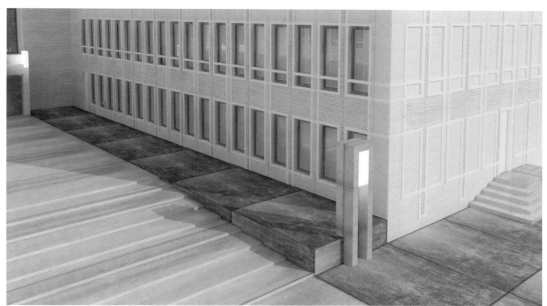

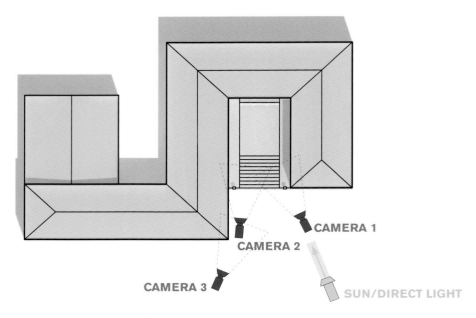

Choice of camera points and sun position on the plan

Once cameras, textures, light sources, skylight and global illumination are set up, you are almost ready to "shoot" the computation.

A few considerations
When placing the camera, perspectival distortion can occur. This is the result of having the wrong relationship between the building, the camera position, the target and the inclination of the projection plane. In principle, a camera without perspectival distortion will better render the building, but in some instances vertical distortion can give more emphasis to the building, like in the case of a skyscraper.
Anyway, to quickly eliminate the distortion, you simply need to move the target of your camera up or down until the projection plane is perfectly vertical. Some professional software has an additional command to do the correction,

allowing to eliminate the distortion without moving the target. Some small adjustments, like moving the target further away, can be necessary to hide some mistakes and make them fall out of the scene. This will make it easier to proceed and will save your difficult post-production.
Before computation, check that you are including the "alpha channel" when rendering the image. The alpha channel is an extra channel for transparency and back-ground, which allows you to quickly select at once all the transparent areas of the image as well as its background. This is quite important if you want to change the back-ground of the image or to add graphic elements behind transparent areas (i.e. persons behind windows). In this case, you do not need to cut out the background manually, but simply select and crop the alpha channel area from the image.

1

Perspectival distortion

2

Vertical correction of the camera

3

Final inclination of the camera

1

Render

2

Alpha channel in black (background)

3

The alpha channel area is cropped out and the building is free

1

Camera 1 (size: 2480 × 3500 pixel 300 dpi, rendering time: 13 hours)

2

Camera 2 (size: 2480 × 3500 pixel 300 dpi, rendering time: 10 hours)

3

Camera 3 (size: 2480 × 3500 pixel 300 dpi, rendering time: 8 hours)

A small size computation will affect the resolution of
the render and the level of details
(left = 2480 × 3580 pixel; right = 500 × 705 pixel)

If you want to render a very detailed image, its size and resolution become important factors. However, it is not always advisable to render a large image, since it is very time consuming and requires powerful computing machines. The correct size to render is determined by the definition of the three-dimensional model and design. If your 3D model is very rough and simple, or if the design is still at a conceptual stage, you should avoid a large render as it will show imperfections and will not appear very convincing to the viewer. On the other hand, if your model and the design are very detailed, then you need to render a large image to show it properly, since computing a small image will blur all the detailed work.

The render is the base of your image, so it is important that you do it right. It is at that point that you fix what you want to show, the way you want to show it and your style. A good render relates the image to the design of the building and to the style of the designer.

Now we are ready to start the computation. This can take several hours and it is often done overnight.

Camera 1

Size:
2480 × 3500 pixel

Resolution:
300 dpi

Rendering time:
13 hours

4. Post-production

The tree was isolated on one layer, then it was mirrored, copied and overlapped many times to obtain the image to the right

Post-production includes all processes that follow the computation (or production) of the render, every modification to the image to improve on the result of modelling and image computation.
Usually at that point you would leave the modelling and rendering software to adopt a graphic software which allows you to manipulate any image made out of pixels. In this way you can work on the whole illumination of the image and its colours, as well as remark or completely change any unsatisfactory part.

A graphic software is very versatile, but its most useful feature are the layers. Layers are conceptually transparent sheets that can be overlapped to each other. In each layer there is a part of the image, and the sum of all layers produces the final image. Working with layers presents an important advantage, as you can isolate the layer on which you need to work without damaging the others. This feature allows you to transform and move one or more layers independently from the others as if you were composing pieces of images cut out from different photos.

The gull is stretched
to give the illusion of
soaring

Yellow areas are changed
to fuchsia

Transformation of a seagull cut out from a photo and
visibly pasted on a cloudy city sky

Graphic software allows you to work incisively on an image, by changing its shape, contrast or illumination, by adding lights, shines or shadows and by creating blurring or transparency. It gives you the chance to cut graphic elements out of photos and add them to your scene. This is the case with trees or persons, which are often cut out of larger photos and inserted in the scene.

Given that layers are one of the most important features in graphic software, allowing you to work on them as if you were building a collage, it is quite important to point out that is relatively simple to build a library of images and details you can draw from. Thus, it is advisable to collect every graphical element which could be re-usable for other projects (for example people, trees, animals, cars, furnishings, skies, etc.).

Many online image banks let you search and purchase beautiful photos. However, even if it is quite easy to download this material from the internet, it would be preferable if you could shoot the photos yourself,

thus avoiding the risk of infringing copyright which might occur when renders are published and shown to a wide audience.

When cutting elements out of photos for your library, it is important to take them from high-resolution images. Since they need to be scaled and modified to fit in your render, low-resolution elements will cause many problems because they require an enlargement, thus making pixeling very visible.

On the contrary, reducing high-resolution graphic elements will not cause any troubles. Always use digital high-resolution images to cut out graphical elements for your digital library. Definitely avoid scanning and cutting out elements from magazines, newspapers and other printed images. Since they are mostly CMYK offset printed, once scanned your element will reveal the printing pattern and any alignment mistake. This will affect the quality of your image, even if you scan the element with the best possible resolution.

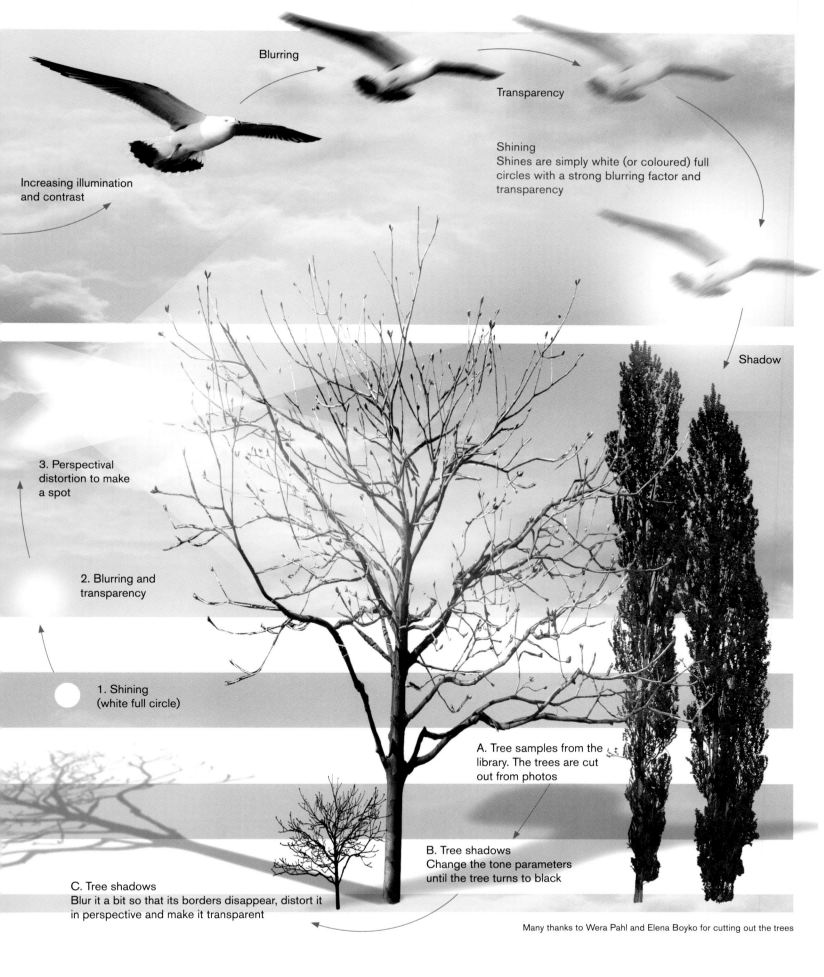

Blurring

Transparency

Increasing illumination
and contrast

Shining
Shines are simply white (or coloured) full
circles with a strong blurring factor and
transparency

Shadow

3. Perspectival
distortion to make
a spot

2. Blurring and
transparency

1. Shining
(white full circle)

A. Tree samples from the
library. The trees are cut
out from photos

B. Tree shadows
Change the tone parameters
until the tree turns to black

C. Tree shadows
Blur it a bit so that its borders disappear, distort it
in perspective and make it transparent

Many thanks to Wera Pahl and Elena Boyko for cutting out the trees

Sometimes original photos are incomplete and need processing in order to reproduce missing parts. This was the case with this tree, which was cut out and reworked to create the missing parts. To do that, small parts of the tree were cut out from the original photo and pieced together. These were then progressively added to the tree until the whole was completed in a realistic way.

1

This was the original photo used as the source.

2

The tree was cut out. This work took a long time and needed to be done very carefully.

3

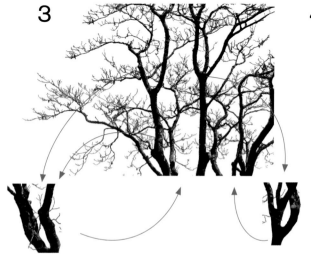

Existing trunks were copied out of the tree and post-processed to recreate missing parts.

4

The parts of the trunk were positioned and added to the tree.

5

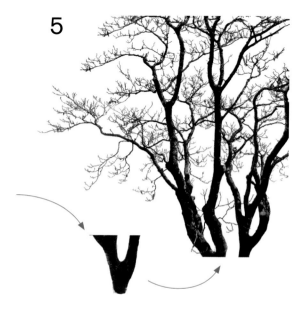

A piece of tree was cut out of another photo to complete the trunk.

6

The new piece was inserted to complete the trunk.

7

The tree with the recreated trunk. Now the tree is lacking some small branches at the top and on the right.

8

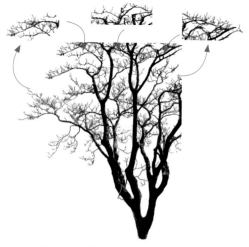

Several small branches were cut out of the tree to complete the crown.

9

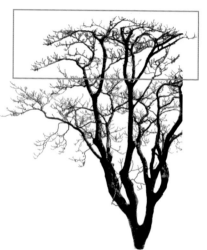

The new pieces were inserted to complete the crown.

10

Again several small branches were cut out of the tree to complete the right side.

11

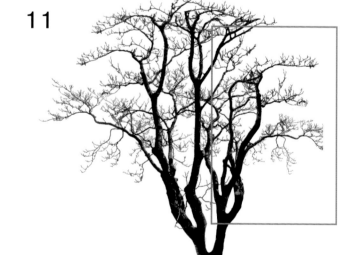

The new pieces were inserted on the right, thus completing the tree.

12

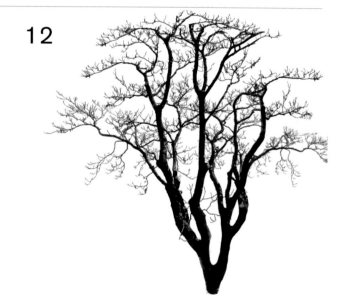

The completed tree: it was hard work, but you only need to do it once – and then you can save it in your library.

Graphic elements chosen for the composition and a "sketch" of the composition

Before working in detail on the post-production, it is advisable to make a "sketch" of the composition: a very fast and rough image containing all the graphic elements is a very good discussion medium for the client and a very useful compositional tool for you when choosing the elements and their placing.

As graphic elements can spoil the focus and emphasis of your image, you ought to focus on your target. If you add graphic elements which are too strong (like two persons fighting or a road accident), the building will disappear on the background and the focus of the overall scene will move to the graphic element. Graphic elements and accessories strongly affect your images, giving them style and credibility, so be careful when choosing and placing them. The viewers unconsciously focus first on them and then on the building.

If needed, you can prepare a board with a selection of your graphic elements to discuss it with your client prior to choosing the final accessories for the scene. It is like a painting board and a compositional tool.

Since the range of accessories reveals your style and taste, choose them to match the building you are rendering. Expensive cars and well dressed people are excellent to recreate a luxury atmosphere, but on the other hand they will clash against a background of social housing. Always remember to "align" the style of the accessories with the design as this will make your image and your work more realistic.

Top: In this sequence of images the trees are used to create respectively a frame for the building, an opposite axis to the viewer, and a symmetrical backdrop.
Bottom: The trees and their projected shadows. This affects the composition except where, on the right, the shadow falls out of the scene.

Placing elements on your scene requires good compositional skills. As the building should be the key visual point in the render, all other elements should fit in and further highlight the building itself rather than create a contrast. It is also important that they have the same illumination of the scene, to complete the picture and add to the realism of the image.

Trees, persons, furnishing can make the building appear closer to or more distant from the viewer, as well as make the scene lively and pleasant. They can also be used to hide mistakes, to fill voids in the scene or to attract the eye of the viewers. Thus you can use a tree for framing the building or a row of them to give the illusion of depth, but do not forget to produce their shadows. Since you are adding accessories after computation, this is not so difficult – if you look at other shadows in the overall scene, it should be easy to produce the new ones with the same orientation.

The graphic software often has a specific command to create shadows, but if you want to have more control, just copy the element, change the tone parameters until it turns black, then blur it so that its borders disappear

Top: Three different background situations, the centre and the right ones contrast with the sunny illumination of the scene.
Bottom: A cloud cut out from another photo is inserted. The original sky around the cloud is erased and adjusted to fit in the scene.

slightly (in respect to the overall scene), and finally distort the layer according to the scene perspective and make it transparent.

The background is something you should use carefully to create the right atmosphere in your scene. As for the accessories, you can use it to add depth or movement to the scene, to blur the border or to focus on the building. As a matter of fact, after computation you often need to change or modify the rendered background. Normally you need to cut it out of the render, but if you have saved the alpha channel after computation, now it is

very easy to crop it at once: select the alpha channel, invert the selection and delete the resulting selected area from the scene.

The background, be it the sky, the city or the landscape, must be chosen according to the illumination of the scene, so that it does not clash with the building. The real site provides the most appropriate background, therefore you should take a photo of the site from the exact position of your camera as this will make things look realistic. If you cannot, use the photo of another similar site or an abstract background, a sky or a neutral landscape.

1 The scene before and after post-production: the steps of the main entrance were visually reinforced with grey colour bands to simulate a darker stone for the head of the steps.

2 A mistake occurred during computation and the steps of the secondary entrance were not properly computed as a result. Steps from the main entrance were therefore applied over the black side steps through the copy and paste technique.

As mentioned, post-production is the stage when it is possible to further correct the rendering following computation. This entails changing the overall illumination of the scene, its tone, saturation or overall contrast. Again you should focus on the final target and on the audience of your image, thus to avoid disturbing the view.

It has been said that now it is the time to add the "human element", just as illustrators did before the advent of computers. This is partially true and it certainly requires sensitivity and technical skills. In this stage, illustrators with an artistic background have better chances of success since they can actually re-draw by hand on the scene, re-marking some details (like joints or lines) or adding shines on some areas to make them more visible. In this phase it is also possible to remedy texture mistakes like repetition or shines which contrast with the overall illumination of the scene.

The scene before and after post-production (from the left to the right).
Visible in the middle the joints which were reinforced by drawing lines on them. This was very important since the building was composed of pre-fab panels and the joints were one of the main aspects of the design. On the right, walls and floor tiles were contrasted and darkened thus giving them more prominence. The overall scene was darkened and saturated to make it appear warmer and recreate the impression of a very sunny day in the steppe.

Camera 1
Before post-production

The overall tone of the render was changed and some details (like the brown floor, the joints and the steps) were highlighted. It was necessary to implement some corrections in the grid on the big window and in the lesenes because following mistakes. Also doors were later added on the left. The cloud, the sky, the tree and its shadow were added for composition.

After computing, it was decided to render the building by night. The overall illumination of the scene was drastically changed from day to night by making the overall tone darker and removing saturation in the render. Furthermore, all significant shadows were deleted and replaced with details without shadow cut out from the render itself. Shining was added to all neon lamps. Shadows of trees and persons were added at a second stage to recreate the effect of a street lamp illuminating the building by night.

Camera 2
After post-production

The overall tone of the render was changed and some details (like the brown floor, the joints and the steps) were highlighted. Some modelling mistakes occured in the staircase on the secondary entrance and a correction was needed. Thus, the first step was duplicated and scaled so to reproduce the other steps. Also some grass was later added on the right. The cloud, the sky, the tree and some shadows were added for compostion balance.

This detail was later cut out of the camera 3 render. The people were hand-drawn by Natascha Meuser and then scanned and coloured digitally.

Techniques and strategies

The making of a render

Over time, through practice you will improve your technical skills, becoming faster and more effective in your work. However, in order to obtain the best result it is also important to choose the right technique and strategy.

In this section you will find an anthology of practical case studies.

Image processing
Perspective construction

Task: rendering the insertion of the Schleich products display (POS) into a photo of a toy store.

The most common problem when inserting an image in a photo is that of perspectival coherence. The display was photographed from various angles and several details were linked together to show the finished POS. The photo of the toy shop provided a clear indication of the two vanishing points of its perspective. These were used to draw guidelines to insert the digital POS in the right perspective.

Project:
Schleich POS System, 2008
....
Client:
Meuser Architekten GmbH, Berlin (Germany)
....
Software / Technique:
Photoshop
....
People involved:
Fabio Schillaci
....
Time needed:
1 day

1

2

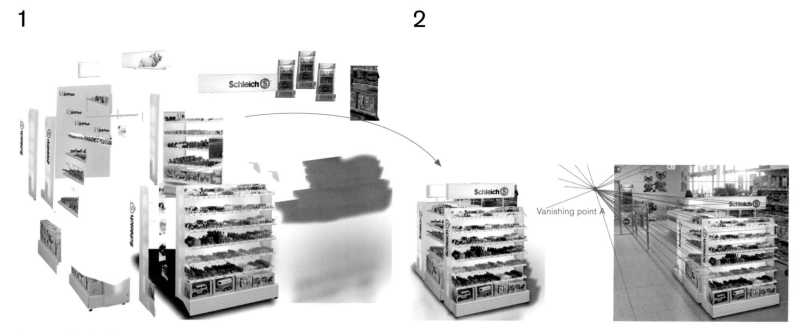

Cut outs used for the collage

The digitally reconstructed POS and detail of the perspective construction

3

Perspective construction of the photo with two vanishing points

4

Final render

Image processing
Colours, tone and saturation

Task: design and render the colours for the new façade layout of the building.

Parts of the almost frontal photo of the façade were selected, duplicated and progressively modified by altering their tone, colour and saturation parameters. This process has the advantage of keeping the new colours coherent with the rest of the photo.

Project:
German Embassy, New Delhi (India), 2008

Client:
Meuser Architekten GmbH, Berlin (Germany)

Software / Technique:
Photoshop

People involved:
Fabio Schillaci

Time needed:
2 days

2

Selection of the areas for the red circles

3

Altering the tone from white to red

5

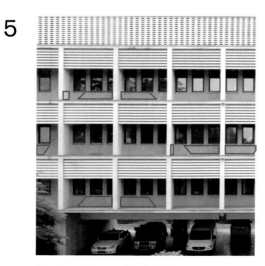

Selection of the areas for the black

6

Changing the tone from white to black

1

Original photo

4

First proposal

7

Render of the final layout

Image processing
The importance of the photo

Project:
Egyptian Embassy, Berlin (Germany), 2009

Client:
Meuser Architekten GmbH, Berlin (Germany)
Thomas Baumann Architekt, Berlin (Germany)

Software / Technique:
Photoshop

People involved:
Fabio Schillaci, Natascha and Philipp Meuser

Time needed:
4 days

Task: rendering the private residence as a golden crown on top of the embassy.

Due to the high quality of the photo, it was decided to process the image in 2D. The new design was rendered using cut outs from the photo itself. This process has the advantage of creating coherence between the original photo and the inserted image.

1

Original photo of the site (photo: Philipp Meuser)

2

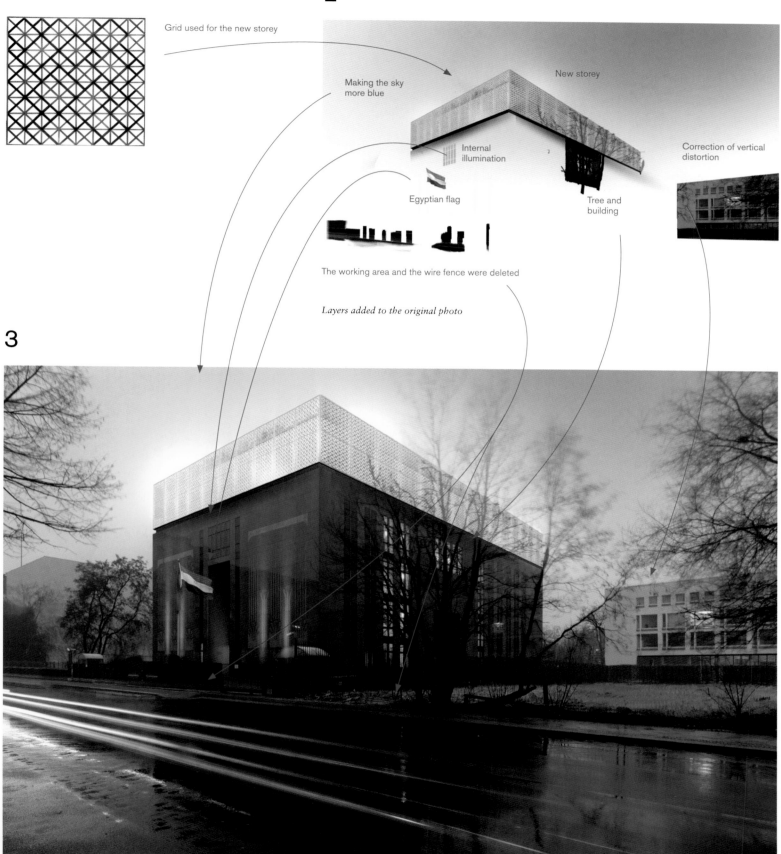

Grid used for the new storey

Making the sky more blue

New storey

Internal illumination

Correction of vertical distortion

Egyptian flag

Tree and building

The working area and the wire fence were deleted

Layers added to the original photo

3

Final render

Modelling
Optimization

Task: to render the insertion of two blocks of town-houses in a historic setting.

In this project it was decided to render only the façades of the 13 townhouses to limit the amount of work needed and to allow the artist to concentrate on the small details. Later on, the render was added to the photo of the site and the overall tone was saturated to recreate an old-fashion atmosphere.

Project:
Molkenmarkt 2020, Berlin (Germany), 2009

Client:
Meuser Architekten GmbH, Berlin (Germany)

Software / Technique:
Rhinoceros, 3ds Max, VRay, Photoshop

People involved:
Fabio Schillaci, Natascha and Philipp Meuser

Time needed:
7 days

1

Photo of the site for the render (photo: Philipp Meuser)

2

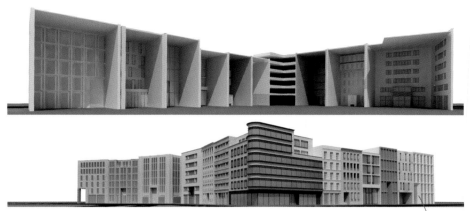

The view behind the façades and the render

Photo

Addition

Modelling
Evolution

Task: to design the interior of a private spa and render its atmosphere.

The 3D model needed to be quickly changeable to help the architects and the client verify their ideas and fine-tune the design. This was achieved by dividing the model into several files: the main file with structural elements (walls, windows, fireplace and sauna) and smaller files containing the individual, unfixed elements (tub, shower, furniture and sink) that could be linked to the first file in successive stages and easily interchanged.

Project:
Private spa, Nuremberg (Germany), 2007–2009

Client:
Meuser Architekten GmbH, Berlin (Germany)

Software / Technique:
Rhinoceros, 3D Studio Max, VRay, Photoshop

People involved:
Fabio Schillaci

Time needed:
Several days

1

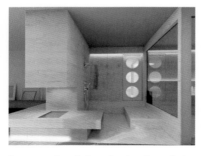

Sequence of renderings showing the evolution of the design

2

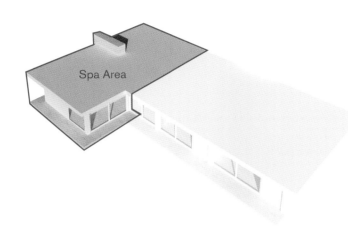

The three-dimensional model holding the spa area (exterior view)

3

Render of the final design

4

Render of the final design

Modelling
Flexibility

Task: to design and render a hotel room.

The 3D model was used as a simulation tool to visualize material cohesion. Even if some minor changes occurred in the furniture, most of the room geometry was fixed and only its texture needed to be changeable. Thus geometrical elements were grouped by material and new textures were assigned to them for every new material added.

Project:
Hotel room, Kühlungsborn (Germany), 2009

Client:
Meuser Architekten GmbH, Berlin (Germany)

Software / Technique:
Rhinoceros, 3ds Max, VRay, Photoshop

People involved:
Fabio Schillaci

Time needed:
Several days

1

Sequence of renderings showing the evolution of the design

2

Render of the final design

Mixed use
More render and less photo

Task: to render the modern elevator tower so that it integrates with the thirteenth-century castle.

Due to the difficulty of working on the original photo, which required removing the waste and reconstructing the ground area, it was decided to render a 3D model of the entrance and combine it with some details cut out from the original photo.

Project:
Schloss Stolzenfels, Koblenz (Germany), 2007

Client:
Meuser Architekten GmbH, Berlin (Germany)

Software / Technique:
Rhinoceros, 3ds Max, VRay, Photoshop

People involved:
Fabio Schillaci

Time needed:
3 days

1

2

3

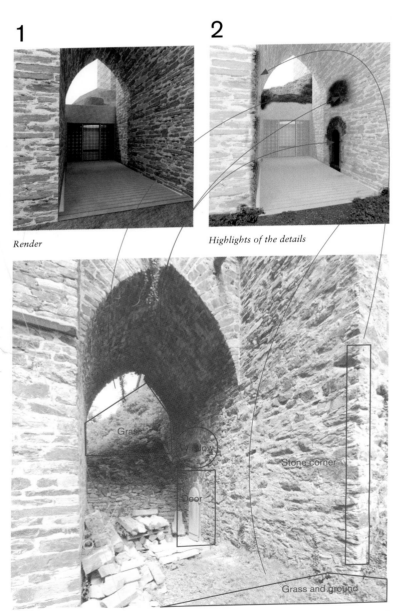

Render

Highlights of the details

Original photo of the site with an indication of the details to be replicated in the rendering (photo: Philipp Meuser)

Mixed use
Less render and more photo

Task: to render the modern elevator tower so that it integrates with the thirteenth-century castle.

The 3D model of the tower was rendered using the same perspective as the photo, to integrate it with the existing building. After computation, the tower was cut out of the render and the overall tone was changed to adapt to the clear illumination of the photo. Later on, some plants (duplicated from the photo) and shadows were added for camouflaging.

Project:
Schloss Stolzenfels, Koblenz (Germany), 2007

Client:
Meuser Architekten GmbH, Berlin (Germany)

Software / Technique:
Rhinoceros, 3ds Max, VRay, Photoshop

People involved:
Fabio Schillaci

Time needed:
2 days

1   2   3

1. Render
2. Cutting out the tower and tone changing
3. Plants and shadows

Addition

4

4. Original photo of the site and position of the tower (photo: Philipp Meuser)

Communication

The making of a render

Rendering means first of all communicating an idea.

Extreme photorealism is not always the best way to achieve that since a certain level of simplification is needed to achieve a message that is both direct and easy to read.

Communication
Manifestation of a strategy

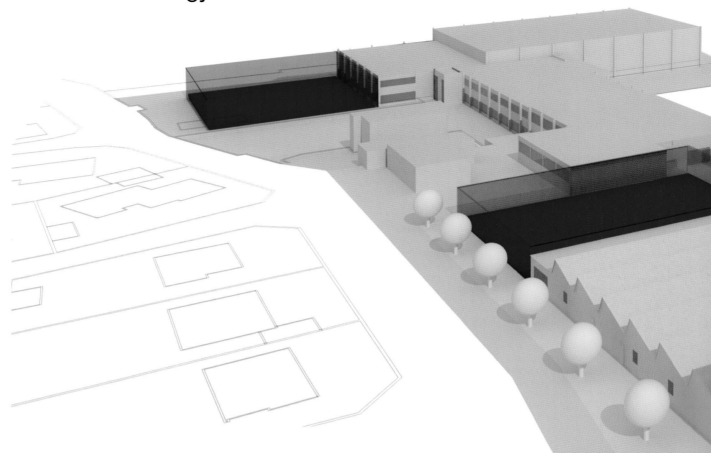

Task: to render the concept for the expansion of the Schleich GmbH headquarters.

Due to the brevity of the presentation, the idea had to be so clear to be understood at a glance. In order to avoid focussing on insignificant details, only crucial parts of the existing situation were accurately modelled and the whole 3D model was rendered with a neutral palette of soft colours, to further highlight the demolition area in yellow and the new buildings in red. The 3D model of the existing site was used as the basis, and only small parts (the demolition area and the new building) were progressively linked and rendered.

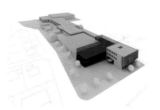

Progressive renders showing the existing site, the demolition area and the new building

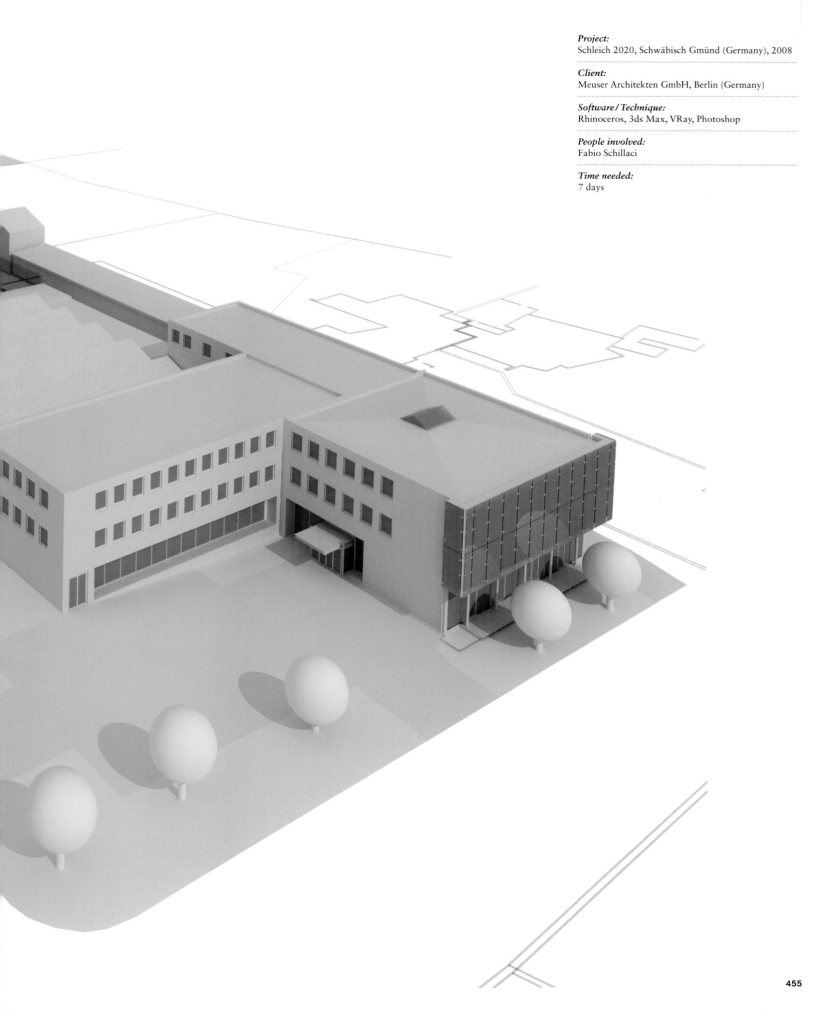

Project:
Schleich 2020, Schwäbisch Gmünd (Germany), 2008

Client:
Meuser Architekten GmbH, Berlin (Germany)

Software / Technique:
Rhinoceros, 3ds Max, VRay, Photoshop

People involved:
Fabio Schillaci

Time needed:
7 days

Communication
Manifestation of an idea

Task: to render the concept for the renovation of a historic building to be converted into a luxury hotel.

As it involved an historic building, the site was modelled to express the wish for its preservation and renovation. The few additions were highlighted with a gentle gold colour. The neighbouring buildings were roughly modelled and rendered in a cold white tone to further highlight the historic building (cream white).

Project:
Monbijouparc Residence, Berlin (Germany), 2008

Client:
Meuser Architekten GmbH, Berlin (Germany)

Software / Technique:
Rhinoceros, 3ds Max, VRay, Photoshop

People involved:
Fabio Schillaci

Time needed:
5 days

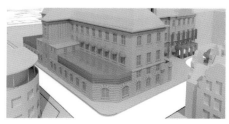

Views of the building

Light sources serve primarily to highlight the design and its main details.

However, as the masters of the past would confirm, the right illumination is key to create the right atmosphere.

Illumination
Daytime, sunlight

Task: to render by daytime using the dramatic effect of sunlight.

When rendering by daytime, daylight and sunlight should always be the main source of light for the scene. Sunlight is often a good tool to create a dramatic atmosphere. Since sunlight projects shadows in the scene (especially if you have grids or frames in the windows), these can be rendered as "volumes" thus giving the impression of fog coming inside the building.

1

2

3

4

5

Project 1:
Hotel pool, Kühlungsborn (Germany), 2009

Client:
Meuser Architekten GmbH, Berlin (Germany)

Software/Technique:
Rhinoceros, 3ds Max, VRay, Photoshop

People involved:
Fabio Schillaci

Time needed:
3 days

Project 2:
Hotel "Die Klause", Koblenz (Germany), 2007

Client:
Meuser Architekten GmbH, Berlin (Germany)

Software/Technique:
Rhinoceros, 3ds Max, VRay, Photoshop

People involved:
Fabio Schillaci

Time needed:
2 days

Project 3:
Monbijouparc Residence, Berlin (Germany), 2008

Client:
Meuser Architekten GmbH, Berlin (Germany)

Software/Technique:
Rhinoceros, 3ds Max, VRay, Photoshop

People involved:
Fabio Schillaci

Time needed:
5 days

Project 4:
Schloss Stolzenfels, Koblenz (Germany), 2007

Client:
Meuser Architekten GmbH, Berlin (Germany)

Software/Technique:
Rhinoceros, 3ds Max, VRay, Photoshop

People involved:
Fabio Schillaci and Philipp Meuser

Time needed:
2 days

Project 5:
Mission Diplomatique France, Almaty (Kazakhstan), 2008

Client:
Meuser Architekten GmbH, Berlin (Germany)

Software/Technique:
Rhinoceros, 3ds Max, VRay, Photoshop

People involved:
Fabio Schillaci

Time needed:
2 days

Project:
Hotel lobby, Kühlungsborn (Germany), 2009

Client:
Meuser Architekten GmbH, Berlin (Germany)

Software / Technique:
Rhinoceros, 3ds Max, VRay, Photoshop

People involved:
Fabio Schillaci, Natascha Meuser

Time needed:
4 days

6

Illumination
Nocturne, moonlight and artificial lights

Task: to render by night using artificial lights and moonlight.

When rendering by night, artificial lights and moonlight are the main sources of light for your scene. Moonlight should normally be used to gently illuminate the overall scene. Artificial lights are the tools to highlight details and to recreate the right atmosphere, be this a grand event or a calm evening.

Project:
Egyptian Embassy, Berlin (Germany), 2009

Client:
Meuser Architekten GmbH, Berlin (Germany)
Thomas Baumann Architekt, Berlin (Germany)

Software / Technique:
Photoshop

People involved:
Fabio Schillaci

Time needed:
1 day

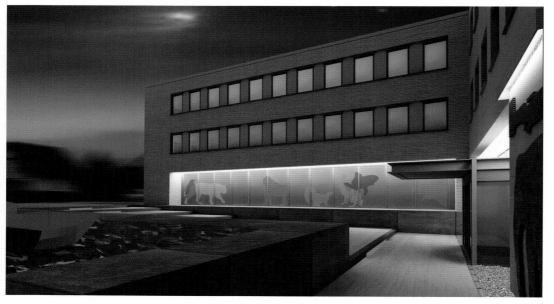

Project:
Schleich GmbH, Schwäbisch Gmünd (Germany), 2008

Client:
Meuser Architekten GmbH, Berlin (Germany)

Software / Technique:
Rhinoceros, 3ds Max, VRay, Photoshop

People involved:
Fabio Schillaci

Time needed:
4 days

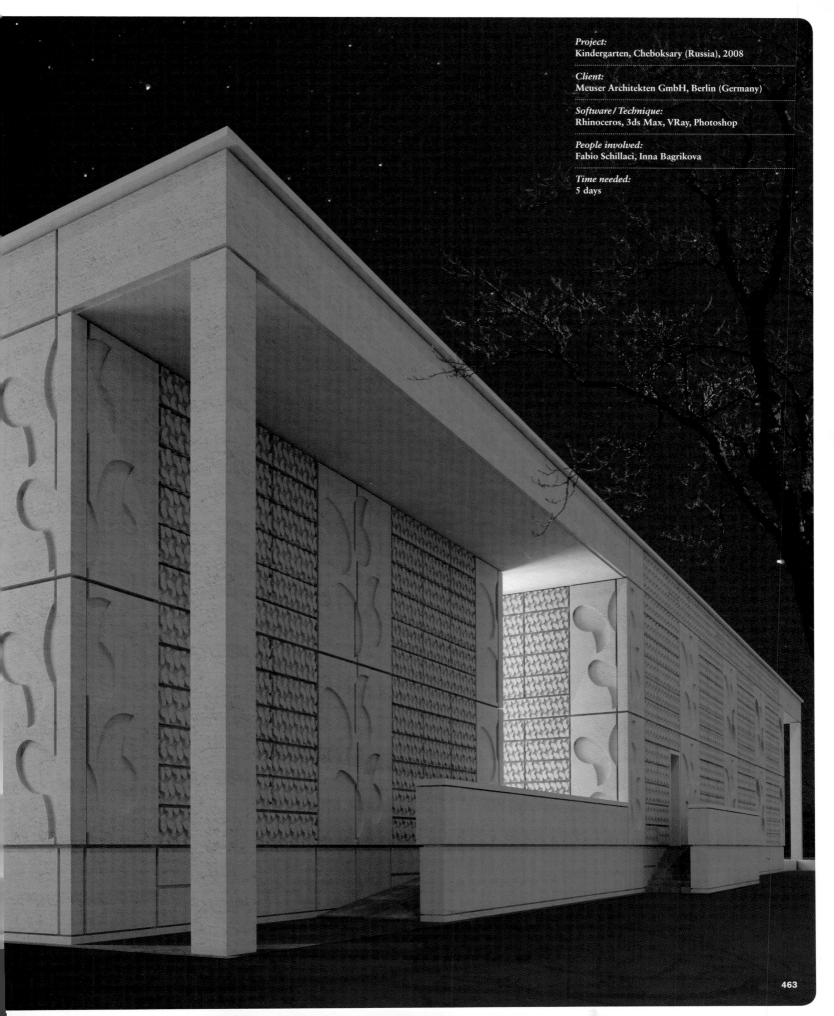

Project:
Kindergarten, Cheboksary (Russia), 2008

Client:
Meuser Architekten GmbH, Berlin (Germany)

Software / Technique:
Rhinoceros, 3ds Max, VRay, Photoshop

People involved:
Fabio Schillaci, Inna Bagrikova

Time needed:
5 days

Illumination
Interiors, artificial lights

Task: to render an interior without windows by the only means of artificial lights.

When you are asked to render an interior without windows (and without any source of natural light), artificial lights are used to illuminate the overall scene and to create an atmosphere. When artificial lights are insufficient and the overall illumination they produce is weak, you can correct the problem by increasing the reflection parameters of the materials and the secondary bounces of light in the global illumination. The overall illumination of the scene will increase and create atmosphere.

Project:
British Embassy, Astana (Kazakhstan), 2006

Client:
Meuser Architekten GmbH, Berlin (Germany)

Software / Technique:
Rhinoceros, 3ds Max, VRay, Photoshop

People involved:
Fabio Schillaci

Time needed:
2 days

Project:
German Embassy, Astana (Kazakhstan), 2007

Client:
Meuser Architekten GmbH, Berlin (Germany)

Software / Technique:
Rhinoceros, 3ds Max, VRay, Photoshop

People involved:
Fabio Schillaci

Time needed:
2 days

Project:
German Embassy, Astana (Kazakhstan), 2007

I wish to thank all those who in different ways contributed
towards the realisation of this book:

Natascha and Philipp Meuser, Mandy Kasek, Uta Keil,
Ralph Petermann, Juliane Kukla, Wera Pahl, Jennifer Tobolla,
Daniel Festag, Inna Bagrikova, Lena Boyko, Nicole Wolf,
Daniela Donadei, Cornelia Dörries, Heiko Mattausch, Paul Angelier,
Alessandra Raponi, Niels Fischer, Andrej Schmidt and Anna Jan,
Omar Jaramillo Traverso, Salvator John Liotta, Alessandra Traina,
Roberto Pelliccia, Carmelo Zappulla, Massimo Tepedino,
Christoph Stinn, Julia Kaulbach.

Fabio Schillaci (Italy, b. 1977) is a licensed architect. Founder of
Architectural Noise (2000) and FAN (2006), he received an honorable
mention at Europan 8 (2006) and a Design Merit Award at Feidad 2005.
His works have been shown and published internationally – in Tokyo,
Warsaw, Quito, Taipei, Milan and Athens. Fabio Schillaci lives and
works in Berlin.

Fabrizio Avella (Italy, b. 1968) graduated in architecture in 1994 and
in 2000 was awarded his doctorate in Surveying and the Representation
of Architecture and the Environment from the University of Palermo's
Department of Representation. Currently undertaking research
and teaching in the Faculties of Architecture at Palermo and Agrigento
Universities, Fabrizio Avella practises as a designer, working with
architects on projects ranging from interior renovation and restoration
of civic and religious buildings, across residential and commercial
buildings, to museum exhibits and landscape design. Fabrizio Avella
lives and works in Palermo.

Augusto Romano Burelli (Italy, b. 1938) is Professor of Architectural
Composition and from 1970 to 2006 taught at the Istituto Universitario
di Architettura in Venice (Italy). Currently Dean of the Department
of Architecture at the University of Udine (Italy), his researches focus
on architectural design and urban planning with a specific interest in
the architectural culture of the city, traditions of settlement, and their
morphological and typological structures. Since 1991 he has been
involved in the critical reconstruction of Berlin and Potsdam (Germany).
Professor Burelli has published widely on the relationship between
architecture and its origins, and that between architecture, its teaching
and its typological codes. Among his architectural works in Friuli
(Italy), Potsdam and Berlin (Germany) are private residences, town halls,
churches and university buildings. Augusto Romano Burelli lives and
works in Udine, Berlin and Venice.

Original edition © 2009 by DOM publishers, Berlin | Germany
www.dom-publishers.com

This edition first published 2010
This English-language edition is published and distributed by
John Wiley & Sons under exclusive licence in the following territories:
the UK, European countries (with the exception of Germany, Switzerland,
Liechtenstein, Luxembourg, Austria and The Netherlands); the USA;
Canada; Africa; and Australia.

Registered office
John Wiley & Sons Ltd, The Atrium, Southern Gate, Chichester,
West Sussex, PO19 8SQ, United Kingdom

For details of our global editorial offices, for customer services and for
information about how to apply for permission to reuse the copyright
material in this book please see our website at www.wiley.com.

Executive Commissioning Editor: Helen Castle
Project Editor: Miriam Swift
Assistant Editor: Calver Lezama
Design: Daniela Donadei
English Translation: Melanie Flynn, Angela Eggers
Proof Reader: Mariangela Palazzi-Williams

ISBN 978-0-470-66410-0

Printed in China by DAMI EDITORIAL & PRINTING SERVICES CO. LTD

A John Wiley and Sons, Ltd, Publication